Britain's Ten Most Wanted

THE TRUTH BEHIND THE MOST SHOCKING UNSOLVED MURDERS

VANESSA HOWARD

JOHN BLAKE

Published by John Blake Publishing Ltd,
3 Bramber Court, 2 Bramber Road,
London W14 9PB, England

www.johnblakepublishing.co.uk

First published in paperback in 2009

ISBN: 978 1 84454 759 3

British Library Cataloguing-in-Publication Data:

A catalogue record for this book is available from the British Library.

Design by www.envydesign.co.uk

Printed in Great Britain by CPI Bookmarque, Croydon CR0 4TD

1 3 5 7 9 10 8 6 4 2

Papers us   :lable
produc   sts.
The man   ental

Every atter   yright-
holders, but   ul if the

To the dedicated members of the British police and justice system and to those who made this book possible.

Vanessa Howard is a journalist and author specialising in real life stories and true crime.

Her first book, *Unconditional Love*, was the true account of a domestic murder and reconciliation. She is married and has two children.

ACKNOWLEDGEMENTS

I would like to thank the following for their help and support: Will O'Reilly, Steve Tolmie, John Clements, Sarah Goodall, Jean Hall, Cheryl Jones, Jonathan Jones, Graham Jones, Stuart Hutton, Greg Lewis, Bruce Kennedy, Vicky Durham, David Howard, Geoff Howard, John Wordsworth, Wensley Clarkson and the staff at the *South Wales Evening Post*.

CONTENTS

CHAPTER ONE
SANDRA PHILLIPS
DEATH ON DILLWYN STREET

On Friday, 14 June 1985, one news story dominated the day. And it was unfolding far away from Swansea...

TWA Flight 847, flying from Athens to Rome, was hijacked by two Lebanese men who'd boarded the plane armed with firearms and grenades. The flight was forcibly redirected to Beirut; later, the world watched on in horror as the body of a passenger was thrown onto the tarmac from the plane. He was 23-year-old Robert Stethem, singled out as he was a diver with the US Navy. Stethem had been savagely beaten, tortured and shot in the right temple before being dumped from the aircraft.

The hijack would not be resolved until the end of the month, when the hostages were exchanged – unofficially – for Shiite prisoners held in Israeli prisons. Fundamentalist terror now defines our age, but this was almost a quarter of a century ago and, in many ways, our day-to-day world is almost unrecognisable from the world back then.

Take pornography, for instance. Now you hear casual references to watching 'porn' on mainstream shows such as *Friends*, schoolgirls buy Playboy pencil cases and pole-dancing is listed as a new type of exercise class, but in 1985 pornography was still a dirty word. Items were sold 'under the counter'; porn was sordid, shameful and only sought out by 'perverts in dirty macs'.

Of course, the truth was rather different. Men from all walks of life bought porn magazines or videos, but this was prior to the Internet domination of porn today. It had to be sought out, mainly through 'private shops' or mail order. Even in 1985, though, porn was big business.

Those working in porn outlets knew it was a less-than-respectable means of income but a wage cheque is a wage cheque. Working in a sex shop might not be the type of job you'd openly brag about, but it was regular work. You'd open the doors, let customers browse, take note of stock levels and work the till, just like any other shop. You'd get to know your regulars too.

Women working in the sex industry know the attendant risks. It is a toxic environment, where sex is overtly on display and customers are actively looking for stimulation. They are not buying groceries. They are buying into a high-octane notion that women are waiting, and willing, to be used by them. In the magazines, in the videos, in the toys out on display, compliant women readily act out any fantasy, no matter how depraved.

For women earning a living in that environment, vigilance is everything. You have to be adept at reading faces and body language, be able to profile and assess a customer in a heartbeat, weighing up who will play nice and who might cause you trouble. It isn't for the faint-hearted – and for the novice, the risks are that much higher.

Sandra Phillips had only been working behind the counter for two months when someone walked in on that day in 1985. Earlier on, the thirty-eight-year-old mother of four had dropped her daughter off at school and her husband, Lesley, off at his job in a city centre Co-op before she parked her yellow Ford Cortina near Dillwyn Street in Swansea and opened up the Private Shop.

Dillwyn Street isn't a main shopping thoroughfare, but it sits between the packed residential streets that surround the old Swansea City Football ground, the Vetch, and the centre of the city. Cars, buses and taxis flow down the street throughout the day as it also links the coast road to the rest of the city. Stand on Dillwyn Street today and you can see the Grand Theatre, pubs and clubs, the Quadrant Shopping Centre and, beyond that, Tesco. Sandra would have been familiar with the location and would have sensed that it was better than being shut away on a back street. Although the windows of the Private Shop were blacked out, everyone knew its function and it was the butt of many jokes. The blackened windows hinted at something unsavoury, but it wasn't menacing, more something to snigger about. Its location – not central, but busy and highly visible – also lent it an air of harmlessness.

But the person who pushed open the door that Friday morning, was wise to its location too. This was a shop people glanced at from buses, from cars and from across the road as they waited to cross. It was sandwiched between an upholsterers and a pub, so the risk of being spotted going in or coming out was high, but clearly, it was a risk worth taking: someone had a brutal desire to kill and a busy road would not deter them. And if it was a calculated risk, it paid off as in the long years that have followed, no one has been able to identify who it was that walked out that morning after committing a hideous crime and locked the door behind them.

Perhaps the location no longer mattered. Perhaps their rage obliterated any rational assessment of whether they'd be spotted. Or perhaps the route was so familiar that getting in while no one was looking was a well-honed skill. They could have used the store for years without suspicion from family, friends or colleagues. This was just another Friday morning, but a murderer was watching and biding his time.

He may have watched as Sandra opened up, some time after 9am. As manageress, she busied herself with the day's tasks. She knew her area manager was due to arrive during the lunch hour with a new delivery and so she double-checked what stock was low.

The best guess the police now have is that it happened just after 11am. The door opened and in walked a man equipped with a can of petrol. He wanted to leave no trace.

Sandra would have had no defence against a man intent on murder. She may have known from the moment she looked up that something was terribly wrong or there may have been a few moments of calm as a regular customer approached her. But it would have been only moments.

The results of what followed staggered the paramedics when they arrived at the scene. Sandra had been attacked with single-minded ferocity. She was found behind the counter of the shop, in a pool of blood and suffering from severe facial and head injuries; the room was doused in petrol. As the ambulance crew crouched down and desperately tried to find signs of life, they began to realise that they were kneeling in a murder scene that no one who worked on the case would forget.

The police were on their way. The emergency call had been made a little before 2pm by Anthony Williams. He was the area manager making a delivery to the shop on Dillwyn Street and had been irritated when he'd found the door locked. He had to return to the van to get a spare set of keys. Why wasn't the shop open? Friday was a busy day, customers wanted to stock up for the weekend and the opportunity to take in money was being lost.

He retrieved his keys and opened the door. It was quiet; it seemed empty. But then he spotted a heavily bloodstained basque, plus another item of lingerie on the floor. Within a few steps, Mr Williams discovered the awful truth. He was desperate to get help for Sandra. There was a phone at the shop, but the handset had been ripped off; this was in the days before mobile phones were widely in use, so he had to run next door to Gwyder Upholstery and make the call for help from there.

Even the most experienced officers aren't immune to the impact of a murder scene. The mind struggles to take in the visual information that floods the brain, it scrambles for an explanation as to what lies before it. The first police officer on the scene, PC David Roach, saw Sandra's head pushed against the bloodstained wall, none of her features recognisable. He also noted that her skirt was above her waist and her tights and pants had been ripped apart. He then had to step out of the shop and continue his duties, organising the cordon and dealing with the members of the public who were slowly gathering.

In the past, officers received an additional payment if they saw a dead body. An attempt at recompense, it is symbolic; it doesn't help meet the true cost of bearing witness to savagery. For men like Anthony Williams and David Roach, that day would mark them forever; you can't forget what you have seen. And neither can a killer. But what they take from the moment is very different.

The killer would have watched Sandra's reaction change from passive enquiry – what does this customer want – to one of paralysing fear. As the first blow connected, Sandra would have known she was in mortal danger. Terror and adrenalin would have flooded through her heart and limbs, urging flight, but she had no chance to escape. She had raised her left hand, instinctively protecting her head, rightly guessing that if she lost consciousness, all was lost. A finger on her left hand was shattered as the attack began.

Forensic experts noted that the attack took place in three areas of the shop – the attacker followed Sandra as she fought for her life. Once dragged behind the counter, she did not stand a chance. The blows rained down with such savagery that she was stunned into submission. Her attacker used a chair or table leg, something wooden – splinters were later recovered from the scene. He also made use of the telephone handset that had been ripped from the wall. He would have watched her helplessness, unable to crawl towards the door and devoid of any hope that someone could save her. But it still wasn't enough for this man.

A cord was placed around Sandra's neck and then she was brutally sexually assaulted. Her face would have been bloated and disfigured, her jaw shattered, her scalp so traumatised that it became detached from her skull. Her attacker had shattered her ribs and now fractured her breastbone as he kicked her and forcibly knelt on her chest. Her clothes torn, Sandra was insensible as the attack ended with strangulation – it is possible that her killer used the phone wire for that, although he may have just used his hands.

This was every violent fantasy about domination realised. Content that his victim was dead, or on the verge of death, the murderer then doused her in petrol where she lay. But the petrol was not lit. The attack may have only taken minutes and yet there is a chance that someone approached the store and stopped the killer in his tracks. He'd already looked through Sandra's handbag, taking a bank card, and opened the till, taking a few pounds. He also pocketed her inexpensive watch. Then Sandra's body was left in a pool of blood and petrol and her attacker melted into the broad daylight of the city streets.

There was a delay. Mr Williams did not arrive at the shop until 1.45pm, and so Sandra could have lain there dead or dying for up to three hours. There were passers-by, there had been customers in the shop, but once Sandra was discovered the scene attracted onlookers, not witnesses.

Swiftly, rumours started to spread that something terrible had happened on Dillwyn Street and shoppers and shop workers came to watch the emergency vehicles and personnel swarm around the building. The gossip going around the market was that there had been a shoot-out. Lesley Phillips heard that something awful had happened in the street. Every other lunchtime he would take some sandwiches around the corner to his wife and they'd sit and share lunchtime together. He liked to spend the hour with her but hadn't that day as he didn't feel well enough to eat. He walked over to Dillwyn Street, unaware that these were the last few moments of his life as he knew it.

He and Sandra had not been married for very long. After Sandra's first marriage ended, she was left in a modest semi in nearby Fforestfach, bringing up her four children. Sandra was well liked, quiet and a good neighbour. Only the two youngest children were at home now and life seemed to be going well. Her hardest years were behind her and although Lesley didn't expect her to work, she had looked for jobs: she wanted to add to the family coffers.

Two months earlier, she had seen an ad in the local paper asking for a shop manageress. Sandra was a little taken aback when the real nature of the work became clear but after hesitating, decided that a job was a job. She confided in her mum, Betty, that she planned to get out of there at the first opportunity. The money was useful, but she would never be happy sitting behind that counter. With her daughter about to sit her O-Levels, though, it would do for now.

Swansea is not a quiet place, it has its share of violence and disturbance; but what happened in Dillwyn Street was different. This was a planned and sadistic attack on a local mum who was simply trying to earn a living. A city today, Swansea is still small enough for a murder such as this to affect many people. So many citizens had some connection with Sandra or her family, either through the school, through work or through the community she lived in. As news of what happened sunk in, there was dismay and anger. Some of it was directed against the shop's owner – Quietlyn, a company that owned several such stores. Local councillors demanded that it be closed for good but a company lawyer for Quietlyn issued a statement stating that no one had ever been attacked in one of its outlets before and that the company wanted to post a £5,000 reward for an arrest that would lead to the conviction of Sandra's assailant. Quietlyn attempted to dampen down speculation that it was the store's pornographic content that had spurred on the killer, pointing out that any shop owner was at risk from robbery, even violent robbery. In the wider community, concerned citizens felt that a killer this violent and depraved must be caught quickly, before any other woman was at risk.

The response, when it came, was quick but it was also unexpected. It happened the very next day, 15 June, and it was not the arrest of one man but two – Wayne and Paul Darvell. Here were two men that would have been seen by many people around Swansea, even if they were more commonly known as the 'Wino Brothers' or the 'Mad Brothers'. Then twenty-four and twenty-five-years-old respectively, the brothers were originally from the nearby town of Neath, two in a family of eleven siblings. The Darvells had eight brothers and one sister and – perhaps because they were born within a year of each other – they were inseparable.

Their childhood was far from ideal and after their father left home when the boys were young, things turned from bad to worse. The younger of the two, whose first name was actually Phillip although he was always known as Wayne, idolised his older brother Paul. It was said that Wayne could be cunning but it was always Paul who dominated their relationship.

It was clear from the outset that the two boys would struggle academically. Ultimately, they were placed in Ysgol

Hendre, a school for children with special needs in Neath, where they soon came to the attention of their head teacher, Gwyn Gower. It was clear to Mr Gower that Wayne had more than academic problems to contend with. He would later say: 'Wayne was always a bizarre character. He was quite unpredictable and was always seeking attention in ridiculous ways. There were certain times when reality meant nothing to him. He would live in a world of his own.'

The Darvells' mother died in 1981 and thereafter the two brothers found it increasingly difficult to stay away from alcohol and life on the streets. By 1985, they were effectively homeless and had had a number of run-ins with the police and prison. They existed on state handouts of £40 every fortnight, which they would spend on cider and occasional trips to the amusement arcade. When that money ran out, they took to petty theft and begging. One of their favourite tricks was to hang around the streets of Swansea and approach shoppers with various tales of woe. Wayne would slash his hand with a razor and Paul would ask passers-by for the taxi fare to get his brother to hospital. When that wasn't enough, they'd try robbery. In 1984, both were found guilty of stealing from a furniture shop employee, making off with the princely sum of 65p after Paul made violent threats towards the poor individual. They'd also been caught after a burglary at a nearby scrap dealer. After serving short sentences, they were released and were offered a place at SASH, a hostel for the homeless in Gloucester Place, Swansea. They had been there for two months, just as long as Sandra had been at the Private Shop.

Although the brothers were known to drink and cause

disturbances, they were seen as a nuisance rather than dangerous. They would make false calls to the emergency services and stay by the phone box to see the vehicles arrive, even following police cars around driving their own 'invisible' squad car, complete with siren sound effects.

The police had picked them up several times over the years, mostly for causing a disturbance when they were worse for wear; few street patrols relished having them in the back of the car as their personal hygiene was not all it could be. In short, the Darvells were trouble and when it became known that they had been spotted hanging around Dillwyn Street on the day of Sandra's murder, wheels were set in motion that would prove disastrous for all involved.

Police officers arrived at SASH at 7am the day after Sandra's murder to pick the Darvells up. Not that the brothers had gone into hiding. They had even hung around the murder scene the day before and at one point, offered their help to set out the police cordon.

Wayne was talkative and always had been. No stranger to police stations, he must have realised at some point during questioning that something wasn't right. He had been on Dillwyn Street with his brother, it was true, but truth was sometimes a slippery concept for Wayne. It threaded through his mind as easily as fantasy and quite often, he could not tell the two apart. He thought he'd done things he hadn't and it had got him in trouble in the past. Wayne had never grasped how bad things could be when he told people lies, as for him, they didn't have the quality of a lie; in the moment, he believed them, he was sure of it. Looking back, he could play out what happened, he could see it and it seemed real enough.

Like the time he'd told the police that he was responsible for a robbery. Or the time that he said he'd kicked over a pile of paint pots, causing a mess. He told the officers what had happened, how he'd carried out the crime, he could see them soaking up what he had to say; it was time to confess, it was good to get back to a clean slate. That way, he'd be out again and he could meet up with Paul and they could see what drink they could get hold of and find somewhere to crash for the long night.

Naturally enough, the officers became angry when they found out that it wasn't possible that he could have committed the robbery, or even caused a mess with those paint cans. The facts didn't fit at all. Wayne didn't like to see people angry, but it happened. He was told he was wasting police time and knew it was best to nod along as, in that way, he'd be out again and he could meet up with Paul and they could see what drink they could get hold of and find somewhere... The loop played out in Wayne's mind over and over. Things happened, best just to go along with them.

There was anger this time too, the day after that lady had been killed, but it was quite serious, Wayne could sense that. There was a tension in the room and it wasn't right. Where was Paul? He would wait for him, he always did. The police were talking a lot about Paul, they were sure he was involved in something, but it was hard to keep track. If he went along with what they had to say, that might be best. Then the questions would stop and he could get some rest and maybe something to eat. There was talk of letting him out on bail if all went well.

Wayne Darvell was twenty-four. His life had never really

begun and now it was about to take a ruinous turn. No one will ever learn the full nature of what happened during the police questioning at that time. By the time it ended, though, not only would Wayne and Paul Darvell face life sentences, but the reputation of South Wales CID would be severely damaged.

Even after two decades have passed, the police refuse to discuss what happened during the initial investigation and why the decision was made to pursue the Darvells for the murder of Sandra Phillips. All attempts to talk about the original investigation are blocked due to 'the ongoing nature' of the case today. There is a reluctance to rake over old ground – understandable to an extent, but the question remains. The police must have had a sound reason, other than the Darvells' proximity to the Private Shop during the day of the murder, to pursue the brothers. Neither had previous convictions for the type of sexual assault and violence that Sandra Phillips had suffered. In town, the rumour spread that the Darvells were simply in the wrong place at the wrong time.

Nevertheless, they were charged and on 19 June 1986, almost a year after their arrest, Wayne and Paul Darvell were convicted of the rape and murder of Sandra Phillips. They had pleaded not guilty but during the course of the thirty-two-day trial, the police had produced a statement, signed by Wayne Darvell, that described how he watched as Paul killed Sandra. It was enough to secure the conviction from the jury of nine men and three women and the brothers began life sentences.

The community in Swansea was divided over the guilt of the Darvells. At the time, the sense of collective shock was considerable. The sight of Sandra's daughter returning to school to sit her final exams provided a particularly poignant moment in the aftermath of her mother's murder. Seeing her courage brought home to many people the burden of grief the family faced. Everyone wanted the killer caught and the speed with which the police acted brought a measure of relief. Even if it would soon begin to ring hollow.

In January 1989, the BBC's *Rough Justice* programme voiced concerns about the safety of the Darvells' conviction. There was sufficient doubt raised in the documentary for the then Home Secretary, Kenneth Baker, and the Chief Constable of South Wales Police to request that Assistant Chief Constable Keith Portlock of Devon and Cornwall Constabulary reinvestigate the case. As a result of this enquiry, the Home Secretary referred the case to the Court of Appeal.

The wheels of British justice move slowly, though, even when the impetus is there to right a wrong. It was not until 15 July 1992 that the Darvells were released, but that was far from the end of the matter for South Wales Police. The Lord Chief Justice, Lord Taylor, described the investigation that led to the Darvells' conviction as 'thoroughly disquieting'.

The Crown Prosecution Service (CPS) did charge three policemen for conspiring to pervert the course of justice: former head of CID Alun Thomas, DCI Jeff Jones and DC Michael Collins. Ironically, Thomas and Jones had been commended by the original trial judge for their 'painstaking work' in the Sandra Phillips investigation.

The three officers now faced their own trial at Chester Crown Court. The main charge raised by the prosecution was that Wayne Darvell's confession had been 'redrafted'. DC Michael Collins was the officer who took notes as Wayne confessed, but a prosecution witness, forensic expert Beryl

Morgan, said that his police notebooks had been 'extensively rewritten and modified'. One page alone, page 62, a page that described a sexual act inflicted on Sandra, appeared to have been rewritten four times.

Beryl Morgan was using a technique called ESDA (Electro-Static Detection Apparatus) but perhaps the most damaging evidence came from a far simpler source. One of DC Collins's notebooks seized by the Devon and Cornwall Police had been signed as completed in June 1985 and yet the batch of books it was from was not issued for police use until August. It appeared that the police had redrafted material to suit their case, and as Wayne's confession was so central to the police investigation, it blew apart the conviction.

The three officers were found not guilty of conspiring to pervert the course of justice on 30 June 1994, some nine years after Sandra's murder. Their defence counsel argued persuasively that if there had been any breakdown in procedure, it was done unintentionally and not with the intent to deceive.

Wayne Darvell maintained that he had been led and prompted during his confession and the original interviews took place before the Police and Criminal Evidence Act (PACE) had been rolled out. This vital piece of legislation was introduced in 1984 and Code E of the act specifies that there should be a tape recording of every police interview and that it 'be carried out openly to instil confidence in its reliability as an impartial and accurate record of the interview'. PACE was not in use during the Sandra Phillips investigation.

With the police officers acquitted, to the relief of their families, the question of who killed Sandra remained. Indeed, there was more at stake than procedure during the investigation. In the pursuit of the Darvells, valuable details were overlooked. Details that paint a picture of the real killer.

After the release of the Darvells, the case was immediately reinvestigated. DCS Phil Jones headed the new enquiry and before long newspapers were widely reporting a possible link to one Michael Pearman. Pearman had been jailed in 1985 for the attempted murder of a thirty-seven-year-old woman from Port Talbot, only nine miles from Swansea. He had bludgeoned the woman with an axe and stabbed her six times in the neck but, fortunately, she survived. Pearman had been living in Swansea and the police must have hoped that they would have a sudden and dramatic breakthrough. But it was not to be. After interviews with Pearman in prison, no link to the Sandra Phillips murder could be established.

So the Darvells had been embroiled in a major murder enquiry, wrongly convicted, imprisoned and released – and yet in some respects nothing had changed. They still struggled to maintain a grip on sobriety and, despite a payout of £80,000 each, soon took to living on the streets once more. It would not be the end of their dealings with the police either and years later, Wayne Darvell would be imprisoned again, this time for indecent assault.

It is worth looking again at the evidence against the Darvells as within it, a picture of the real perpetrator of the crime emerges. At the original trial, the jury arrived at a guilty verdict based on more than Wayne Darvell's confession. Both brothers had been spotted on Dillwyn Street; one witness was an off-duty police officer, who saw them standing opposite the Private Shop. There can be no doubt that they were on the street at several points during the day, and crucially the off-duty officer saw Paul Darvell holding a can. This was an important detail, of course, as after the murder petrol had been used to douse the scene.

The police also produced a witness who worked at a nearby car body repair shop. He stated that Wayne Darvell had walked in and asked for a can 'to put petrol in' at between 10.45am and 11.15am on the day of the murder. He positively identified Wayne and was sure that Paul was also waiting outside on the forecourt. He also gave an accurate description of Wayne's clothing at the time – dark trousers, a dark jacket and a white shirt.

A final piece of damning evidence came when the police cleaned the patrol car Wayne had travelled in after his arrest. There, under the back seat he'd sat on, they found a gold stud earring with traces of blood on it. Sandra Phillips owned earrings that matched the stud and the detectives were sure that Wayne had tried to dispose of it during the journey to the police station. Unfortunately, there was not enough blood present to make an identification of whose blood was on the stud, though the possibility that it had been taken from Sandra after the attack could not be ruled out. When Wayne's confession was read out to the court, it rounded off the prosecution's case and the brothers were found guilty.

Let's now look at each of those points in turn. The Darvells were known to hang around the Private Shop and had even tried to steal from the store in the past. But they had also been spotted at several other points in the town during the day of the murder, including St Mary's Church, where they'd talked to the vicar as they often did. Reverend Jonathan Barker said that he had spoken to the brothers at the start of the day, around 9.30am, but also later, between 11.30am and 12.30pm. This is significant, as the time of Sandra's death was believed to be shortly after 11am. A warehouseman had called the store at 10.45am and spoken with Sandra but could not get an answer some fifteen minutes or so later. It was likely that this was the time of the attack.

St Mary's is about a ten-minute walk from Dillwyn Street. Conceivably, the brothers could have left the store at 11.30am and strolled over to talk to Reverend Barker. But what of their clothes? Forensic scientists are adamant that an attack on the scale inflicted on Sandra would have meant extensive blood staining on the perpetrator's clothing. Both brothers had been wearing black trousers, Wayne wearing a white shirt and Paul a blue shirt and jacket. Their clothes were examined after their arrest and no DNA evidence linking them to Sandra Phillips was found. One forensic expert went further, stating that either he had not been given the clothing worn by the Darvells at the time of the murder or they didn't do it.

The police changed tack and said that the brothers had simply disposed of their clothing and changed. But it is unlikely. No one at the SASH hostel was allowed back in their rooms until 5.30pm and no one saw the Darvells carrying around a bag or spare clothes during the day. That scenario would also rely on the brothers having a sufficient grasp of the likely outcome of an attack – in essence, their actions would have been premeditated. And if they'd planned to commit a serious crime, why would they not have carried something to disguise themselves, a mask for example, as both were well-known faces about town? In fact, not only did this murder fly in the face of the Darvells' previous felonies, but it contradicted the police assertion that this was a robbery which had suddenly erupted out of control.

What about the petrol can? The car repair employee was sure Wayne had asked him for a can and the off-duty policeman had seen Paul holding a can too. The police officer was in a car and caught a glimpse of something in Paul's hand; indeed, he had been walking around the town holding an item – but it was actually a large novelty radio in the shape of a can. Crucially, on the same day a Jet garage employee had sold £2 worth of petrol in a can to someone, but was not able to identify them. Pre-CCTV, the police could not be sure of finding out who this was. Also, Wayne had helped a motorist who'd run out of petrol the day before the murder, probably hoping to be rewarded financially by showing a willingness to help, and the car body repairman could simply have been mistaken about the date.

As for the earring, there was too little for the forensic techniques of the day to establish what blood group it came from, let alone whether it belonged to Sandra. Gold studs are very common and as the police vehicle had carried other detainees in the days after the murder, it can't be established for certain that it was Wayne who dropped the earring.

As Wayne's confession later came into question too, the prosecution case effectively unravelled. It is at this point that the original evidence yields vital clues – and once more, clothing is key.

The police had suggested that the Darvells must have changed their clothes and yet it seems highly unlikely that they would have had the opportunity or the wherewithal to do so. Crucially, clothing had a part to play in the crime scene but it was evidence not raised at the trial. On the day of her murder, Sandra was wearing a cream checked skirt and a pink blouse. It was on her blouse that Forensics found a blood mark, an imprint in blood of another fabric. Sandra's ribs were broken, probably as her assailant knelt on her chest with considerable force. It left a partial imprint and that allowed the material to be identified; it was denim. Sandra's attacker had been wearing jeans. The Darvells both wore black slacks made of a different fabric.

Sandra's clothing revealed other vital clues. A small number of hairs were found on them that belonged neither to her or the Darvells.

On a more disturbing level, perhaps the biggest single piece of incriminating evidence was a partial bloody palm print that was visible on the wall above where Sandra died. Forensic officers got to work on the print but once it became clear that they were unable to make out enough characteristics to identify a killer, yet enough to show that it could not have belonged to the Darvells, work stopped.

The hand-print could yield nothing more when it was analysed during a reinvestigation of the case years later. It is likely, as with many cases of murder during the 1980s, that the original chemical work carried out to try and enhance the print inadvertently destroyed any intrinsic DNA.

What do other details from the crime scene reveal? Sandra's watch, not an expensive piece, was taken, as was her Williams & Glyn bank card, but not the cheque book that was also in her purse. If this was a straightforward robbery, the police are sure that it would have been taken too. The till was opened at 11.02am, a silent witness to what was unfolding in the store, but no sale was registered. It is possible that the till was opened so any cash could be taken but, again, other aspects of the crime indicate that this was not simply an ordinary robbery that spiralled out of control. This was a murder driven by ferocious sexual violence.

Other items missing from the shop included Sandra's set of keys and the handset from the telephone receiver in the shop. They have never been recovered. The pathologist who examined Sandra believed that the handset could well have been used to attack her, but it was clear that another weapon had also been used. Small shards of wood were found in the shop as well as on Sandra herself; she could have been hit with an item such as a wooden chair or table leg. There was no sign of broken furniture at the shop, so it is likely that the weapon was brought to the store by the murderer. Again, the weapon has never been recovered.

If these clues give us some insight into how events unfolded during the murder, it is important to try once more to pin down the time frame. The last customer to come forward to the police was in the store at 10.15am; he chatted to Sandra and left without purchasing anything. The warehouseman called at 10.45am and spoke with Sandra; she seemed unperturbed and they talked about stock issues. Either the killer was there at this point on an ordinary Friday morning, or he was about to enter the shop.

At 11.02am, the till was opened but no sale rang up. At 11.15am, the police learned that a man passed the shop and said that the door was locked. Asked to explain what he was doing there at that time, he explained that he was walking his dog and 'leaned on the door to remove a stone from his shoe' when he noticed that the door was locked. In reality, he was probably a customer, as leaning against a door seems an unlikely thing to do – why not just lean against the wall?

We know the door had been locked, as by 1.45pm area manager Anthony Williams had to return to his van to find the spare set of keys to open it. By then, the scene was drenched in petrol – the shop owner next door was aware of the smell. So at some point after 11am, the killer was inside the shop. Did the dog-walker disturb him? Did the attempt to open the door halt the attack and stop the murderer from setting the shop alight? Perhaps the attacker feared that a fire would attract immediate action. Perhaps he reasoned that petrol would be enough to chemically contaminate the scene and that he should now make good his escape.

Walking out of the back of the shop leads on to several alleyways that link the terraced streets. Some of the streets have long been a mix of homes and commercial units, and at the back of Dillwyn Street there is even an alleyway that widens to form an area where some employees leave their cars. It is not that obvious from the street, but if it was known to the killer it would be the perfect place to leave a vehicle to step into and drive away.

The police have conducted thousands of interviews and taken hundreds of statements; more than 160 sets of fingerprints were taken from the scene alongside scores of items from the shop. By the time that Albert Kirby reviewed the case in 2003, key suspects had emerged. Kirby was the Senior Investigating Officer in the murder of Jamie Bulger and he recommended a reinvestigation be launched, as there were significant sightings of three men the police wanted to speak to. They are as follows:

> White male, 25/26 years old (would now be 49/50 years old), 5ft 10in tall, athletic build, dark brown curly hair with a fringe cut over the ears but not shoulder length, pale face which was clean shaven. This person was seen talking to Sandra in the doorway to the shop and this is the last reported sighting of Sandra Phillips alive.

> White male, 35/40 years old (would now be 56/64+ years old), 5' tall, portly build, described as smartly dressed and wearing a trilby-style hat. This man was carrying a brown parcel under his arm when he left the shop and is believed to be the last customer served by Sandra Phillips.

> White male, late fifties early sixties (would now be in his eighties), hefty/stout build, about 16 stone, approximately 5ft 6in, neat short grey hair, wearing three-quarter length coat, dark clothing. This man was seen leaving the shop and a witness believes he locked the door from the outside.

The first two men were customers but despite repeated appeals, including a plea from Sandra's daughter on *Crimewatch*, for the men to come forward, they have failed to do so. It could well be that any initial reluctance to admit to family and friends that they used the Private Shop has become more resolute over the years. Why come forward now? Would it not look suspicious? It is probable that they are entirely innocent, but their memories of the day, even over a quarter of a century later, could still prove invaluable. It is often seemingly mundane and inconsequential details that lead to the identity of the real suspect. Had they seen anyone in the store that day? Anyone waiting and watching?

The third suspect may well prove crucial. An employee of Welsh Water was walking down Dillwyn Street on the day of the murder when he noticed a man in his fifties or sixties trying to lock the door of the Private Shop. Odd thing to do in the middle of the morning, he thought. Looking at his watch, he noticed it was about 11.15am. The man's clothing did not appear to be stained with blood, but as he wore a three-quarter-length coat and had his back to the witness, any such stains could easily be missed.

There might be an entirely innocent explanation, of course. Perhaps, like the dog-walker, this man was just trying the door. But any ordinary customer might turn a handle or rattle the door – it's unlikely that they'd fumble with the lock. Could this be the killer, already disturbed by the dog-walker trying to get into the shop? Had he pulled on his coat and taken Sandra's keys to lock the shop behind him? There again, surely the killer would have locked the door from the inside, and left at the rear of the shop?

The killer would have needed a large coat or bag, as items had been taken from Sandra's bag and the telephone handset was missing along with a long wooden implement used in the attack. This was mid-June, a heavy coat should have marked the man out in the street, but no other witnesses came forward with a sighting of someone acting in a suspicious manner. It would be easy to walk away from the city centre, heading down Oxford Street towards Little Gam Street or down Western Street. One man was even spotted running down Western Street that morning at around the time of the murder, but the witness believed that he was only in his twenties.

Bearing all this in mind, it is easy to see why the trail is so hard to pick up for any investigation team after all these years. Are they looking for a man in his fifties or his eighties? Is the perpetrator even alive now? Witness accounts are notoriously sketchy and with so much time having elapsed, it is doubtful that anyone has anything new to recall unless it is specific and incriminatory. The police are sure that someone knows the suspect; someone will have seen a change in behaviour in someone they know and may well still be protecting their identity.

As Detective Superintendent Simon Clarke, heading a new investigation, says: 'There may be a good reason why these persons have not come forward – whether they were in relationships and may have found it embarrassing, or for other personal reasons.' The hope exists that over the years, the killer has felt the need to confide in someone about the murder. DS Clarke believes that someone has been told, even if they did not know the killer at the time of the murder. He says: 'If that is the case, I would ask them to examine their consciences, think of the family of the victim and come forward with what they know.'

The wall of silence remains in place, but the team have not given up hope. In 2005, they hoped for a forensic breakthrough when it became apparent that a wooden partition built in the shop after the murder may have helped preserve evidence left by the killer. Painstaking work was carried out behind the false wall in the hope that new DNA material would emerge. It wasn't the crucial step the team was looking for, but it raised the profile of the case once again.

The killer was still out there somewhere. So why had he not struck again? Men who sexually assault and murder will have built a pattern of abuse and an escalating path of violence. This type of offender cannot control his violent fantasy life or his desire to act on his evil impulses. A murder this extreme may have been the first one the perpetrator carried out, but it is highly unlikely that it was his first act of sexual and physical violence and equally unlikely that it was his last. If he stops, it is because he is either imprisoned or dead.

Later that same year, it seemed that perhaps a prisoner in Yorkshire could prove the link needed. Robert Black was a serial rapist and killer who had been imprisoned in 1994 for the murders of Susan Maxwell, Caroline Hogg and Sarah Harper. He had a long history of sexual violence; as a van driver delivering posters, he had travelled all over the UK. After his arrest, police uncovered a vast collection of pornography and photographs taken by Black himself. One of them featured a phone similar to the one used to attack and kill Sandra Phillips. Black had confessed to a long-held obsession with inserting items into his anus and among the photographs, pictures were found that he'd taken of himself: one showed a telephone-handset hanging out of him, yet another, a table leg. He said he took them because he wanted to know 'how much he could insert into himself'.

Clearly, the items were significant to the Sandra Phillips investigation, but there were too many key differences in the profile of Black as a killer. Sarah Maxwell had been eleven when she was abducted, Caroline Hogg was five and Sarah Harper was ten years old. In the main, serial rapists tend to stick to a certain fantasy and Black had a long history of targeting young girls, not women. Black abducted children; even his attempted abduction of a fifteen-year-old girl in 1988 was probably motivated by the fact that the teenager was petite and looked far younger than her years.

His attacks on young girls bore other similarities. They would be taken from public places, usually when riding a bike, held in a van and driven miles away before being attacked and killed, but none bore significant bruising or broken bones. The offender profile simply didn't add up. South Wales Police had to continue their search for Sandra's murderer.

Robert Black does provide other valuable insights into how to track a predatory killer. In many ways, Black's life mirrors that of many dangerous sexual serial attackers. Born in 1947 to a young unmarried woman, no name was entered onto his birth certificate and he was quickly put up for adoption. It was the beginning of an unstable childhood, marred by abuse, that would shape him. Unpopular and bullied at school, he often appeared covered with bruises, but no one in authority intervened to understand why.

By the age of five, he was displaying inappropriate sexual behaviour, hinting at the possibility that he had been abused. His stepfather died and by the time he was eight he was experimenting sexually, inserting objects into himself. He developed an obsession with young girls and, once his stepmother died three years later and he was taken into care, he took part, with two others, in a sexual assault on a girl in care. He was moved to another establishment, where he was sexually abused by a male member of staff over the next two years.

As the years passed, Black took part in over thirty sexual molestations of young girls; he was first caught, aged seventeen, after luring a seven-year-old girl to a derelict building. He strangled her until she passed out and then masturbated over the unconscious body. The girl survived the attack, however, and Black was later charged with 'lewd and libidinous' behaviour. He was not imprisoned and would go on to abuse at least two other girls under the age of ten before he received his first custodial sentence in the late 1960s.

By this point, the pattern of his predatory abuse was long set but very often, parents who discovered what had happened to their daughters were reluctant to go to the police, choosing instead to warn Black off. He moved from town to town and it was not until the late 1980s that police began to piece together evidence against him.

It seems extraordinary now that someone so dangerous to children, and someone who in all likelihood had killed other young girls, was allowed to slip below the radar for so long. And yet it can be argued that sexual offenders did not, and do not, attract tough sentences. An armed robber can expect a sentence of fifteen years, even if no one was seriously injured in the crime. If he commits more than one offence, it is automatically raised to eighteen years. Someone found guilty of rape can expect a sentence of five years. Only if they carry out a campaign of rape on a number of different women or girls would a fifteen-year sentence be thought of as appropriate.

In the 1980s, it was not a widely recognised fact that men like Robert Black are repeat offenders whose use of violence escalates over time. Today, we have a better understanding of what drives men to become serial sexual offenders, we are better at profiling and hopefully better at monitoring. Yet men like Ian Huntley – someone who was a suspect in an act of indecent assault, four acts of underage sex and three rapes – was still able to gain employment in a Soham school as recently as 2001.

The police need to renew their focus on sexual offenders as too often, predators are allowed to slip through the net. Men like John Worboys. From as early as 2002, fourteen women reported a black-cab driver who had drugged and assaulted them yet the attacks remained unlinked until 2008. Chef Kirk Reid had also come to police attention on twelve separate occasions but it took four years before he was arrested for a string of sexual assaults and found guilty in 2009. A serial sexual offender, he had been attacking women for at least twelve years.

The man who assaulted and murdered Sandra Phillips would undoubtedly have a history of sexual violence against women, even if he had not been found guilty in a court of law. So where is this man today? Perhaps he is in prison, awaiting release after serving a sentence for another crime. Perhaps he moved abroad and is now an elderly man, nursing the sick truth of his destructive nature. Wherever he is, somebody knows, someone will have encountered him before. And DNA science advances every day. Even those who've carried on with their lives for decades after committing a serious crime can be caught. Men such as Ronald Castree.

In 2007, Castree was found guilty of sexually assaulting and killing eleven-year-old Lesley Molseed. The young girl, who had learning difficulties, had been abducted, driven to moors near Oldham, attacked and brutally stabbed twelve times. In an eerie parallel to the Sandra Phillips case, the wrong man was arrested and imprisoned for the crime. Stefan Kiszko served sixteen years before he was cleared and released in 1992.

Castree was caught when he was arrested after another sexual assault, this time on an Oldham prostitute, although he was cleared of involvement in that crime. As part of that investigation, a DNA swab was taken and it led his arrest for the murder of Lesley Molseed. Even though the schoolgirl had disappeared some thirty-two years earlier, the chances of the DNA found on the semen of Lesley's underwear belonging to anyone but Castree are a billion to one. Castree is known to have molested at least one other young girl and yet he remained free for over thirty years. But he didn't remain free forever.

The Forensic Science Service are confident that as time goes on, suspects will be found, even beyond the grave. As forensic scientist Jim Fraser says, 'The long arm of the law is getting considerably longer – there's really no hiding place now.' No hiding place. Not behind a three-quarter-length coat, down a back street and out of a city or even through the best part of thirty years.

In 'cold' cases, time was once an enemy. But no longer. As the Forensic Science Service revise over 450 unsolved crimes and techniques are refined and become ever more sensitive to capturing DNA profiles, time is now on the side of justice and the Phillips family.

CHAPTER TWO
JANET BROWN
THE UNSOLVED BREAK-IN

It is the first few hours that matter. Standing at a murder scene, it can even be the first few minutes. No matter the carnage, a picture of the events can swiftly emerge.

Detectives rely on the findings of immensely detailed hard work carried out over the first forty-eight hours of an investigation. If they are thorough, a trail of events takes shape and it leads to a suspect. Take this scenario, for example: a woman working in medical research, in her fifties, doesn't return her family's calls and fails to show up for work. At her parents' insistence, the police make a call to her home and, unable to get an answer, they break in. They find her body, punctured with multiple stab wounds and a jumper tied around her neck.

There is no sign of forced entry and so the first piece of the puzzle is gathered. Other facts are established. She was home alone. She opened the door and so may well have recognised her attacker. The scale of the injuries inflicted means that the perpetrator walked away knowing that he has left his victim for dead. There is no sign of sexual assault. What was the motive for the attack?

At first glance, this could be the outline of the murder of Janet Brown yet this was the scene that greeted detectives called to the home of Dr Barbara Johnston, eleven years after the date of Janet's murder, in 2006. Both were women in their fifties, both had backgrounds in medical research at Oxford University and both were alone at home. But there the similarities end, because the investigation that followed Dr Johnston's murder uncovered a trail that led to her killer. It is worth looking at how he was identified, as it reveals a good deal about how murder cases are approached.

Police procedures are standardised across all forces and are followed to ensure that vital evidence is not missed. The scene is sealed, all necessary forensic studies are made, exhibits are taken away, exhaustive statements are gathered and bank and phone records checked. Each part of the investigation is mapped out and overlays the others and, in doing so, a detailed picture of someone's life and last few hours emerges. 'Show me how someone lived,' says DCI Steve Tolmie, who led the investigation into Dr Johnston's death, 'and I can show you how they will have died.'

The team of officers from Thames Valley Police established that Dr Johnston was comfortably well off, that she recently had the windows replaced on her flat and that there was a team of four men working on her property in the weeks leading to her death. There was no sign of a forced entry at the property so it was likely that Dr Johnston recognised the perpetrator and opened her door herself. Later that day, withdrawals were made from her bank account using her card at a cashpoint. After an attempt to withdraw £300 was refused, two separate withdrawals of £200 were made successfully. Someone had Dr Johnston's card and PIN.

Dr Johnston had been subjected to terrible violence. She had been beaten and stabbed a total of forty-nine times; some of the cuts were shallow, others deeper. Someone had tortured her and officers suspected they had done so to force her to reveal her bank details.

Over the next three days, DCI Tolmie's team found out that one of the glaziers had been made redundant by the window company three weeks before Dr Johnston's death. This man, Michael Humphries, had mounting debts. His Peugeot 206 van was picked up by two traffic cameras entering Oxford from the direction of where he lived. An hour later, it was filmed again, this time at a petrol station near Dr Johnston's flat and where the first of the £200 cash withdrawals were made. Although the point at which cash was withdrawn was not filmed, there was no CCTV footage of Dr Johnston visiting the garage that day. Humphries also bought tequila, cigarettes and paid the overdue rental fee on his van.

Police were able to piece together a sequence of events and identify an all-too-common impulse for the attack, as DCI Steve Tolmie says: 'Humphries' motive was money and greed.' Michael Humphries was tried and found guilty at Oxford Crown Court in December 2006 and jailed for thirty years.

What happened to Dr Johnston was a salutary reminder to women everywhere that they are still at risk even in their own homes. The case was all the more poignant as Barbara Johnston had only returned to the UK, after many years working in New Zealand, to help care for her elderly parents.

She'd arrived back in Oxford in 2005 and may well have read about Janet Brown's case. Her story had been widely covered in the press once more as it marked a decade since her brutal murder. Her family had made a fresh appeal for help in catching her killer and, at the same time, DCI Steve Tolmie had been tasked with reviewing the case.

Having met with the family, DCI Tolmie was well aware that no matter the length of time that elapses, the family still bears a heavy burden of grief. It is made harder still if the killer remains at large. Thames Valley Police remain committed to finding the murderer, but even with advances made in forensics every year, picking up the trail after ten years is far from easy.

Yet every detective also faces cold cases with a glimmer of optimism. Fresh eyes may spot something. New leads can surface. And so the file is picked up and questions are raised, the first and most obvious being: why was Janet Brown killed?

Motive is important. It is as essential to understand why someone was killed as it is to discover how they were killed, if you are attempting to pick up the trail a suspect leaves. Often, motive becomes immediately apparent. Greed is a common trigger, another is rage as a relationship breaks down, evidenced by the fact that two women a week are killed by a violent partner. If you are a murder victim, you are likely to know your killer; if you don't, it is likely your killer is driven by greed or sexual violence.

Dr Johnston fell victim to a man driven by greed. Yet even with all the available facts gathered and hundreds of police hours dedicated to solving the crime, DCI Tolmie was about to discover that Janet Brown's case didn't seem to fit in anywhere at all. It remains a genuine mystery.

Few cases produce so many strands with so few suspects. At the time of Janet's death in April 1995, the investigation was led by Detective Superintendent Mick Short, an experienced officer from Thames Valley Police. Yet thirteen years later, the same questions that faced Detective Superintendent Short's team over the first few days of the enquiry remain unanswered.

The original investigation quickly built up a picture of Janet and the way she lived her life. They learned that she was born in January 1944 in Southampton and was an only child. She grew up on the Isle of Wight and after leaving school, trained as a nurse at St George's Hospital in Tooting, London. It was in London, aged twenty-two, that she met Grahaem Brown and four years later they married. Grahaem became an army doctor and their early married life saw a good deal of travel with time spent on overseas postings.

Throughout her life, Janet was well respected. She was generous with her time, kind to friends and colleagues and clearly devoted to her three children, Zara, Ben and Roxanne, all born within a few years of each other. Like any mum of three, Janet's life was busy but no matter where they were posted, she worked hard to make sure that her children always enjoyed a happy home environment. By 1985, Grahaem was ready to leave the army and take up a role in civilian life, working for the pharmaceutical company Glaxo, and it allowed the family to settle in the quiet village of Radnage.

Radnage immediately inspires a sense of safety and security. It is an ancient village, tracing its origins back to the twelfth century, and is tucked away in the picturesque Chiltern Hills. Although quiet and unspoilt, Radnage is still close enough to High Wycombe, Oxford and the M40 into London to attract commuters. Affluent professionals are drawn to the village not just because of its good road links but also because of the many period properties and a genuine sense of privacy.

Those who grow up in a village will know that a quiet setting does not necessarily mean a quiet acceptance of newcomers. Villages don't always warm to 'outsiders', but Radnage avoids the claustrophobic elements of village life as it has no 'centre'. There is no village green with a church, post office and pub to act as the heart of the community. Instead, Radnage is spread over several hamlets in the valley, linked by winding country roads. They have names that hint to a lost and simple past: Bennett End, Green End and Town End. Perhaps the most notable landmark is the church, St Mary's, yet even that stands alone on Church Lane, on the way to neighbouring Bledlow Ridge.

Grahaem's career was well rewarded and they were fortunate to find Hall Farm. As the name suggests, it is a former farmhouse and is an impressive property set in eleven acres with outbuildings attached. The pretty wisteria-covered home seemed to have everything a family could wish for. That is certainly what Grahaem and Janet Brown hoped and once they moved in, they were relieved to see how quickly the children settled in at the farm and their schools in High Wycombe.

Janet went back to work at the end of 1991. The children were more independent and Janet felt that with less demands on her time at home, she would enjoy returning to nursing.

She began working as a research nurse at John Radcliffe Hospital and that led on to a project at Oxford University's department of public health and primary care. The department is part of the University's Medical Sciences Division and employs around 150 people working in teaching and research. Although not based at one of the many picturesque and ancient buildings of Oxford, it is a prestigious department with a worldwide reputation for research. Janet was working on a project examining the health of women who had undergone treatment for infertility. In vitro fertilisation is not only an expensive procedure, but is also invasive. During a course of IVF, ovaries are hyper-stimulated through the use of fertility drugs, which could imply long-term health implications for women. The research underway at Oxford was just one of the studies designed to establish just what, if any, the risks were to women hoping to conceive artificially.

Janet enjoyed her work and was well liked by her co-workers. But while work was proving more and more rewarding, her marriage was faltering. Grahaem and Janet had been married for over twenty years, but by the early 1990s Grahaem's new role at chemicals firm Ciba-Geigy Ltd meant that a good deal of his time was being spent abroad. Despite their best intentions, the couple had drifted apart. Their focus had always been on providing for the children, but with Zara leaving for college and the other two children likely to follow, it was hard for Grahaem and Janet to avoid the feeling that the marriage had run its course.

There is enormous sadness when any marriage begins to fail. They'd worked hard for all they'd achieved, yet like many couples facing up to the realities of life in an 'empty nest', a shared past no longer seemed enough to sustain them for the future. Both accepted that the marriage was at an end.

This was no longer about just about two people, though. Grahaem had met someone else. While Janet was not angry – they had been effectively living separate lives for some time – it was still a big step to have to acknowledge that her husband had moved on. There was no one else in Janet's life.

The children were aware that their parents were planning to end the marriage. By this point, Ben was at Exeter University and with Grahaem away too, Roxanne grew ever closer to her mum. It was a time of sadness, but practical decisions had to be made. Grahaem lived and worked in Switzerland with his new partner but would return on alternate weekends to see the children. Hall Farm would be sold and Janet would have the chance to buy somewhere for herself, still close enough to work and to allow Roxanne to finish her A-Levels at Wycombe High School.

It was a taxing time but in quiet moments, Janet was relieved to see how well her children were doing. This was to be a new chapter in her life and at least she was not being faced with the urgent need to move. Grahaem and Janet had decided jointly that they could take their time and see if a buyer came forward with a good offer. The house had been on the market for almost a year and they were ready to accept an offer of £345,000. One of the outbuildings, used as a garage, needed some work on the roof. A local builder, Nick Marshall, was employed to replace the red brick tiles, a fairly minor project, and as Janet worked in the daytime there should be very little disturbance.

It was an ordinary Monday evening in April. Grahaem was

away and Janet was planning what to prepare for the evening meal when Roxanne called with some good news. A friend had passed her driving test and, to celebrate, her family wanted to know if Roxanne would join them for a meal out in neighbouring Marlow. Janet thought it a lovely idea and looked forward to a quiet night in alone.

Being at home alone as a mother has its advantages. There is something indulgent about a night in with the TV, eating what and when you want and knowing that no one will ask where a favourite skirt is or whether you can arrange to pick them up: it is its own kind of pleasure. Yet it is only a pleasure if you know that the next day the rhythm of family life and all its demands will return. The next day, a Tuesday, should have meant Roxanne would be back at Hall Farm, the builders would arrive and life would plough on as normal. None of us know the moment that everyday life will be snatched away, few of us guess at its fragility. Life for the Brown family was about to be irrevocably shattered.

The last person to talk to Janet was a friend of Roxanne. She called a little after 8pm to speak to Roxanne, unaware that she was out in Marlow. She and Janet chatted briefly. At around 8.30pm, Grahaem phoned from Switzerland, but no one picked up. At 9pm, Nick Marshall called with a question about work on the garage, but again, there was no reply.

No one knows what unfolded within the space of just two hours after Janet last spoke to Roxanne's friend. Except two people: Janet Brown and her killer.

Hall Farm is a big property, but it was home and Janet had always felt safe there, even when alone. It had an alarm and even a personal alarm that could be activated from upstairs, although there had never been cause to use it. But it was set off at some point that night: a passing motorist heard the external alarm ringing after 10pm, although not later that same night on his return past the property. The external alarm was designed to ring for twenty minutes and then cut out. The alarm inside would ring until someone stopped it manually. It rang all night.

Janet was found the following morning. Builder Nick Marshall and his teenage son had arrived at 8am to resume work on the outbuilding. At first they did not hear the alarm as they unloaded the van for the day, then Mr Marshall became aware that it was sounding from inside the house. He knocked and when no one came to the front door, he looked through the window. There, at the bottom of the stairs, he saw Janet lying naked in a pool of blood.

Although this was only fourteen years ago, mobile phones were not yet in common use and Mr Marshall had to drive back to his own house to call the police. They arrived shortly afterwards and the house was sealed. Forensics began to process the scene and everything was documented, from the broken glass formation to the blood patterns on the walls. A fingertip search of the house and grounds began and over 1,200 exhibits were taken away.

Typically, it takes at least three days of painstaking work to examine a murder scene and the team were hopeful that a picture would begin to emerge to explain what had happened and why. To the detectives at the scene, however, a series of baffling questions were immediately apparent.

Most of us would hope that an alarm would alert

neighbours, though the homes nearest to Hall Farm were set too far apart to hear it. How had the alarm been set off? Had someone triggered it by breaking in to the house, or had Janet activated it herself at the sound of breaking glass?

Glass was broken. It was the central pane of the patio doors, set to the side of the property but out of sight from the road. Tape had been stuck to the glass – an attempt, perhaps, to dampen the sound made when hitting it, or to dislodge the pane without it shattering and crashing to the floor.

If this was a burglary, it was already far from a routine approach. If glass-cutters are used, only a space small enough to slip a hand in and undo a lock is cut. The attempt on the patio door was cut large enough to walk through. Only one pane had been cut, the double glazing meant that the second pane was simply smashed through. What really puzzled the investigators was that more glass appeared outside than inside. They could not rule out that the door may have been smashed from inside the house. That would suggest that it was done once the perpetrator was already inside and perhaps chose to smash the second pane to make it look like a break-in. If that was the case, though, how did he get in?

The idea that the intruder had chosen to break in with tape, glass-cutter and through double glazing didn't feel right to police. The windows would have been an easier option for most burglars. In addition, the vast majority of house break-ins happen not at night but in the daytime, typically around 3pm, when thieves expect most households to be empty. Thieves do no look for confrontation; they look for an easy entry and easy escape route, focusing on valuables that are easily portable. And if it was a burglary at Hall Farm that night, the first of a series of questions arose. Not only was the thief not deterred by the alarm going off, he took nothing of value from the property.

Instead, someone got in to Hall Farm and confronted Janet. She routinely went to bed early and it is probable that she was woken by a disturbance. It could have been as early as 8.20pm, as Grahaem called around ten minutes later and Janet did not pick up. The intruder may already have been holding his terrified wife captive. When her body was found, she was still wearing all her jewellery, items she'd usually remove, so perhaps she had not yet gone to bed. Yet the duvet was turned down and there was an imprint of a body on the sheets. Perhaps he forced her onto the bed? Perhaps he forced her to put on her jewellery? Incongruous details were mounting up.

Janet was found at the bottom of the stairs, so she may have walked down or may have been ordered downstairs. The police had a handful of certain facts. Mrs Brown had been bound, her arms were handcuffed behind her back, she was naked and her mouth was heavily taped, with the same tape used on the patio window. Restrained, defenceless, placed face down, she was then savagely attacked.

A long, heavy, blunt instrument was used to inflict severe head injuries, the blows reigning down from two different angles. This could mean that more than one attacker was involved, but it is just as likely that it was a lone assailant who simply changed his body position. Unable to breathe because of the tape, Janet died from a combination of asphyxia and traumatic head injuries. Beyond these facts, the who and why of the situation were still very unclear.

Grahaem was informed of his wife's death and subjected to intense questioning. Understandably, he was very distressed and only gradually came to realise that he was a suspect himself. But it became apparent that although their marriage was at an end, Grahaem had no reason to wish his wife harm. There was no financial gain to be had from her death, the separation was amicable and he had been living a separate life in Switzerland for some time. Interpol checked and confirmed his alibi. Grahaem was cleared of suspicion and continued to cooperate fully with the police at all times.

With no clear suspect, theories began to sprout, only to fail to take root. The possibility that Janet was victim of a contract killing was raised, but then ruled out. Contract killers aim to kill efficiently and within the briefest period of time, they do not stay inside a property, restrain and repeatedly hit their target, as they run a greater risk of being caught. The manner of Janet's death – a hands-on and rage-filled attack – suggested that it was personally motivated.

The team once again examined the details of Janet's personal life. She was close to her daughters and friends and had not given any indication that she had become involved in a new relationship. If Janet had become intimate with someone, her friends are certain that she would have told them, even if she wanted to keep the early stages of a love affair from her children.

Phone records from home and her office supported the fact that no one new had entered her life. If the murder happened today, mobile phones and personal computers could also be checked, both of which can be invaluable in uncovering any private preoccupations. As it stood, the police had to accept that Janet had not become involved in a new and possibly dangerous relationship.

Perhaps, then, an unknown figure had been watching her? Again, family and friends are certain that if Janet had felt that she was being watched or followed, she would have told someone. A few years earlier, she had become involved in a Neighbourhood Watch scheme after a few local properties had been hit by house break-ins and she would not have hesitated to contact the police if she felt unsafe. Police checked that there were no other similar crimes in Radnage or the surrounding areas, checking all aggravated burglaries and assaults to see if there were any noticeable similarities, but drew a blank.

The fact that there had been no sexual assault surprised some involved in the investigation as the attack could fit the profile of an opportunist. Serial rapists do not require a personal link to their victim and the fact that Janet was home alone would have been sufficient reason to attack. This would go some way to explaining why she seemed to have been targeted out of the blue; but she had not been sexually assaulted. In addition, an opportunist would have been deterred by similar factors to burglars. There was an alarm at the property and two cars in the driveway, suggesting that more than one person could have been at home. There was even a 'Beware of the Guard Dog' sign and the assailant would not have known that the family dog had died a year earlier.

The murder scene continued to haunt investigators. Janet did not fall down the stairs or suffer an accidental death, perhaps pushed over by an unsuspecting thief. This was an orchestrated, prolonged and terrifying attack on a defenceless woman. Despite weeks of detailed investigation, however, no openings emerged.

News of Janet's murder spread quickly and upset the community a great deal. Radnage was thought of as a safe enclave and many locals assumed that Janet had become the victim of a botched robbery attempt. But the details at the scene gave lie to that. Detectives knew this did not fit with the profile of a burglary. Thieves don't take handcuffs to a robbery and strip their victims. The house had not been turned upside down in the hunt for valuables. The one focus had been Janet, a desire to humiliate and control her. It had to be personal.

The team began to split in their response as to who could be responsible, a worrying sign in any investigation. It was suggested that Janet had simply heard an intruder and came downstairs to investigate. Yet what would be the first reaction of a woman alone at night who thinks she hears a break-in? The overwhelming majority would call the police or a neighbour. Few would leave the room; most would lock the door if possible.

There was a panic alarm in Janet's room, which she may well have set off. It seems highly unlikely that she would choose to go downstairs naked to investigate the noise. Clothing yourself is instinctive, a protective measure against what you might find. Detectives found two dressing gowns on the back of the door and so it is unlikely that Janet would have left the room without putting one on. But it is plausible to imagine that she was ordered out of bed and then moved downstairs. It is possible that she set off the alarm and waited, terrified, only for her attacker to open her bedroom door. Janet preferred to sleep naked. Her attacker would then have kept her that way – her vulnerability and stress rising to extreme levels, she would be easier to control.

If this was the sequence of events, why was she taken downstairs? There were no notable valuables at the property – a safe, for example, that Janet could be forced to reveal or open. It seems more likely that the attacker enjoyed Janet's vulnerability and moving her around the house was one way to demonstrate it. The pathologist's report also revealed that Janet's ankles had been bound at some point in her ordeal, but not at the point when she was found. Changing handcuffs takes time and may give the victim the chance to fight back, so the motivation to play with Janet in this way and render her helpless must have overridden any desire to minimise the risk of being caught.

With Janet unable to move, naked and aware that no neighbour had heard the alarm, the attacker then spent some time in Hall Farm. The police discovered this through Roxanne, who had noticed that some items in the house had been moved. To rearrange household objects is an oddly intimate act, demonstrating the intruder's need to exercise control over the space as well as the victim.

Janet must have known her attacker. Yet thousands of words in statements from those that knew her best and all available records suggested that she did not. And so the lines of enquiry came full circle again.

Any hope that Forensics could provide a breakthrough were soon extinguished. All available tests had been run on fingerprints found at the scene, but nothing emerged. Some parts of the scene were too blood-soaked; other partial prints did not reveal anything when exposed to chemicals designed to enhance the findings. There were prints on the light switches, but they were diluted. That meant that the attacker took the time to wash his hands before looking around the house.

One development came when the 'cast-off' blood pattern from the blows inflicted were studied. They revealed that the instrument used to attack Janet was long, such as a chisel. Still, a fingertip search of the property and grounds had not turned up anything the attacker might have abandoned.

There was a man's bathrobe on the floor in a bathroom too. The head height of the shower was raised high, well beyond where the 5ft 4in Janet may have placed it. As the external alarm was not heard until after 10pm, perhaps it had been set off at a later point in the attack too, perhaps when the perpetrator was ready to leave, smashing his way through the patio window to suggest a break-in. The attacker could have even taken a leisurely shower after the attack. The case threw up more possibilities at every examination.

Police appeals were made and a few people came forward to share what they knew with the investigating team. There was frustratingly little to share, though. Some neighbours had not heard the alarm at all; some thought they might have. No one had seen anything or anyone suspicious on Sprig Holly Lane, the road that Hall Farm stands on, yet this seemed the most likely route the attacker took. There was no sign that anyone approached the house on foot through the grounds and only two vehicles were identified as possible leads during the house-to-house enquiries: a brown Ford Escort and another small car, possibly a Metro or a Fiesta.

Those that knew Radnage and the location of Hall Farm

felt that the attacker had to have some knowledge of the area. As Hall Farm was for sale, the team looked closely at all the prospective buyers and when that drew a blank, widened enquiries to newcomers to Radnage in the previous twelve months and any tradesmen working in the area. In total, over 2,700 people were spoken to during the course of the enquiry but as the statements mounted, so did the concern that answers were not forthcoming.

Janet's family were desperate to understand what had happened. Any sudden loss to a family is traumatic but the extreme circumstances of Janet's death were harrowing. It made no sense. Everyone who knew and loved her was faced with the same question: why? They looked to the police for answers. If Janet had been the victim of a serial killer, they would have to accept that she was targeted at random. If her attacker had been known to her, there was hope that he would be caught and brought to justice.

The possibility that Janet was the victim of a serial attacker was examined closely. A profile of the murder was drawn up and the Home Office Large Major Enquiry System (HOLMES) was employed to try and match details with other solved and unsolved murders. HOLMES was a computer-based system set up after the Yorkshire Ripper case. Over a quarter of a million names were logged during that investigation and 30,000 statements taken. Investigations were paper based at the time, and the floor of the enquiry room had to be reinforced due to the sheer weight of files generated by the case.

Any high volume of data is open to misfiling and human error – plus, it becomes impossible for any one officer to read the all statements that stream in. HOLMES was designed to allow officers to input data accurately, retrieve information quickly and make vital links between pieces of seemingly random markers. HOLMES works rather like an Internet search engine: type in 'brown Ford Escort' and the search pulls up the files that contain matching words. Previously, officers had to look for the same piece of information manually. In 1995, the Thames Valley investigation team were able to access any cross-searches they wished to make quickly. If there was a serial killer targeting lone women in the way that Janet had been targeted, the search would throw up similarities.

Other local murder cases were examined and hopes were briefly raised when a link was established with another victim. Dr Michael Meenaghan had been murdered in his home in nearby Blackbird Leys five months before Janet was killed. Like Janet, he had also worked on a medical research project at Oxford University. But there the similarities ended. Dr Meenaghan had been killed by a single shot fired through his kitchen window. It was reported that Dr Meenaghan had been conducting affairs with more than one woman and that his death could have been a revenge killing by an angry spouse or partner; the idea was also floated that the murder could have been a simple case of mistaken identity. Whatever direction that enquiry took, however, it became clear that there was no firm link to Janet Brown's death.

No other cases seemed to provide a link and the investigation started to stutter. The dreadful fear that something had been missed, or something crucial remained unknown, started to trouble the team.

Taking a step back, Dr Paul Britton, a forensic psychologist, was asked to look at the case. Years later, Dr Britton included the case in his book *Picking Up The Pieces*. He provided the team with some insights and even drafted an appeal for *Crimewatch* but ultimately, no progress was made.

The question remained as to why Janet was tormented and killed. It is sometimes of use to look elsewhere at other cases and research carried out by forensic psychologists. Looking at certain studies, some light is shed on the mind-set of serial killers. Patterns and motivations emerge. The behaviour of individual killers changes over years, their behaviour escalates.

Typically, as children, serial and mass killers suffer serious abuse and their fear and rage becomes internalised. They spend hours alone, excluded from the outside world, and an elaborate fantasy world is created. It is a form of escape, where they become the ones that orchestrate pain. They are no longer the victim; now they are in the driving seat. The fantasy sustains their existence for a while, but in time it begins to lose its potency. Slowly, the idea that it could be enacted for real begins to dominate. It is very common for incarcerated serial killers to admit that they tortured animals in their adolescence, in the main targeting neighbourhood cats and dogs. These savage acts satisfy the perpetrators for some time, but the novelty fades and gradually their thoughts turn to human victims.

This behaviour takes years to accumulate. Fred West, for example, had a history of sexual assault long before he turned to ever-worsening acts of sexual violence, torture and murder. It was possible that Janet's attack may not have been one of many acts committed against women, but rather the first act of murder carried out by a burgeoning serial killer. That was why tracking other serious assaults, as well as acts of aggravated burglary, was key to the case.

Experienced officers are also aware that serial killers share another characteristic beyond a compulsion to escalate their acts of violence. They cannot stop. Once the threshold has been crossed, one murder is never enough. They only stop because they are caught or because they die. Serial killers are compelled to repeat their crimes as any plateau and emotional fulfilment they reach after a murder slowly begins to wane. The only way to revisit that sense of excitement and invulnerability is to kill again.

One recent case in Mexico City perfectly illustrates the point. Juana Barraza was abused and neglected by her mother and her rage and desire for retribution escalated to the point where, in the late 1990s, she followed an elderly women back to her home then knocked at the door, posing as someone seeking work as a maid. Once inside, Barraza savagely attacked and murdered the old woman. Yet that was only the start. Police believed that by the time of her arrest, she may have been responsible for the death of forty women. Some of her victims were as old as ninety-two and ultimately, Barraza was convicted of sixteen counts of murder. When asked about why she targeted old women, she merely replied: 'I got angry.' Rage fuels fantasy and the act of murder.

Thames Valley Police were conscious of the fact that the death of Janet Brown could mark the start of a killing career and all efforts to track a suspect were re-doubled. Yet as the months passed, the trail went cold. No other force reported attacks on women that shared similarities with the manner of

Janet Brown's murder. It was as if a killer had arrived and disappeared without trace on a single night at Hall Farm.

The case was not closed, though. It was periodically reviewed and officers waited to see if a link would emerge elsewhere. Two years later, almost to the day, another woman in her fifties who had been at home alone was found bound and beaten to death by an assailant. Carolanne Jackson lived some twenty miles or so away from Radnage, in another village called Woodburn Green. She ran an antique dealership called Kings Chase Antiques from her cottage. But once more, initial similarities did not lead to anything more substantial. In February, two months before her death, Miss Jackson had contacted the police after she spotted a prowler outside her cottage. Two months later someone, possibly with an accomplice, beat her until she revealed how to open the safe in her home, which held a substantial sum of money and jewellery. Although she was bound, she was found fully clothed; the motive seemed clearly to be one of robbery. The intruder she spotted in February may well have been assessing her cottage for security measures and planned the theft after tracking her home.

By the time DCI Steve Tolmie reviewed the case, it was clear that despite the best efforts of Mick Short's team, Janet's family and her community, nothing had emerged that pointed to a suspect. The case appeared on *Crimewatch* and Janet's family again appealed for information from the public. The hope was that with scientific advances in identifying DNA, the forensic work could be reviewed and a profile could be created. It is a strange coincidence that Dr Meenaghan had been an expert in genetic fingerprinting and it was fingerprint evidence that was the particular focus of the review. DCI Tolmie had witnessed huge leaps in forensic science during his years investigating serious crimes and the team were hopeful that a breakthrough was possible.

Yet they were to be disappointed. The chemicals used during the initial investigation that attempted to enhance the fingerprints found had unfortunately destroyed the DNA needed. It was a setback and yet the hope was that the public appeal would still prompt someone to come forward. The reason was simple. As DCI Tolmie said: 'I think there is a high probability the killer lived locally at the time. When the killer returned home he would have been covered in blood. The level of violence was despicable. Whoever he was living with would have had suspicions.'

So many years had elapsed since the murder and yet this time-gap can throw up good things as well as bad. Relationships break down. If anyone was in an abusive relationship with a man they sensed was capable of horrific violence, if they had seen clothes hidden away that were bloodstained, or spotted a change of clothing on the night in question, perhaps their sense of loyalty would have diminished over time. Perhaps someone had broken away from their partner and had come to understand how unfair it was to leave Janet's family lost in anguish for any longer. DCI Tolmie's request was simple: 'Search your soul.'

His team also wanted to explore another angle. What if Janet was not the target? What if the intruder expected to find Roxanne at Hall Farm that night? After all, her decision to go out was a last-minute arrangement. It was a chilling moment for Janet's youngest daughter. She was only seventeen at the time of her mother's death and she had to look again at her past. Had someone been watching her or been behaving in an obsessive way towards her? Roxanne had shown unflinching support to the police throughout the enquiry and was determined that her mother's killer should be brought to justice. She reviewed every possibility but, again, was left with nothing of substance to help the investigation.

The longer you look at the details of this case, the more they begin to blur. Janet could have opened her door to the killer, someone she knew and trusted. Yet no link existed to any acquaintance, no matter how casual. So this was a random attack, but no link existed to other crimes; the killer appears to have disappeared from view. 'I've never known a case so wide and so open,' DCI Tolmie admits.

The investigation remains open and Thames Valley Police are determined to bring Janet's family answers, no matter how much time elapses. Even after a decade, the family's feelings remained high. In one statement, they admitted: 'It tortures us that after ten years, we still don't know who did this or why. The biggest worry is that her brutal killer is still out there, free to do the same thing again.'

Killers don't disappear. It is hard to imagine how, yet they sometimes remain in the community, leading ordinary lives, working and even settling down and enjoying a family life for themselves. But a darkness remains beneath the surface. If someone is protecting a killer, they cannot do so forever.

Forensic science had made huge breakthroughs, as DCI Tolmie attests: 'I would not have imagined how far modern policing has been advanced by science. All it takes is a few cells to build a profile and who knows what's around the corner.'

During another serious crimes investigation, an unexpected angle arose that might shed light on the case. While reviewing unsolved rape cases, DCI Tolmie was told that enough DNA existed to build a profile of an offender. Years had passed and yet now there was enough evidence to track down the man. It was the type of breakthrough officers welcome – yet it proved another blind alley: they soon learned that the suspect had committed suicide.

Sometimes justice does not catch up with offenders, but these men are not always able to outrun their own demons. Could that have happened to Janet Brown's killer? It would go some way to explaining why there were no repeated attacks of a similar nature. Also, if the killer was socially isolated, if they lived alone, their disappearance would not be reported. And if the murderer was living alone, that could explain why no one had come forward to report that they had seen bloodstained clothes.

If this was a loner – someone who watched Janet, who built up an obsession with the life they imagined she lived at Hall Farm, who felt an irrational rage as they watched this pretty, successful and affluent woman – he could have been watching Roxanne too. Two vulnerable women. He knew their routines; knew Janet liked to go to bed early; knew how to leave a car out of view; knew that Janet's desire to protect Roxanne was so overwhelming that he could play with her as he wished. It would explain why Janet had no defence injuries – she may not have attempted to fight off her attacker; perhaps she was forced to bide her time, to ward off any harm to her daughter by obeying his orders.

Janet may even have heard the attempt to cut through the

glass, set the alarm and put on a dressing gown to go down and investigate. If the perpetrator made threats against Roxanne, saying that he was holding her, for example, Janet may then have simply opened the door to him. Once inside, he could have manipulated her in any way he chose.

He didn't need to penetrate her – very possibly he was unable to maintain an erection, which may have further enraged him. Total control was enough, enough to fuel his fantasies for some time.

Other psychotic killers have spoken about the desire to destroy 'perfection'. One killer is on record as stating that other people seemed to have a light around them, as if they were filled with love and joy, which only served to fuel his hatred. Profoundly damaged by a life of neglect and abuse, this killer began to fantasise about turning his rage outside himself; watching someone else endure pain would act as a release.

From the outside, Janet Brown did seem perfect; and someone wanted to get inside and destroy that. That's why they spent time at Hall Farm, humiliating and controlling her, moving her around like a rag doll at whim, moving family ornaments, controlling the house and for a few minutes, creating torment inside the perfect home. Yet perhaps it wasn't enough to appease any sickness he harboured; perhaps it overwhelmed him in the end. Not every killer faces justice, but not every killer escapes the consequences of his or her crimes.

Time may still provide an answer. The family deserves some measure of peace. They have tried to rebuild a life without Janet: Grahaem has remarried and the children now have careers and their own home lives. But every time something good comes of life and work, each of them wishes they could let the one person who cared about them most know. Janet was devoted to her family and she would be proud of the way they have coped after losing her.

No one is under any illusion that life today is free of risk. There are enough stories of violent attacks in daily newspapers to ensure that few of us would walk city streets at night without a second thought. But some of us are lucky enough to live out our lives sheltered from deprivation and the threat of urban gangs, of muggings and vandalism. Out of the city, distanced from urban poverty, we imagine that our families will be safe. Perhaps it is a state of mind that can leave us vulnerable. Wealth and success bring certain privileges, but they bring certain dangers too. Janet Brown may not have known her killer, but her killer may have built a fantasy world in which he believed he knew her. Those two worlds met at Hall Farm. No idyllic country lane would ever look the same again.

CHAPTER THREE
LIEUTENANT COLONEL ROBERT WORKMAN
MURDER IN THE VILLAGE

Robert Workman was an avid reader. Tolstoy's *War and Peace* was his favourite book – in part because Tolstoy, like Workman, had served his country during times of war: Tolstoy fought at Sevastopol; Workman served in the British Army throughout the Second World War. Yet it wasn't wartime that proved the old gentleman's downfall, but a quiet and peaceful village in the English countryside. There, on 7 January 2004, Robert Workman was gunned down on his doorstep.

Furneux Pelham is in Hertfordshire, approximately forty miles north of London. It is one of three 'Pelhams', mediaeval villages that form almost a triangle in this part of the county. The other Pelhams – Stocking Pelham and Brent Pelham – are connected through their history as much as geography, as they all made up parts of an old estate belonging to the Furneaux family.

The 'a' was dropped from Furneaux over time. It still appears on one village sign, but locals spell the address as Furneux and pronounce it as 'Fur-nicks'; it might wrong-foot outsiders, just as nearby Braughing is pronounced 'Braffing'.

It is this kind of minor detail that always allows locals to spot outsiders.

Furneux Pelham looks quintessentially English, lined with pretty thatched cottages, rambling lanes and Grade II houses, but it is not quite the quiet country retreat it first appears to be. It is close enough to London to make it 'commutable' – something reflected in its property prices. With rail links to London's Liverpool Street only a few miles away, and a commute of only forty minutes, larger Grade II properties in the area are now valued at over £1 million. Creating the illusion that your life is lived far from the city can be an expensive undertaking.

Yet perhaps it is this proximity to London and the commuters it brings that has led to a strong sense of pride in the community. Furneux Pelham has regular history group meetings, parish council events, arts-and-crafts exhibitions and a village hall available for children's parties and celebrations. For a smallish village of around only 240 properties, it is thriving but it also respects a great English tradition: privacy.

Like many English villages, there are two sides to Furneux Pelham. If you wish to live in anonymity there, you are able to do so. Some people retreat behind wisteria-covered walls and enjoy peace and quiet; others make their village their own with an active involvement in parish life. It would be fair to say that Lieutenant Colonel Workman preferred the quieter life. Although by no means unfriendly, he kept a low profile in the village. He did not drink at the Brewery Tap, the local pub on Barley Croft End, and by the end of his life he was virtually housebound, unable even to climb the stairs to the upper floor of his cottage and relied on a home help to deliver day-to-day basics and prepare meals.

Even before the infirmities he endured when he reached his eighties, Robert Workman found himself confined to his home for another reason. His wife of thirty-five years, Joan, who was known as Joanna, was suffering with arthritis and ill-health and after a back operation in 1994, her condition worsened. She became effectively bedridden and Robert Workman became his wife's full-time carer. It was a role he carried out for the next nine years. Some villagers were aware that an elderly man was caring for his wife over at Cock House, and if they asked him, he would have introduced himself not as Robert but as Riley. It was one of his middle names, the name his family had known him by for as long as anyone could remember; a niece and nephew in Australia had only ever called him 'Uncle Riley'.

Joanna and Riley bought Cock House in 1977, but they did not move in until 1984, after they returned from working in America. In a somewhat unusual move for a retired lieutenant colonel, Riley took a position as a housekeeper for a large and wealthy household in Massachusetts, alongside Joanna, who worked as a private nurse.

Joanna had been nursing when the couple met in the late 1960s. Not many people who came to know the couple knew that they had met because Riley had himself advertised for a 'private nurse'. Joanna was one of the applicants. Riley was not thought to be suffering from ill health; there was a suggestion that as he reached his late forties, this was a way of meeting a potential bride.

Three years older than Riley, Joanna was divorced and had

a daughter, Anna. She lived in Massachusetts until her marriage broke down and then returned to the UK with her daughter. The couple married in 1968, when Riley was forty-eight. Although they lived in Furneux Pelham for twenty years, they acquired no close friends in the village. Perhaps the closest was their nearest neighbour, Edward Davidson, a barrister, and his wife. Riley would spend time talking about his army career to Mr Davidson although he was always guarded about what went on at Cock House and never criticised his wife or stepdaughter. Mr Davidson thought Riley's care for Joanna 'saintly'. There can be no doubt that attending his wife's every need for nine years was taxing, yet he never complained.

In short, anyone who encountered Riley knew him to be polite, caring and reserved, in fact, a gentleman typical of his generation and background. All were sympathetic when news of Joanna's death became known in April 2003 and with a sister in Guernsey and a brother in Australia and no children of his own, many people wondered who would care for Riley in his old age.

The Davidsons made sure that Riley was not left alone at Christmas-time and invited him to share Christmas dinner with them. All in all, Riley's spirits seemed to improve throughout 2003 and his Australian relatives were relieved to hear that he was making plans to rebuild his life after the death of his wife. Riley had even talked about taking a trip out to Australia to see his brother Cecil and he was in good form during a brief visit from his nephew, Kenneth Workman, in October of that year.

But any hopes for a happy future for the old man were to

be cruelly snatched away one Wednesday evening. It was a murder that continues to haunt Riley's family and the village of Furneux Pelham to this day.

Josette Swanson found Riley's body. She was his carer and would call on him three times a day to check that all was well and help with basic household chores. During her last visit of the evening, her husband Brian often accompanied her and he'd share a nip of whisky with Riley. It was the old man's favourite tipple although Josette had kept an eye on his consumption. Since Joanna's death, she was concerned that Riley was drinking too much. Yet she understood how difficult things were for her patient: he had long stretches of time on his own and found it increasingly difficult to get around the house. He used a stick now and had resigned himself to sleeping downstairs.

That Thursday morning, she made her way to Cock House and thought it odd to see the hall light on. She had left Riley at about 8pm the previous night, after setting out a few biscuits, a cigar and a glass of whisky. It was early January, so it was still dark at 6.30am. Perhaps Riley had forgotten he'd left the light on?

She made her way to the side of the house and then saw his body, lying across the entrance of his doorway. It was a sad sight, the old man slumped in the hall, his hand raised as if in shock. Riley's health was not good and Josette thought that he must have suffered a heart attack. She called Brian and the Davidsons and they contacted the police in the hope that they could trace Riley's next of kin.

Any death brings a swarm of activity. A doctor would need to provide a certificate, undertakers would need to transport the body to a chapel of rest before funeral arrangements could be agreed and the police wanted to call at the property too. By around 9.30am, a number of people had been at Cock House, some three hours after Mrs Swanson had raised the alarm.

It was not until Riley was moved by the undertakers that the true nature of his death was revealed. As his shoulder was moved back, a huge wound to his torso was exposed. It was a shock to everyone gathered at Cock House and the police realised to their considerable discomfort, that they'd failed to put into place the procedures that follow all suspicious deaths. It was only then that the scene was sealed, Forensics swung into gear and a fingertip search of the property and grounds began. A murder enquiry was up and running but it was already possible that some clues that could have been picked up during those vital early hours after the murder, the 'golden' hours in terms of policing, had already been lost.

Locally, many people had sympathy with the police. No one expected a violent death in Furneux Pelham, this quiet and refined village, and yet it was not the only violent murder set to tear the village apart. And both cases were to involve the same suspect: Chris Nudds.

Nudds was well known in the farming community around the Pelhams. In fact, the year that Joanna died, he'd become something of a local story in his own right as a champion mole catcher. 'I catch moles for football players and for members of bands such as The Prodigy and Iron Maiden,' he said when interviewed about his unusual career. He was travelling all over Hertfordshire, Cambridgeshire and into London, ridding lawns and greens of moles. It was more than a quirky story: Nudds was able to earn up to £4,000-a-month from his talent. He also rid properties of wasp nests, which was how he came to Cock House.

Nudds, twenty-five at the time, was called out twice by Riley to deal with wasp nests in his garden. He was known to have access to shotguns, the weapon used to kill Riley, and the decision was made to arrest him later that day. But within twenty-four hours, he was released without charge, his solicitor stating: 'Mr Nudds was arrested in relation to this murder, and was questioned by the police. He was released with no further action. He categorically denies any involvement in this incident.'

In the meantime, the post-mortem confirmed that Riley had died from a single round fired into his torso at close range. Forensics established that the murder weapon was a 12-bore shotgun, a common weapon used locally with forty-five licences held in Furneux Pelham alone. The shot used was rather less common: it was a cartridge containing nine pellets, 8.44mm in diameter, the largest shot in use legally, and primarily used only by gamekeepers for destroying large game, such as deer.

The plastic wadding around the shot revealed that it was manufactured by a company in Bologna, Italy, but there were several specialist shops in the UK where it could be purchased. The cartridge itself was not recovered, which suggested to the police that either it was picked up by the killer or it had not been discharged from the gun.

While gathering ballistic evidence was important, the key question remained: who would want to kill Riley in cold blood? Was this a botched robbery attempt? Before taking up his position as housekeeper in America, Riley had been a successful antique dealer. Edward Davidson was aware that Riley was a very knowledgeable collector, particularly of silverware. Riley still read about antiques for recreation and he had a sizable collection at Cock House. But nothing was stolen. What was more, the killer had not even set foot in the property.

It is rare for thieves to use firearms and rarer still for them to confront a householder. They might, if they know that there is a safe in the home that would require the householder to reveal how to open it and a weapon can be used to intimidate the victim. Riley was in his eighties and unlikely to put up a fight, even an old soldier would hesitate when faced with a shotgun – plus, he knew that he was adequately insured against theft. But this scenario did not fit the sequence of events as they became known. Nothing was stolen; the case simply did not have the hallmarks of a robbery. Whoever confronted Riley had simply knocked on his door that Wednesday evening, waited and then shot him in cold blood.

Mrs Swanson confirmed that it would have taken a minute or so for Riley to open the door. He had difficulty rising out of his favourite armchair, he'd use his walking stick and make his way slowly to the door. The killer waited. The hall light went on and as the door opened, he took aim and would have known that the eighty-three-year-old would be dead before he hit the ground.

Robbery could not have been the motivation, so what did that leave? Sadly, those who have the misfortune to become victims of a murder with no immediate suspects have their lives scrutinised after death. It can be distressing for families to have their loved one's past pulled apart and become subject to theory and gossip. With no obvious motive or suspect, Riley

Workman was to prove as vulnerable to speculation after death as he had been defenceless on the night of his murder.

The police began to examine his past and at first the picture appeared unremarkable enough. Robert Riley Workman was born in April 1920 into a comfortably well-off family from Gloucester. He was the youngest of three children and was close to his brother Cecil and sister Mary. After public school, he gained a place at Queens College, Oxford and began his studies there in 1938. The following year, war was declared and Riley enlisted with the Oxford and Buckinghamshire Light Infantry.

He was finally posted abroad in 1942, serving as a lieutenant in India and later in Burma, where he acted as an aide-de-camp for Field Marshall Slim. Riley continued to serve after the war and saw many overseas postings, including Canada, Nigeria, Germany and Cyprus. He returned to England in 1958 and five years later was promoted to the rank of lieutenant colonel and commander of the Royal Green Jackets Brigade. He retired in 1965. Although his military career was not exceptional, Riley had always enjoyed steady promotion and earned a good deal of respect for his diligence from his fellow officers.

With his army career at an end, Riley returned to Gloucestershire and set up an antiques business with his sister Mary. It proved successful, but with Riley now entering his late forties, Mary hoped that her brother would settle down and start a family. There is some suggestion that it was Mary who placed the advertisement for a 'private nurse' in the paper on Riley's behalf and no doubt she was pleased that her brother had found someone he felt he could share his life with.

Joanna was not wholly approved of, however. Mary may have had reservations about Joanna's status as a divorcée, she may not have been entirely comfortable with her social background either, but whatever the case, their personalities jarred. Joanna would make herself absent in Mary's presence and seemed a poor match for Riley's convivial personality, retreating upstairs and taking no part when her brother entertained. Nevertheless, they were married in 1968 and Riley honoured his vow to care for his wife, for better or for worse. Worse was to come in the shape of Joanna's daughter, Anna.

Anna was no longer a child when her mother remarried, she was a woman of twenty-four, and yet she was deeply unhappy with the union. Over time, Anna would develop an alcohol addiction and regularly gave full vent to the antagonism she felt towards Riley. Verbal sparring turned to abuse and as her mother's health failed, Anna's rage increased. Why she loathed Riley was never clear, but it became a source of great concern to his family.

Her appearances at Cock House became more and more erratic, and as Anna became more unstable, she began to subject Riley to more than just verbal abuse. Raised voices were heard by neighbours and Anna attacked Riley physically on more than one occasion. She slashed his clothes and threatened him with a knife. The police were even called to Cock House during one violent incident, but Riley chose not to press charges.

By this stage, his life must have been intolerable. At a time when he should have been enjoying a peaceful retirement, he was housebound through his dedication to his wife's needs and subject to attacks when his stepdaughter was intoxicated. As she lived nearby in Bishop's Stortford, Anna could land without a moment's notice. Yet Riley made no complaint and carried on to the best of his abilities, hiding alcohol whenever Anna arrived and seeking solace in his garden.

He must have often wondered how his life had become so reduced in this way. He and Joanna had had great hopes for their retirement and had even purchased a camper van, which sat on the driveway of the house. Yet any trips Riley took were few and far between – mostly to visit his sister in Guernsey, alone.

Edward Davidson thought his neighbour saintly, but he can only have had mixed feelings when news of Anna's death reached him in February 2002. Although it was terribly sad that a woman aged only fifty-eight had reached the end of her life, it was clear that she had drunk herself into an early grave. It was an awful blow for Joanna but perhaps Riley felt a measure of relief, as Anna could no longer terrorise him or upset his invalid wife.

The realisation that she had been able to do nothing to halt her daughter's addiction was hard for Joanna to live with, though. In a little over a year, she too gave up the fight for life and Riley now found himself entirely alone.

Few people make it into their eighties without reflecting that life is full of unforeseen events that can prove highly distressing. Riley had lost his stepdaughter and wife within fourteen months and faced an uncertain future. Josette brought vital care that would allow him still to function and live in the downstairs of his home – but for how long? It was a worry: Riley cherished his independence and wanted to live at Cock House for as long as possible. As it turned out, he would do so for only nine more months.

Something happened. Something within that short time span triggered a catastrophic end to Riley's life and it was a puzzle the police were left with after the 8th January.

Had Anna not died, she would have been a prime suspect. In the overwhelming majority of cases, victims know their killers and she had a volatile relationship with her stepfather. As it stood, the police had very little to go on. This was evident when Detective Superintendent Richard Mann gave a press conference on Friday, 9 January, the day after Riley had been discovered and the day Chris Nudds was released without charge. 'We have got no reason or motive for that at this stage,' Mann stated. 'From all the people we have spoken to, no one has had a bad word to say against him.'

But people aren't gunned down for no reason. There had to be something in Riley's past – a grudge held, a relationship turned sour – that would lead to a suspect. The police appealed for those who knew Riley to come forward. They began to piece together his life history and made enquiries to see if there had been any bad blood during his time as an antiques dealer. His army career offered another avenue for exploration. Had he caused any resentment during his years of service? There was his time in Massachusetts too... in fact, over the course of a long life, surely he must have aroused some antipathy in someone?

The questions raised would require answers from many corners of the world, but the first breakthrough for the team came from no more than three miles away – from a phone box in Braughing. At 4.57 on Thursday morning, someone dialled the emergency services and asked for the ambulance service. All such calls are recorded and the police soon had the transcript in full:

Operator: 'Hello, caller. Hello.'

Caller: 'Hello.'

Operator: 'The Ambulance Service. What's the address you want the ambulance to come to?'

Caller: 'Ambulance. It's Hollyhock Cottage.'

Operator: 'Holly...'

Caller: 'Hollyhock Cottage.'

Operator: 'Can you spell that for me?'

Caller: 'H.O.L.L.Y.C.O.C.K.' [*sic*]

Operator: 'And what road is it on?'

Caller: 'It's The Causeway.'

Operator: 'The Causeway.'

Caller: 'Yes.'

Operator: 'In what town?'

Caller: 'That's Furneux Pelham.'

Operator: 'Can you spell that for me?'

Caller: 'F.U.R.N.E.A.U.X. P.E....'

Operator: 'Is that S for "Sierra"?'

Caller: (*Pause*) 'F.U.R.N.E.A.U.X. Pelham – P.E.L.H.A.M.'

Operator: (*Long pause*) 'Bear with me a moment.'

Caller: 'That's near Buntingford.' (*Caller puts receiver down.*)

Operator: Furneaux Pelham... Hello?

In all, the caller was on the line for less than two minutes, but the call was highly significant: at that point, no one knew that Riley was lying dead or dying in his doorstep. Except the killer. Yet the call was not made immediately following the shooting. The post-mortem revealed that Riley had been shot at some point during the evening before and local residents told the police that they had heard a gunshot at around 8pm.

The timescale was narrowed further still when a caretaker told the police that he heard a shot just before setting the school alarm. The alarm was set at 8.17pm, so it was likely that Riley was killed at 8.15pm. That was only half an hour after Josette Swanson's visit came to an end. It was possible that Riley's house was under surveillance. Someone watched as Josette drove away and remained vigilant to make sure no one else approached.

The killer might have watched as villagers poured into St Mary's Church on the Sunday following the murder. Representatives from the seventy-strong investigation team were there to pay their respects and many believed that this was a local matter, that someone close to hand knew Riley and had elected to kill the old man.

The police released the tape of the call made to the ambulance service and voice experts confirmed that the caller was likely to be aged fifty or older and had a local east Hertfordshire accent. Hundreds of calls came in to the incident room, but the investigators were to be disappointed: none led to the caller being identified.

There were other subtle clues left by the caller. Initially, he gave Riley's address as 'Hollyhock' cottage. The house was always known as Cock House, in reference to the weathercock on the roof. There was only one occasion within recent memory when the name was changed. Briefly, in the early 1980s, it was called 'Hollyhock', but the name did not stick and Riley preferred its original title. The person who'd campaigned to change the name was Joanna.

The caller then refers to the house as 'Hollycock', perhaps wrong-footed once he's asked to spell the name that the call handler is trying to locate, and he stumbles on to a blend of the two names. It suggests that the caller knew the cottage under both names.

The next clue comes with the misspelling of 'Furneux Pelham'. The caller inserts an 'a', spelling out F.U.R.N.E.A.U.X. As you exit the village, a sign appears on which the village name is indeed spelt this way, but no villager uses the 'a'. The caller pronounces the name correctly as 'Furnix', though. As the caller is under pressure, knowing that Riley is dead or dying, such mistakes are easily made. Again, however, the implication is that the caller is familiar with the area but may not live in the village.

Above all, the caller clearly wants an ambulance crew to attend to Riley but sadly, the confusion over the house address meant that Cock House was never found. Paramedics travelled up and down The Causeway but never reached the intended destination. The grim discovery would have to be made by Josette Swanson, some ninety minutes later.

The investigative team felt they needed to know far more about Riley's life but before detectives could leave for Australia to talk to Cecil about his brother, a new theory arose: had the murder been a case of mistaken identity? As nothing had been stolen and there no obvious suspect had come to light, could Riley have been mistaken for someone else?

Senior District Judge Timothy Workman was one possible candidate for the intended victim. He lived within a few miles of Riley, shared a last name and in his role as a senior magistrate had been involved in some very sensitive court cases. Two that caught the attention of the press involved his decision to turn down extradition requests from Russia. The Russian government asked that Akhmed Zakayev, the Chechen leader then living in London, be flown to Moscow. Justice Workman refused on the grounds that Zakayev faced, a 'substantial risk' of torture or death in Russia. The Kremlin were far from pleased but were to cross swords with Workman again over a request that Boris Berezovsky be flown back to Russia to face charges of fraud and political corruption, charges he has always denied. Berezovsky had successfully claimed political asylum in the UK in 2001; once again, Justice Workman refused the Russian request.

The police examined the possibility that the judge had been the intended target, but they found nothing to substantiate it. Justice Workman merely commented: 'I think this is just one line of enquiry and I think it is not a matter that is causing me undue concern.' While the judge may have appeared unperturbed, Russian exiles speculated on the possibility that the FSB – the Russian secret service – had had a role to play in the murder. After the death of Russian dissident Alexander Litvinenko, the conspiracy was given renewed attention. Critics of Putin's Russia claimed that not only were the FSB involved but that the organisation is sufficiently incompetent to have identified the wrong 'Workman'.

One theory is that the Russian secret service would assume Workman had a military title, as many Russian judges do, so simply seeing the name Lieutenant Colonel Workman in any phone directory could have led to the mistake. The problems with a theory of international espionage and a revenge attack on a British judge become immediately clear, though. Firstly, it would be hard to think of a crime as diplomatically explosive as killing a foreign judge. That the FSB may have had a role to play in the poisoning of Alexander Litvinenko is plausible, which is why the UK has asked for the extradition of an ex-KGB officer. But there is a great deal of difference between the death of an ex-Russian agent on UK soil and the assassination of a British judge. Such an act would cause an irrevocable rift in Anglo-Russian relations and have huge international repercussions. The refusal of Russia to allow the ex-KGB officer to be questioned by Scotland Yard can be seen as part of a 'tit for tat', allowing Russia to show her displeasure with the UK's refusal to hand over Berezovsky, and far more typical of an inter-governmental spat.

Secondly, Justice Workman's decision to allow Berezovsky to stay was not a personal one. He was adhering to British law and any other judge could have turned down Russia's extradition request. It isn't credible to imagine Russia assassinating British judges, and neither is it likely that such acts of intimidation would alter judicial decisions.

Leaving the conspiracy theories aside, the fact remains that Riley's death did not have the hallmark of a professional killing. A shotgun is an unlikely weapon of choice. Professional assassins look to discharge multiple shots to the head from a semiautomatic pistol, ensuring that the job is finished, not fire buckshot into a target's torso. There are those who have stuck to the theory of a Russian conspiracy and have asked why Riley's case has not been rolled into the Litvinenko investigation – but they have overlooked an obvious clue. This was personal. Adam Gregory is a senior Behavioural Investigative Advisor (BIA) and works with senior investigators to build a profile of offenders. In his view, the killer had a deeply felt grudge against Riley that was probably long held. To Gregory, the manner of Riley's death smacked of a calculated act of anger and revenge.

BIAs are careful to point out that their advice should be categorised as intelligence, not evidence, but their work does help senior investigators review what information they've gathered and to examine new routes. The volume of information compiled during a murder investigation can be overwhelming and run to thousands of pages in statements alone. Every local in Furneux Pelham over the age of ten had been spoken to by police officers and some 2,000 statements were taken. Physical evidence is also extensive: the phone box where the call was made was even removed entirely from the village and each millimetre pored over for signs of DNA.

Despite all the efforts put in by the team, however, no firm leads were established. As January drew to a close, the decision was made to make an appeal on *Crimewatch* and air the 999 call. The incident room took around sixty calls in response and the police hoped that someone had come forward with information about a person in Hertfordshire who was known to use the type of buckshot used to kill Riley.

In Furneux Pelham, villagers were anxious that the murderer be found, but the general mood was not improved by the way the story was being treated by the media. The picturesque village was caught up in a real life 'Miss Marple' or 'Midsomer Murder', a perfect English mystery where a retired lieutenant colonel was shot on his cottage doorstep with the murderer still at large. While news crews from around the world filed 'whodunnit' reports, it was easy to lose track of a very real human tragedy.

It took the arrival of Ken Workman, Riley's nephew, to remind everyone that the old soldier was a beloved relative, not a character in a TV mystery. Mr Workman spoke movingly about the deceased late in February, revealing: 'My uncle was trying to regain his purpose in life after the recent loss of his beloved wife Joanna, or "Nan" to us, whom he was totally devoted to caring for. This reflected the quality and commitment of the man I am proud to have called my uncle.'

The police press conference was a timely reminder that Riley was much missed, but it was also designed to prompt anyone with knowledge of who the killer was to come forward. Detective Superintendent Mann felt that the killer would be known in the local community.

On 28 February, a memorial service was held at St Mary's and over 150 people attended. Ken Workman read a eulogy and a rifleman from the Royal Green Jackets, Riley's regiment, sounded the Last Post. It was a moving occasion, but it was also discreetly filmed by the police, in the hope that something or someone would be revealed on the tape. Nothing was.

Calls were still coming in to the incident room and the police were still filling in gaps in Riley's life when a routine enquiry unexpectedly led to an arrest. As part of a process of elimination, the team took voice samples from local men over the age of fifty. One gentleman refused to cooperate. He was in his sixties and from east Hertfordshire, but was unwilling to commit his voice to tape. He was arrested but later released on bail. It was not the breakthrough the police were looking for.

By June, a reward of £10,000 was offered for information leading to an arrest. Riley was in the news the following month when it was revealed that he'd left close to £1 million in his will. The police did not consider this fact relevant to the enquiry, but it ensured that the case made the headlines once more, and if the killer was still in the area, that would have an effect. The hope was that his or her family would have noticed a change in behaviour and would speak out.

But the next wave of headlines took everyone – even the investigating team – by surprise. In December 2004, a prisoner at the high-security Parkhurst jail on the Isle of Wight asked to speak to detectives hunting Riley's killer. The press statement, when it came, was a sensation. A spokeswoman from Hertfordshire police said: 'Detectives have spoken to a prisoner but, for reasons of confidentiality, we cannot divulge what was said. We can confirm that an active line of enquiry is around the strong suggestion that Colonel Workman was a homosexual.'

She also added: 'It's the last thing we expected to turn up.' In reality, for a man of Riley's generation, leading a double life as a gay man wasn't unusual. Homosexual acts between two consenting men over the age of twenty-one were not legalised until the Sexual Offences Act of 1967. But even then, homosexuality itself remained socially unacceptable. Many gay men of this era married and had children as they struggled to reconcile their sexuality with expectations of friends, families and colleagues. Trying to live as a homosexual in the armed forces was a particularly fraught experience. The police hoped to speak to anyone who served with Riley during his career. Those who did come forward, however, said that they never heard any suggestion that Riley was gay and indeed, recalled a number of girlfriends.

Were the police being misled? The team felt confident enough not to dismiss it as a line of enquiry and it would go some way to explaining a 'long-held' grudge that could lead to murder. Perhaps someone had been rebuffed with the end of an affair; perhaps Riley had refused to leave Joanna. Riley took his wedding vows seriously and remained devoted to his frail wife. Joanna's long-term ill health could have created both the desire for an extramarital affair and also the setting for such a relationship to turn sour.

It may be significant that Riley was killed after Joanna's death. Is it possible that Riley had used care for his wife as grounds to end an affair? Could an ex-lover have pressurised Riley after her death and found himself further scorned? This could have had more than a sexual aspect to it: Riley was elderly and may not have wished to continue an affair, but he was wealthy and an ex-lover would have known that. He was vulnerable to blackmail.

The idea that Riley may have been gay raised the possibility that his life was far more complex than the police had first imagined. They appealed to older members of the gay community to come forward with any information that they may have had about Riley's life and acquaintances and hoped that it could lead to a possible suspect.

At the same time that this development was unfolding, Hertfordshire police were dealing with another murder case. On Tuesday, 30 November, twenty-one-year-old Fred Moss had gone missing. Fred was part of the traveller community and had left his aunt's house that day, telling her that he was going hare coursing. When he failed to return home, his family feared he'd fallen victim to an angry farmer as he'd already picked up a conviction for illegal coursing the year before. The following day, he was formally reported as missing and travellers poured across the countryside hoping to find him.

Fred had set off in his yellow Astra van and that was missing too. He didn't always go coursing alone, and on hearing of his disappearance someone who regularly accompanied him joined the search. It was this friend who found Fred's missing van. He called the police and Fred's family to let them know he'd found it reversed against a hedge in Hay Street car park.

This helpful gesture would backfire, though. The caller fell under the suspicion not only of the travellers but of the police too. On 4 December, a group of travellers asked to meet him and it is alleged that he was abducted and driven to an isolated location. The caller claims that he was then beaten and threatened at gunpoint to reveal Fred's whereabouts.

Badly shaken, he reported his abduction the following day to the Hertfordshire police, but instead of investigating this complaint he was arrested for the murder of Fred Moss. The reason was simple. After he denied that he'd been with Fred on 30 November, the police produced CCTV footage showing them in a car convoy together. At this point the caller, Chris Nudds, must have realised that he was in serious trouble.

Chris was a good friend of Fred's: they shared an interest in coursing and spent a good deal of time together enjoying the countryside. Although Fred called himself a traveller, in fact he lived in a static caravan on a site in nearby Sawbridgeworth. He'd spent time in France, tarmacking drives, and spoke French fluently.

Chris later admitted that they had met up that morning but that Fred told him he was not coursing but involved in a drug deal. This was why Chris was reluctant to disclose that they had driven off to a meet together as Chris feared not only the police but retribution from the travelling community. He told the police that the last time he saw Fred, he was a passenger in a Mercedes that drove away from the meet for the drug deal. Chris acted as lookout at the side of the road and he saw Fred being driven away. When Fred did not return, he was concerned but went home to wait to hear from him.

After a series of interviews, Chris was remanded in custody in HMP Bedford on 13 December. He was originally placed in a cell on his own but was subsequently moved into a cell with another inmate, Darren Horner. On 16 December, Horner asked to see the Governor and reported that Chris has confessed to killing Fred Moss. Horner said that Nudds had said the killing was 'personal' and that Fred had been shot, dismembered and his remains burnt.

The police still had no body but with this information, they returned to Chris's home and searched it thoroughly, along with his vehicle. They found bloodstains that matched Fred Moss's DNA on a large knife and hacksaw at the home and a blood spots in the boot of the car. On 20 January 2005, Chris Nudds was charged with the murder of Fred Moss.

His case came to trial early the following year at Northampton Crown Court. He was found guilty of murder on 27 February and was sentenced to thirty years in prison. A 'Justice for Chris Nudds' campaign was soon established.

His supporters believe that he has suffered a miscarriage of justice and that the evidence against him can be explained.

For instance, the blood spots in the boot of the car could be a result of a bite Fred suffered when breaking up a fight that two of his dogs began in the back of Nudds' car.

Nudds denies that the hacksaw and knife were his and questions why, if he burnt Fred's dismembered body, no evidence of ash or smoke had been found on his clothes or vehicle. Moreover, why would he not dispose of a knife and hacksaw at the same time as the body?

He is now serving time in Durham Prison and is fighting his conviction, but his support is not unequivocal. A good deal of anger exists in the traveller community over the disappearance of Fred Moss and the hunt for his remains goes on.

At the time of Nudds' conviction, Riley's case was examined again. There was a huge age difference between the two men, but could it have been possible that they had a homosexual affair? As Riley moved to the village in the 1984, it is possible that the lieutenant colonel could have known Chris Nudds as a boy. But throughout extensive investigation into Riley's past, there had never been an allegation or suggestion that he was a paedophile or, for that matter, that Nudds was a homosexual.

The suggestion that Riley had gay affairs did persist, however, and if this has some basis in fact, it is possible that his stepdaughter Anna, who lived within a few miles of her mother, knew something about Riley's other life. Could it have fuelled some of the rage she felt against her stepfather and could it have contributed to Riley's reluctance to prosecute her after she assaulted him? He was unquestionably devoted to Joanna and would not have wanted to hurt her through revelations about the life he hid from her.

Anna was vicious enough to cut up Riley's clothes, a very personal form of attack, but Riley chose not to disown or threaten her. Perhaps a sense of guilt and fears for his marriage forced him to restrain any anger he may have felt towards Anna. But if Anna knew, who else did? Enough people for the rumours to spread and enough to make Riley vulnerable to blackmail?

Listening to the 999 call made after Riley's attack, it is clearly not the voice of Chris Nudds on the line. It is a much older man, someone who was acting almost nine hours after Riley had been shot. Perhaps it was not the voice of the killer at all – what if it was an older friend of the killer's, for instance? Could this man have nursed his friend through a confession but, in the cold hours of the morning, wanted to salvage some humanity and help for the old man?

In some ways, the call fits that profile. There is a note of distress, of confusion, in the voice and a certain irritation when the call handler does not recognise the address the caller is giving. It is easy to imagine that this is someone that has driven past the address many times but has never given it his full attention. When it came to trying to save the old man's life, a sketchy familiarity was not enough. Listening to the recording, there is a note of caution in the voice, there is the fear of being caught.

The phone line went dead and with it any hope that the police had to establish a link with the killer. The call is still central to the enquiry for one simple reason: the caller had to be involved. If not, he would simply have called the police and emergency services the moment he found Riley. Even if for some obscure reason he wanted to remain anonymous, few people would evade a direct appeal from the police in a murder enquiry unless they had something to hide.

But until the voice is matched, the motivation for the call remains only guesswork. The police spoke to Chris Nudds once again after his conviction but admitted that their interview did not help to progress the case.

Three years after Riley's death, the case passed through the hands of yet another detective chief inspector and landed on the desk of DCI Bill Jephson. Jephson is a very experienced officer and has made the news leading large and complex cases such as the hunt for Phillip McHugh, the out-of-work tax inspector who blackmailed Tesco. In 2007, McHugh threatened to contaminate food in various stores unless his demand of a payment of £1 million was met. He was arrested at his home in Clitheroe on 23 July, the culmination of diligent police work, and sentenced to six years' imprisonment.

As part of the Bedfordshire and Hertfordshire Major Crime Unit, DCI Bill Jephson aims to bring Robert Workman's killer to justice. Although he is the third senior investigator to head up the case, Jephson is well placed to unpick the case that has so far confounded all those who have looked into it.

Much as it was for his predecessor, the need to establish motive is essential. Motive will lead to a suspect. The phone call placed on the morning of 9 January is undoubtedly part of the puzzle. Here is someone who knew what had happened to Riley. An ex-lover perhaps, who'd waited for Joanna to die, believing that Riley was now free to resume a relationship. Did Riley's rejection cause him to snap?

The caller was an older member of the community,

someone who may also have grown up conflicted about his sexuality. He could also have married and had a family and been forced to live a double life. The psychological strain of long-term duplicity is often more than the human mind can bear. Facing old age, did Riley's rebuff cause that unknown figure to turn first on himself and loathe his situation only to then externalise his rage and lash out? In killing Riley, did he think he could kill what he hated in himself? Such theories must remain pure speculation, of course, until the police have a breakthrough.

The voice of the man on the police tape is that of someone confused and defeated. The only note of resolve arrives at the end of the call. The call-handler asks 'Bear with me a moment' but it is a moment too long for the caller. He says: 'That's near Buntingford' in a very different tone from that which begins the call. He has no intention of waiting a second longer. Perhaps he's waited long enough.

Drive through Furneux Pelham today and you would never dream that anything untoward could have happened there. The pretty village has resumed its aura of affluent calm and most villagers accept that whatever it was in the retired lieutenant colonel that drove someone to shoot him, it was a personal matter and will not affect them. It's sad but it is over. They are safe in their beds.

As an English village with a darker side beneath its postcard loveliness, Furneux Pelham is by no means alone. DCI Bill Jephson now heads the investigation into the murder, assembling the pieces of Riley's life to create a picture of what might have led to his death. Some of those pieces are proving very difficult to discover.

But if Jephson has read *War and Peace*, as Riley did often, perhaps he'll appreciate Tolstoy's advice: 'The strongest of all warriors are these two – Time and Patience.'

CHAPTER FOUR

ADAM

A SACRIFICIAL VICTIM

December can be a difficult month. The streets are bright
with lights and tinsel but the piped carols that greet
shoppers do not cheer every heart. The police are accustomed
to this being the month in which incidents of assault, suicide
and domestic violence all rise. But that wasn't on the minds
of the officers who gathered in a quiet cemetery in east
London one December day in 2006. All had families and each
knew what Christmas should mean for children. Under grey
skies, it was the worst time of year to say goodbye to a child.

Detective Chief Inspector Will O'Reilly stood and watched
as the small pastel-blue coffin, decorated with teddy bears, was
lowered into the ground. It had been a non-denominational
ceremony and he knew he would have to speak for all those
gathered as he prepared his eulogy. What he said struck a
chord: 'Like the unknown soldier, his death should not be in
vain – some resulting good must be his epitaph.'

The officers and forensic scientists who attended the funeral
had lived with the case for five years and knew that the words
'unknown soldier' were apt. They had vigorously investigated

the murder of the young boy being buried that day and yet they were no closer to knowing his name on that cold December morning than they had been on the first afternoon, when a child's mutilated body was pulled from the Thames.

It began, as murder cases often do, with a passer-by. Crossing Tower Bridge on foot at around 4pm on 21 September 2001, a commuter noticed something floating down-river. Could it be a barrel? It had something bright orange attached to it. As it passed under the bridge, it began to look more like a body. It was probably a mistake, a trick of the light, but the witness called the police to report what he had seen. No one would have guessed that this was to trigger one of the most extraordinary and ground-breaking investigations ever carried out at New Scotland Yard.

Following routine procedure, the Metropolitan Police dispatched a marine search unit to investigate. Travelling upstream past The Globe Theatre on the banks of Southwark, the team slowly approached the object and carefully brought it on board. It was the torso of a young black child wearing a pair of orange shorts, although the legs were missing.

The members of the marine unit were accustomed to seeing bodies in the Thames and knew what damage boat traffic can do to a corpse, but this was not like anything they'd retrieved before. As well as the child's legs, both arms were severed and the body was headless.

The remains were taken to the nearest police station and a call was made to DCI O'Reilly. He was making his way home when his phone rang and as the senior officer covering the area where the body was found, he made his way to the station. He said later: 'I knew the moment I saw the remains, from the nature of the injuries, that this was a homicide.' If that was a certainty, so was the belief that they would quickly identify who the boy was. As DCI O'Reilly explains: 'Murder is a rare occurrence in London but a body remaining unidentified is even rarer. In fact, I can't think of a case where we haven't found the deceased's identity.'

The body was taken to Poplar Mortuary in Tower Hamlets and the routine enquiry began. Pathology had to determine the cause of death and the investigative team began to search through records of missing children. The Home Office pathologist began work the following morning and quickly established that the child had been male, Afro-Caribbean and between the ages of four and seven. Identification beyond that would be problematic as there was no head. No picture could be released, no dental records checked.

But, as the marine unit suspected, the autopsy also revealed that this was no accidental fatality. The cause of death was given as a violent trauma to the neck area. In the starkest of terms, the boy had had his throat slit and his blood drained. After death, a sharp precision knife was used to cut the skin, peel back the muscle and cut the bone. It was concluded that the orange shorts were then placed on the child, as it would not have been possible to remove the legs if they had be worn.

The stomach was almost empty – the child had not eaten for between twelve and eighteen hours before his death. There were traces of a cough medicine, however, so apparently the boy had received some level of care. That jarred uncomfortably with the facts of his ultimate fate; unsurprisingly, the pathologist admitted that this was a case unlike any other he'd dealt with.

Detective Superintendent Adrian Maybanks was the senior officer appointed at the start of the enquiry to field press questions. It was difficult to know how to address the case at the outset, but he made it known that a boy of about five years of age had had his head and limbs removed before being tossed into the river, yet no one had come forward to say he was missing.

No matter the length of time an officer has spent dealing with serious crimes, any case where a child has been deliberately and cruelly harmed never fails to be distressing. At a press conference held two days after the torso had been found, DS Maybanks stated frankly: 'The child died a very violent death. It's very tragic and traumatic. At this stage I would like to reassure members of the London community that we will not rest until the person responsible has been apprehended.' This wasn't press conference rhetoric – every member of the team assembled had privately vowed to move heaven and earth to track who was responsible for the little boy's brutal death. But where to start?

Although no longer the heart of its commerce, the Thames still dominates the city's geography. From the air, you can see how clearly it divides north and south, two sides of the river that can feel like different worlds rather than just two parts of the same city. Jokes abound about taxi drivers refusing fares if it means 'going south of the river' but a closer understanding of London reveals that the city is less divided by north and south than by zones of tightly packed and very diverse villages. Pockets of depravity rub up against streets of staggering affluence across London's sprawl. It is common for sink estates to butt up against multi-million-pound period homes. The streets of London aren't easy to navigate unless you know them well and neither is its river.

As well as dividing the city, the Thames also shapes its neighbourhoods, from west to east. The river has an overall length of 215 miles, but it is the slow and wide flow through London that is most familiar. Its estuary opens onto the North Sea and the marine unit estimated that it would only have taken two more tides before the torso they retrieved near Tower Bridge would have been pushed out into the North Sea. In doing so, it would probably have remained undiscovered.

The Thames is tidal up to Teddington Lock, about fifty-five miles upstream from the estuary. The pathologist estimated that the child's body had been in the water for up to ten days and so the police team knew that it could have been disposed of at any point from Teddington to Tower Bridge, a huge area to search. The appeal went out for people to contact the incident room if they had seen anyone acting suspiciously near the water's edge in the previous two weeks. The incident room had been set up at Catford Hill police station and initially police hoped that someone would come forward with key information about a missing child. The days passed, however, and no one did.

Of all our citizens, children are the most vulnerable. About every ten days, a child will meet a violent death, but that will be at the hands of a parent or step-parent. When a child's body is found outside the home, it implies that the murderer comes from outside the family. Between five and seven children are abducted and murdered by strangers each year in the UK. The numbers are dwarfed by those of accidental deaths or road fatalities, but they are the ones that haunt the public consciousness most deeply.

Police initially speculated that a paedophile had snatched this child and disposed of him after a sexual assault, but the pathology report cast doubt on that. There were no signs of sexual assault. Also, no one had reported a missing child. Checks had already been made but not every child that goes missing is reported. The majority of the unreported cases are teenagers running from broken homes or care; it is rare for children under ten to leave home. As the first crucial seventy-two hours passed, it seemed more likely that the boy had died at the hands of someone he knew.

It was on 24 September that the investigation took its first twist. A police team from the Netherlands contacted their Metropolitan Police counterparts to say that they too were investigating a case where a child had been dismembered and had been found in water. But there were crucial differences. The Dutch child was a girl and she was white. Her body had been found floating in a lake at Nulde the previous August; her head was not discovered until later, by a fisherman in the Hook of Holland.

Both investigation teams met and shared what they knew and although it seemed unlikely that a firm link would be established, it had brought Europe into focus. A European connection had been suggested by the washing label found on the orange shorts the boy had been wearing. It was in German. Also, 'Kids & Co', the retailer of the clothing, was not a British brand. It was possible that the child was not born in the UK. He may have been brought to these shores and that would mean the search for his identity would have to widen farther still.

The search for the boy's other body parts had continued in

the Thames, but nothing more had been discovered. With no name or even country of origin to work with, the team looked again at possible motives for the child's death. A number of theories arose. Could it have been a 'mercy' killing? Probably not: if the child had been terminally ill, it seems unlikely that a carer would choose such a violent end. Was this a 'stranger' or paedophile abduction? If it was, and children are frequently killed so they cannot reveal the abductor's identity, shouldn't there have been some evidence of sexual assault? This had been a brutal and deliberate beheading and dismemberment. What was to be gained from the violent death of a young child?

Ritual murder. Two words that would take the team into wholly new and very disturbing territory. This possibility was first raised by the Home Office pathologist, who'd read about 'muti-murders' in southern Africa, and wondered if the body he examined could have been used for a sacrificial killing. Two weeks in to the investigation nothing was being ruled out, but as officers made tentative enquires about the role of human sacrifice in 'muti' (traditional medicine) practised in southern Africa, alarm bells began to ring.

Even raising the possibility that a boy had been 'sacrificed' was a cultural and political minefield. The press immediately led with the fear that 'black magic', 'witch doctors' and 'medicine murder' were being imported from Africa into the UK. With the media intermittently stirring up anxiety over immigration, the investigative team was loath to be dragged into any tabloid hysteria. But the fact remained that a five-year-old boy was dead and no lead could be ignored.

By mid-October, the possibility that the boy was the victim

of a muti or medicine killing was being openly explored. The team had been approached by Colonel Kobus Jonker, a South African police officer and member of the Occult Related Crimes Squad in his home country. He was in the UK attending a conference about Ritual Abuse Information and Network Support (RAINS). Colonel Jonker had wide-ranging experience from his time serving as a police officer in Pretoria but the British team was wary of being dragged into any kind of Satanist scare story. Nevertheless, it was clear that the team needed to find out more about muti and unscrupulous religious practices.

Muti is a Zulu word meaning 'tree', and many of the remedies practised as part of one of Africa's oldest healing traditions come from trees, bark and indigenous plants. Predominately found in Southern Africa, it is on the whole benign and has been used for centuries to treat common medical complaints. Practitioners are called 'sangomas'. Most sangomas act as counsellors as well as herbalists and even when modern Westernised medicine is available, the majority of communities still consult traditional practitioners.

Difficulties, should they arise, are twofold. First, those who practise this age-old form of medicine are prone to spreading misinformation. Sangomas believe that illness can result from contamination from witchcraft, angry spirits or impurities. Much focus is given to communicating with ancestors and placating or recruiting them to fight sickness. With illnesses as life-threatening as HIV, misplaced beliefs can hinder health campaigns.

With around 80% of southern Africa consulting sangomas, combating misinformation surrounding the spread of HIV was a major hurdle facing health workers. One breakthrough came when sangomas were enlisted as part of health campaigns, imparting safe sex messages directly as part of their roles as counsellors. When sangomas work alongside health specialists, they prove highly effective.

The second problem arises when a small minority of sangomas choose to use their skills for a far darker purpose. The overwhelming majority of sangomas work for the benefit of their patients, but as with any belief system, there are charlatans and crooks at work too. Some advertise their services claiming to offer guaranteed lottery wins, job promotions or enhanced sexual prowess. Others boast that they alone know the route to business success, power and influence. With their 'power of sight' into the spirit world, they promise rewards if the right sacrifice is made, and the more powerful the potion, the more powerful the outcome.

Sangomas use animal remains as well as herbs and plants, but there is also an underground market that deals in human body parts. Despite denials and an emphasis on the good work carried out by the vast majority of sangomas, the belief persists that human remains make the strongest medicine. The rarer the ingredient, the more it is imbued with notions of power. It is an ancient belief and it is not as bloodthirsty as it first sounds. Many civilisations have built belief systems in which sacrifice is central if the gods are to be appeased or celebrated. For the Aztecs, the ultimate gift was a human life – they understood that the gods sacrificed themselves so that the universe and mankind could exist – and so by offering the heavens what was most precious, i.e. human blood, life could continue.

The scale of human sacrifice carried out by the Aztecs is

still staggering today. At the reconsecration of the temple at Tenochtitlan, it is estimated that 4,000 human sacrifices were made over the course of a single day – and the most powerful of offerings was the life of a child. Nothing was held more dear, no greater gift could be made to guarantee a happy and prosperous life. It is easy to dismiss primitive faiths, but human sacrifice so others can live even has echoes in the formation of Christianity: Christ gave his life so we may live. Receiving the Eucharist, through eating bread and drinking wine, is symbolic of Christ's body and blood.

Ritual killings have always played a part in our attempt to understand our place in the universe and to control our destiny. But ritual killings are no longer the preserve of archaeologists. As the Metropolitan Police were to discover, they still play a part in the worst practices of muti today and they are no longer confined to the shores of southern Africa.

It is safe to say that stories of muti murders eclipsed anything the investigation had ever come across. Recent incidents recorded in South Africa include cases such as that of the six-year-old boy, Fezeka Maphanga, who was taken from his bed at night and found by his neighbours the next morning, dumped in some bushes near his home in Bushbuckridge. His head, arms and genitals had been hacked away and have never been recovered. In another case, the body of a young man believed to be in his twenties was found near Limpopo with his right eye gouged out, his nose and lips sliced off and five fingers of his right hand missing. Over the course of the mutilation, the toes on his right foot had also been hacked off as well as the palm of his left hand.

Then there were the brutal deaths of two girls out on errands for their families. Mapula Lonkokile, fourteen, and Tshiamo Dominica Gaope, ten, were reported missing when they failed to return home. Their bodies were later found on the outskirts of Phokeng, near Rustenburg. Tshiamo's hands had been tied behind her back and part of her big toe had been cut off. Mapula's body was found with her skull cracked open and her brain removed. Her right ear had also been cut off. The list of atrocities believed to be part of muti killings is horrifying. But what do those who commit the murders hope to gain? The answers, when they come at all, are no less disturbing.

Recently, the body of a seven-year-old boy from Durban, Vuyani Nqulunga, was found yards from his home after he had been stabbed, decapitated and his genitals removed. Unlike many muti killings, this time the killer was apprehended and brought to trial. Vuyani's killer was only seventeen years old and he had lured the boy back to his room after they had watched a video together at a nearby shop. The accused remained anonymous during the trial at Pretoria because he was still a minor, but was eventually sentenced to 23 years in prison. What emerged as part of the teenager's confession gave a chilling insight into the world of muti.

He said he had killed Vuyani on behalf of another man. This man offered him R20,000 for the head of a child, a considerable sum of money for the teen, who was only earning R70 a day and who had to send home R500 to support his family every three months.

The teen said he was not told why the man wanted body parts, but Advocate Bekhi Manyathi stated that it could have been only for muti. Greed is the motivator. It is probable that the man who hired the teen was seeking business success and believed that a corrupt sangoma could guarantee it through powerful muti.

Other cases bear this out. A hairdresser and a sangoma she had consulted were arrested after the disappearance of a four-year-old girl. The police searched the salon after a witness came forward to say that the girl's body parts were buried in the wall, as part of a spell to ensure the business would thrive.

Criminals are known to consult corrupt sangomas too, hoping for spells that will make them undetectable to the police. The more powerful the concoction, the more protected they feel, some even believing that they are invisible in the presence of police.

Greed, ignorance, criminality and even mental illness have all had a part of play in southern Africa's muti murders and the lines of motivation often become blurred, as was revealed during the trial of Khayelihle Dlamini. This twenty-four-year-old admitted murdering his four-year-old brother and drinking his brain fluid because he believed that the muti would help him win the lottery. But he also believed he was possessed by a tokoloshe, an evil spirit. Dlamini was sentenced to 20 years.

This was the world that the team from the Met found themselves plunged into; the complexities of the darker side of muti were difficult for the officers to comprehend. They consulted Professor Hendrik Scholtz, Head of Pathology at the University of Witwatersrand in South Africa. Professor Scholtz agreed to carry out the second statutory post-mortem on the mutilated body for the Met. The team no longer wanted to see their case featured in the news as 'the Torso in the Thames' and took the decision to call the boy in their care

Adam. They made it clear that until he and his family could be identified, the police would act as his family and that he deserved a name. He had been a defenceless young boy; he should not be reduced to a macabre headline.

If creating an identity was not enough to stir the conscience of someone holding back key information, in December 2001 a reward of £50,000 was also offered for information leading to a conviction. It was the highest reward offered for a murder in the UK, but still no one came forward.

Professor Scholtz carried out tests and concluded that the nature of the wounds were consistent with ritual homicide. He also raised the concern that not only are children often the targets but that parts can be removed while they are still alive, as this is believed to increase the power of the muti. His findings made news not just in the UK but around the world. The Met's commander, Andy Baker, proved himself a model of British understatement when he declared: 'We have learnt things that they don't teach you in police college in London.'

But there were key differences between this case and incidents of muti killings in South Africa. The boy's genitals had not been mutilated, for a start, and furthermore, the boy had been circumcised, a feature of boyhood in west or central, not southern Africa, Professor Scholtz informed the police. He agreed to continue to assist the Met with a broader understanding of ritual killing and also to attend a police conference early in the New Year of 2002. Yet it wasn't South Africa that was to lead to the next major development but the Thames once more.

In January, seven half-burnt candles were found wrapped in a white sheet and washed up on the banks of the river. The name Adekoye Jo Fola Adeoye was written on the sheet and the name Fola Adeoye was inscribed on the candles. The police were cautious but gave a press conference at which DCI O'Reilly stated: 'We know with some certainty that the candles and the sheet form part of a ritualistic ceremony. We can't say if they are connected, but at the moment we are linking them.' Quietly, the team was hopeful that this would prove a breakthrough.

The names found on the candles and the sheet were not traditional southern African names either, they were far more likely to be Nigerian. Before too long, the investigation was to dramatically swing away from South Africa, but not before the most influential figure in Africa, and arguably the world, spoke out on Adam's behalf.

Nelson Mandela, former president of South Africa, made a global appeal for information about Adam. Deeply moved by the young boy's plight, he stated: 'It seems likely that the boy might have come from Africa... I wish to direct my appeal specifically to people in Africa.

'If anywhere, even in the remotest village of our continent, there is a family missing a son of that age, who might have disappeared around that time, 21 September 2001, please contact the police in London, either directly or through your local police.'

Of course, Mandela's appeal was hardly likely to prompt the killers, or those who knew them, to come forward, but once again it demonstrated how committed the Met was to exploring every channel in its attempt to track the guilty party. It also unequivocally showed the world that muti murders were repellent to all law-abiding Africans and there was no better person than Mandela, or 'Madiba', as he is known in his homeland, to articulate that.

Back in London, any hope that had sprung from the discovery of the burnt candles and sheet discovered in the Thames was ruled out. Adekoye Jo Fola Adeoye had been found and he was living in New York. He was interviewed by detectives from the Met alongside officers from New York's Police Department. Adeoye confirmed he was the person referred to on the sheet and candles and, in a strange collision of worlds old and new, said that the candles and sheet were part of a prayer service friends in the UK had held seeking to protect him following the 9/11 terrorist attacks. What was written on the candles and sheets was no more than a good luck charm from well-wishers. Detectives may not have been closer to establishing Adam's identity, but they had a renewed sense of how traditional practices from Africa travel with immigrants even as they carve out new lives in cities thousands of miles away from their homeland.

The media were quick to trade on stories of voodoo and ritual medicine thriving in the UK, particularly in London. One Radio 4 journalist from the *Today* programme went undercover and witnessed a ceremony where a young girl with a speech defect was wrapped in a black sheet and chanted over by a group of men wearing white robes. Practitioners advertised their services in London newspapers and it wasn't long before more tales of horror were being reported.

At the same time that the Met were trying to get the investigation onto a neutral footing with Nelson Mandela's plea for information, BBC 2 aired a documentary called *Nobody's Child* about Adam's case. In the programme, Helen

Madide, from Thohoyandou in South Africa, told the BBC that her former partner, a sangoma, had once forced her to hold her toddler while he slit its throat and then dismembered the child. He insisted that the sangoma's ancestors had instructed him to kill the child so that he could be rich. The man was arrested and imprisoned but stories such as this fuelled fears that children could be subject to ritual abuse in the UK.

For the Met, the focus remained on establishing facts. 'I must stress we are not judging any cultures,' stressed Commander Andy Baker. 'We are investigating a crime, the crime of murder.' Existing DNA tests confirmed that Adam was from Africa, but pinning down where in that enormous continent outstripped the techniques forensic scientists had at their disposal.

When a high-profile murder isn't solved quickly, a committee is set up to oversee the enquiry; in this case, it was called Gold Group. The group was used to review findings and suggest new approaches. The biggest stumbling block in tracking the killer or killers had not changed since that first day: Adam's identity. Until officers had a name, tracing his movements, associates and vulnerabilities would be next to impossible.

The team had been in touch with forensic scientists in the US hoping that the techniques that emerged during work to identify victims after 9/11 might be of use. Unofficially, the FBI thought Adam's case was unsolvable and US Forensics did not offer anything new. Adam's case could have been filed away as unsolved, but DCI O'Reilly's team were determined that if all avenues had been explored, they'd find ways to open new ones.

Gold Group invited other homicide detectives and leading forensic scientists to a meeting and DCI O'Reilly made his pitch. He ran through the information gathered to date and asked what could possibly be done to identify Adam. The hope lay with Forensics. If there was a new technique being developed, could it help pin down where Adam was from? The method did not have to be published, peer reviewed or validated. This was an opportunity to act as pioneers.

The response was extraordinary. 'Investigations of this nature can be very expensive,' DCI O'Reilly revealed, 'forensic bills can soon run high, but we were very fortunate, the scientists gave their time and effort without charge. They were committed to doing what they could to help Adam.'

As the forensic teams began their work, Dr Richard Hoskins stepped in to advise Gold Group in his capacity as a specialist in African religions, then lecturing at King's College, London. He told the team that the nature of Adam's murder suggested a corrupt form of practice in west Africa. In Nigeria, there are over 400 'Orisha' or ancestor gods and Oshun, a Yoruba goddess of the river, is associated with the colours red or orange. That might go some way to explain why orange shorts were placed on the child's body after death and also why his remains were put in the Thames.

Dr Hoskins again stressed the fact that Adam was circumcised, a procedure that happens shortly after birth in Nigeria but not in South Africa until after puberty. And as his genitals were intact, it again pointed strongly to west Africa. In South Africa, genitals are taken for their 'power' but in the west, it is the blood rather than the genitals that are key. This cultural insight was valuable but needed to be backed by scientific evidence. Ray Fysh is a specialist advisor to the forensic science service. He recognised that current methods had failed and, after scouring through research papers and journals, was sure that a new approach was required.

While chromosomal DNA had produced little in the way of progress, researcher Andy Urquhart suggested that the team look at mitochondrial DNA, which is passed straight from mother to child. The signature stays unchanged, so those with the same mitochondria would share a female ancestor. It was the first time this approach had been used in a criminal investigation, but it indicated that it was highly probable that Adam was from west Africa. There are no extensive databases to help narrow down the search further – however, it still left a huge land mass that took in Nigeria, Togo and Benin. Once more, it seemed an avenue was coming to an end.

The breakthrough, when it came, was inspirational and it all started with a conversation between Ray Fysh and Professor Ken Pye, a forensic geologist from the University of London. Professor Pye was discussing the role of Strontium isotopes with Fysh – at its most basic, the idea that 'we are what we eat'. The ratio in these isotopes does not alter from rock, to soil, to water, to plants. Animals eat the plants and we eat the animals and in doing so, store a signature of them in our bones. What's more, it takes many years for the isotopes in our bone chemistry to change. As Adam was so young, these isotopes could act as a clear indication of his place of birth.

It would demand a leap in scientific attempts at 'bone mapping', as no isotonic map of the world existed. The team was able to find the same signature in Adam as in rocks that were more than 2,500 million years old – rocks of the Pre-Cambrian era. The areas of this rock type were shaded in on a map of Africa, and Nigeria immediately suggested itself as a prime location. But the area was still vast and encroached on neighbouring countries. The team could proceed no further without a more detailed isotonic database so, with typical tenacity, they decided to build one themselves. DCI O'Reilly joined Ray Fysh and Andy Urquhart as they spent almost three weeks collecting samples in Nigeria. Around 150 items were sourced, including soil, rocks, plants, animals and even human tissue. The three men travelled hundreds of miles and returned to London to deliver what they found to Professor Pye.

Their efforts were not in vain. After analysis, Professor Pye was able to rule out northern Nigeria and other stretches of the country. The closest matches came from one place alone: Benin City. From the discovery of a boy's body in the Thames two years earlier, DCI O'Reilly now knew he could return to Benin City and canvas to find the boy's family.

It was a huge achievement for the forensic teams, though it would prove to be just one of the breakthroughs they would pioneer. Original pathology revealed that there was little in Adam's stomach contents other than cough medicine. He had effectively been starved prior to his death. Now the team looked at his upper and lower intestines to see if they would yield more evidence about his final hours.

The upper intestine revealed little, but the lower showed that the boy had been given clay pellets that contained traces of gold and quartz. It seemed likely that they were part of a ceremony before the sacrifice was made. This notion was fully backed up after another substance was identified by botanical experts at Kew Gardens in London. Adam had been fed Calabar bean. This is a highly toxic substance that is found growing on vines in southern Nigeria and is also known as the 'ordeal' bean, as it is used in witchcraft rituals. If someone is suspected of a crime, they are fed an extract and in an alarmingly simple test, if they reject it through violent vomiting and survive, they are innocent. If they die, it is a sign of guilt. But the bean is also known for its ability to paralyse a victim if used in smaller doses. Just as the team felt that they were starting to understand what had happened to Adam, they were faced with the terrible scenario that the young boy would have been conscious but unable to move during his final moments.

Traces of pollen found would provide another key insight – namely about Adam's movements. Had he been brought to the UK and killed immediately, or had he been kept in the country for some time? Dr Nick Branch from Royal Holloway uses pollen analysis in archaeological digs, for example in connection with bodies preserved in bogs for thousands of years. He identified pollen spores in Adam's lower intestine that are only found in the UK or north-western Europe.

Firstly, Dr Branch carried out tests to see if the spores could be found in food, such as cereal. No sign of the spores were found – but they are found in the air too, and Dr Branch concluded that the pollen had been breathed in. 'Food takes about seventy-two hours to pass through the body,' he explained later. 'Because there was food material inside the large intestine you could confidently say it had been fed to

Adam roughly seventy-two hours before his death. That meant that, in all probability, Adam had been in Britain for at least three days.'

The police were now able to piece together a more detailed picture of Adam's background. In all likelihood, he was from Benin City, he lived there until shortly before being smuggled into the UK where he was held for a few days and then used as a human sacrifice.

DCI O'Reilly travelled back to Benin City with flyers about the missing boy and asked for anyone with a missing relative that fitted his description to come forward. DNA swabs were taken of those who did but, sadly, no match was made. A reward for information about Adam produced nothing either. The police had to accept that it was possible that Adam's family knew he was missing and did not want the police to become involved.

He could, of course, have been an orphan who fell between the cracks of any organisation in Benin City equipped to deal with his case. He could have been snatched from the streets, a forgotten child among many who live perilous lives on the poverty line in the city. Benin City is a ramshackle metropolis with a population of over a million but it is estimated that up to 90% of adults are unemployed. For those born there, it can be a desperate existence and it is not uncommon to see signs offering children for sale. That might sound barbaric, but a family is forced to weigh up the fact that by selling one of their number, perhaps their other six or seven can be saved. Families imagine children are bought to be servants or workers elsewhere, yet some are also aware that their daughters will be trafficked into a life of prostitution in the

West. The families hope that whatever the children's fate, money will be sent home that will improve life for them.

Joyce Osagiede was a woman who knew all about how harsh life could be in Benin City. In fact, she had managed to flee from Nigeria but when she was interviewed by immigration services in Croydon, she told them that she and her two daughters were from Sierra Leone. She also said that she was escaping persecution from a cult who had been responsible for the death of eleven children, including her eldest child.

She became of interest to the police investigating the Adam case, but the Forensic Science Service found that her DNA did not match Adam's. She was handed over to immigration and, after a claim for asylum was turned down, she was deported back to Benin.

Her ex-husband, Sam Onojhighovie, was also investigated, although it took a year to find him. He had previously lived in Germany but had fled following charges of fraud in relation to human trafficking and, in his absence, had been sentenced to seven years. When he was finally tracked down to Dublin; he'd been hiding there for some months in a local authority home. The house was searched and documents and a computer removed. But, after his DNA was tested, no connection to Adam was found.

DCI O'Reilly, who took part in the press briefing, said: 'This is the trafficking side of the Adam investigation and it is significant and important to that enquiry as a whole.' On a chilling note, he added: 'We don't know how many children are involved in this operation but it's certainly in the hundreds, if not the thousands, coming from mainland Africa into the UK.'

Again, the media went into a tailspin over the spectre of missing children. One report stated that the police knew that hundreds of children were missing from school records, but DCI O'Reilly later stressed that the situation was far more complex than it first appeared and that the police were at a significant disadvantage when identifying a child's whereabouts. Firstly, children move, parents separate, some are taken care of by a different set of relatives and former schools and GPs' surgeries are not always informed of the change of circumstances. Another disadvantage that the authorities face is that a child can leave the country to return home permanently, but no formal record of these departures at ports and airports exists. Children are trafficked in, mostly by desperate parents hoping that their offspring will enjoy better life, but some, like Adam, will encounter hardship, cruelty and even murder.

Someone who would have been well versed in the life that awaited those smuggled to these shores is Kingsley Ojo. The 35-year-old Nigerian's home in Stratford was raided by police; he was suspected of being a people trafficker. Indeed, it emerged that he was part of a gang that had charged immigrants up to £20,000 for a new life in the UK. Among many other cases, he is believed to have aided Joyce's entry into the country.

He first came to the notice of the authorities in 1997, claiming to be from Sierra Leone and seeking asylum. During his trial, he showed little remorse for his actions, even when it came to light that he had stolen the identity of his girlfriend's dead baby son. He was jailed in 2004 for four-and-a-half years.

The Met had successfully broken up one people-trafficking ring, but knew that others would spring up in their place. Operation Maxim was highlighted as one response, to target organised immigration crime within London. Yet even while the authorities step up their efforts to tackle trafficking crimes, children slip through the net.

Those involved in Adam's investigation will have read with dismay the case of an eight-year-old girl brought to court only one year after Ojo was sentenced. The girl remains unnamed, to help protect her identity. She was brought to the UK from Angola after her father died in the civil war and her mother went missing. Her 'aunt' posed as her mother and moved her into the family home in Hackney, east London. Another eight-year-old, a boy, accused the girl of using witchcraft and this proved to be the start of a fifteen-month ordeal that went unnoticed.

She was starved, beaten with belts and cut; chilli peppers were rubbed into her eyes. At one point, the girl was stripped naked, cut with knives and forced into a plastic bag, which was then zipped up. The plan was to throw her into a canal and it was only halted by the intervention of Sebastian Pinto, a brother of one of her tormentors, Sita Kisanga. He explained that if the body was found, the individuals involved would be investigated and might get a prison sentence.

Street wardens in Hackney found the girl sitting barefoot and with facial injuries on the steps outside Ms Kisanga's flat. She had already been returned to her 'aunt' by social workers after being removed for a month and the prosecution at the Old Bailey trial made it clear that the girl would have died if the abuse had been allowed to continue any longer.

As well as shock that a child could be abused this way came the uncomfortable realisation that witchcraft is real for a minority of those who have settled in the UK. Sita Kisanga gave an interview to the BBC in which she maintained that she had challenged the 'aunt' about the girl's treatment but that it became clear why she was being beaten and tortured. Ms Kisanga explained that the girl 'went to Africa' in the night-time to do bad things: 'I know that it is not easy for people to believe,' she acknowledged, 'but those people with a spiritual belief, they will know that what I am saying is true. There is the spiritual world and the material world.' Her words fell on deaf ears as Kisanga was jailed for ten years. Her brother, Sebastian Pinto, was jailed for four year and the 'aunt' (who cannot be named) was jailed for ten.

The BBC set up a talkboard to canvas views on this controversial subject; many of the respondents provided revealing insights into muti. One resident of Zimbabwe claimed that witchcraft is practised throughout Africa and that the only person immune to it is Robert Mugabe, as 'he can afford stronger potions'. Someone from Nigeria condemned the fact that a five-year-old girl was tied upside down and tortured for hours, accused of the death of her mother. Another posted the fact that people could travel from Malawi to the USA in seconds: 'There are no planes which can travel from UK to USA in seconds, but ordinary people here can do it. In Karonga in the northern part of Malawi you can be removed your bones if you are rude and when you apologise they are returned. Anyway, don't be shocked.'

John Azah is vice-chairman of the Metropolitan Police Independent Advisory Group. Originally from Ghana, he has helped the investigation walk a difficult tightrope – not condemning cultures and concentrating on focusing all eyes on the crime committed. But he has been candid too and summed up the concerns of many when he said: 'In promoting cultural diversity we import the good and the bad... as bad as it may sound, we have imported those aspects of culture into mainland Britain.'

Mr Azah hoped that this kind of behaviour would not travel to these shores, but it has. In 2006, five years since the discovery of Adam's remains, the decision was made to bury him. With hundreds of lines of enquiry and millions of words spent, the team were as determined as ever not to cease in their hunt for Adam's killers. DCI O'Reilly called Adam an unknown soldier and he fell in a little-known war, carried out on the fringes of society and fed by criminality, superstition and greed.

The police in the UK are better equipped than ever to tackle any ritual abuse of a child in this country. DCI O'Reilly admits that in 2001 no one had ever had to deal with this sort of offence and few people in the police force would have been aware of the cultural nuances at play. It is very different today. The investigation will continue and every trafficker will be aware of the Met's remorseless efforts to track them down. 'We will keep going,' DCI O'Reilly says. 'Sometimes I think of what that poor child went through and it drives me on.'

In fact, the determination of all involved in the investigation has already born fruit. The forensic techniques pioneered during the course of the case have resulted in prosecutions elsewhere. A man who raped three teenage girls in Llandarcy, south Wales, in 1973 was tracked down using Ray Fysh's pioneering work, with the help of a relative's DNA. The suspect, Joseph Kappen, had since died, but his body was exhumed and a DNA match made.

Craig Harman was responsible for the death of Michael Little, who died after a brick thrown from a motorway bridge smashed through his lorry windscreen. Harman was finally tracked down when DNA left on the brick was examined and found to be similar to those of his close relatives; he admitted manslaughter in 2004.

In 2006 James Lloyd was jailed for life for raping four women and attempting to rape two others. He had kept his victims shoes as trophies after the attacks, which took place in the Rotherham and Barnsley area. Although these offences all dated back to the 1980s, Lloyd was eventually identified after a family member provided a DNA sample in connection with a driving offence some twenty years later.

The work with strontium isotopes also provided a vital link in the prosecution of the four men involved in the botched bomb attacks of 21 July 2005. Only two weeks after the devastation of the 7 July attacks on London's transport network, Muktar Ibrahim, Yassin Omar, Ramzi Mohammed and Hussain Osman, planned to detonate explosives on three tube trains and a bus in London. Fortunately, the devices strapped to them failed to detonate. During the investigation, Forensics used isotopes to trace the men's movements, revealing they had spent time abroad at terrorist training camps. We are what we eat. In 2007, all four men were jailed for life.

That said, the forensic developments that the Adam case

pioneered bring little solace when we are reminded of his last few hours. This was a five-year-old boy, an innocent, and a victim of a barbaric ritual. His legacy lives on, though: the 'family' who adopted him in death will continue to pursue his killers. And it is hoped we are no longer blind to the evil carried out in the name of a corrupt faith.

CHAPTER FIVE
SUZY LAMPLUGH
'LIFE IS FOR LIVING'

A million words. That is a rough estimation of the word count held in the police files on the disappearance of twenty-five-year-old Suzy Lamplugh. And yet what happened to the young woman still remains unknown. Except in the mind of one man – one man the police are seeking to this day.

Each year, there are almost 1,000 recorded homicides in the UK and thousands more go missing. Not all will be covered widely in the press and fewer still are remembered as the years pass. People still remember the name of Suzy Lamplugh, though, in part through the huge efforts her family have made to find out what happened to her and to help others, and in part because something about Suzy's story spoke to a fear in each of us.

She was young, attractive, well loved and happily establishing her life in London, working hard at an estate agents in Fulham, south-west London. The photograph of her that became famous after her disappearance is particularly memorable – it is a picture of a pretty, carefree young woman. Although it might sound unfair, it is widely accepted that an attractive victim will achieve a higher profile than a less personable victim, both in terms of media coverage and in terms of the general public's ability to remember them. If Suzy Lamplugh had been a 'typical' runaway – someone involved with drugs or prostitution, someone from a broken home – it's doubtful her story would have made a single column of print. We are all guilty of forgetting the vast majority of people who go missing. It shouldn't be the case, but at some level we are programmed to respond to attractive open features and a wide smile, such as Suzy's. At a more disturbing level, those qualities may well be what attracted her killer.

The contrast between light and dark, the bright young woman and the shadowy figure that hunted her, inevitably haunts us. Abduction and murder is very rare in the UK and yet Suzy Lamplugh's story struck a chord that reverberates still. How could a young woman disappear on an ordinary working day, on a busy London street? There is a great deal to be learned from her story – both good and bad.

Suzy was one of four children in a close-knit family from Richmond, south-west London. At the time of her disappearance, her sister Tamsin was twenty-four; Lizzie, the baby of the family, was aged sixteen and Tim, the first-born, was twenty-six. Suzy's parents – Paul, a solicitor, and Diana – knew their daughter wanted to make the most of life and supported her fully. Academically, Suzy had not achieved as much as she could have, as she struggled with dyslexia. She'd got through her O-Levels, but found the workload of A-Levels too demanding and opted to begin work after failing English Literature.

'Life is for living,' Suzy would say, and she'd enjoyed seeing the world, at one point working in a beauty salon on board the luxury cruiser the QE2. She'd enjoyed her time on the Southampton-based liner but had come back to the area of London where she grew up to set up home with Tamsin and explore new career avenues.

At first, she returned to the world of beauty therapy, working in exclusive London hotels, but part of her felt that this was not the career she should settle for. Suzy moved with an ambitious group of friends in Putney; they expected to attend spa days, not to administer them. She considered opening up her own salon and a client, the wife of a banker, talked about backing her, but in the end, at the age of twenty-five, she settled on a new path.

In 1986, property was booming and there was money to be made buying, developing and selling homes. Fulham was a popular suburb. The streets were dominated by Victorian and Edwardian period properties that made for ideal renovation projects. Shorrolds Road was typical. The location was good, as it is within a ten-minute walk of both Fulham Broadway and Parsons Green tube stations. The houses that line the street are impressive Victorian terraces, with high ceilings and large reception rooms. The homes are big but garden space is limited and an obvious option was to convert them into flats. In 1986, a typical home, such as No.37, would cost around £130,000. Today, one-bedroom flats on Shorrolds Road sell for over £300,000, so developers with an eye to the future were on course to make a good deal of money.

Estate agents had also benefited from the property boom. A number of new agencies had sprung up and as there are no formal qualifications required to become an estate agent, it was a good route for younger people with ambition to join a profession and earn a good wage. Agents work on commission and Suzy had the qualities any successful agent would need: she was well organised, personable and committed to following through a deal from viewing to completion.

Suzy walked into one agency, Sturgis, and immediately impressed the branch manager. She was offered a position as a negotiator and quickly settled into the role and the team. Suzy enjoyed her new job and would often eat lunch at her desk, rather than opt for a long break, to make sure that she was taking calls and potential commissions. When a call came thought late in July, she was happy to set up a viewing at No.37 Shorrolds Road. It was empty, as the owner was working overseas, and a set of keys was kept at the office so Sturgis could show prospective buyers around at short notice. Suzy finished the call and made a note in her appointment diary: '12.45pm, Mr Kipper, 37 Shorrolds Road, o/s'. The note o/s was shorthand for meeting the buyer outside and Suzy should then have filled out an index card listing Mr Kipper's details, his current address, whether he was a cash buyer, had a house to sell or had secured a mortgage offer and so was in a position to move quickly. But she didn't. It was a busy office and she could always fill in the details later.

It was a Monday afternoon, a warm and bright July day, as Suzy set off at 12.40pm. The house was less than a mile away, but she'd be there in good time as she was driving. Picking up her purse, taking the keys off the board, she headed out, saying goodbye to her work colleagues. And that was the last time they saw her.

We are forced to speculate as to what happened next. One witness claimed that Suzy arrived at the property, just a few minutes' drive from the office, on time; if so, she would have parked the company-owned white Ford Fiesta at the side of the road. That afternoon, two white Fiestas were seen in the street – but they were a popular model back then, and relatively common.

One resident of the street described seeing a woman, fitting Suzy's description, with a smartly dressed man outside No.37, sometime before 1pm. Later, another witness would come forward to say that he remembered seeing the couple; as he was running late, he checked his watch and noted it was 12.50pm. It was a sequence of events that made sense until something incontrovertible turned up later that evening – something that has muddied the investigation to this day.

Suzy's car was found over a mile away, badly parked on Stevenage Road, as if it had been abandoned with some haste. It was left facing the opposite direction to Shorrolds Road. One witness noted that it was blocking a garage and wondered how long it would be parked there; she was walking her dog back home and was sure this was about 12.45pm.

How could the car be in two places at once? Did Suzy drive to Shorrolds Road or not? This was just the first of many questions that would tax the enquiry as the weeks, and years, unfolded.

The investigation had begun simply enough, when Suzy was reported missing the day of her disappearance. Her colleagues were puzzled when she didn't return to the office after the viewing and concern turned to worry by 3.30pm – it was most out of character for her. Calls were made to her flat and friends and then to local hospitals, but no one had seen her. When she failed to show up at a pub at 6pm, her colleagues knew something was amiss. Not because the pub was a social call: two nights earlier, Suzy had lost her chequebook and diary and had spent part of Monday morning phoning venues she'd visited over the weekend to see if they'd been handed in. They had, at a local pub; a relieved Suzy told the landlord she'd call in at 6pm to pick them up.

The Metropolitan Police deal with a large number of missing persons calls – over 20,000 every year – and happily, most are resolved within the first forty-eight hours, without the intervention of the police. Of those who disappear, a very small percentage become victims of homicide – just one in every 7,400 of those reported missing. But as Suzy was alone when she made the appointment to meet Mr Kipper, there was a small chance that some harm had befallen her.

Of course, there are cases of adults choosing to walk out on their lives and all who know them. Commonly, they are in a state of emotional crisis, perhaps after the break-up of a relationship or because of an inability to cope with mounting debts, and they choose to go missing. Depression is certainly a factor in such cases and each year many families face uncertainty and distress as they try to trace a loved one. The police checked Suzy's background, though, and were satisfied that there was nothing that could have encouraged her to walk out on her life. Having spoken with her family and friends, they began to worry that she had been abducted.

When Suzy's car was found abandoned on Stevenage Road, near the Thames, the police feared the worst. The driver's door was unlocked, the handbrake was off and Suzy's purse had been left in the driver's door pocket. If the vehicle had been stolen, it is unlikely that a car thief would have missed the opportunity to steal a purse. It also seemed unlikely that Suzy would have left her car in such a state and walked away without her purse.

With no progress made in the first forty-eight hours, the police and Suzy's family appealed to the public for information. Suzy's mother Diana emphasised that this was not in her daughter's character, explaining: 'There has never been a time in the past when I did not know where she was.' A photograph of a smiling Suzy was released to help prompt any potential witness to come forward, alongside a description of what she had been wearing that day: a grey skirt, dark jacket and low stiletto heels. The Senior Investigating Officer, Detective Superintendent Nick Carter, gave his own blunt assessment of the situation: 'Everything leads us to believe she has been abducted.' It was 30 July, a particularly poignant date as it was Diana Lamplugh's birthday. Suzy had known that she wouldn't be able to spend it with her mother, as she'd be at work, but ever the thoughtful daughter, she'd arranged for Diana to visit the theatre.

By now, forty officers had been assigned to the investigation and the River Police carried out a search of the Thames. Searches of gardens, towpaths, lockups and drains were also carried out. Nothing was found, which was something of a relief to the family. They were still certain that Suzy was alive and appealed for her abductor to contact the police and let them know where she was being held. Life without her was simply unimaginable for them.

The police were encouraged by the initial reaction from the public. Not only had the case attracted nationwide attention, but enough witnesses came forward from Shorrolds Road to create a Photofit identity of the man seen standing outside the property waiting for Suzy. He was described as around 5ft

8in, with dark swept-back hair, aged around twenty-five to thirty years old and wearing an expensive, well-fitted suit. In fact, he looked every inch the prospective and well-heeled developer, but the police were concerned that this was part of a front designed to lure Suzy into believing that this was an ordinary appointment.

What happened to Suzy had an immediate impact on young working women everywhere. It seemed impossible that a grown woman could be snatched in the middle of a working day and it emphasised just how vulnerable they were, no matter the time or place. Despite police efforts to stress how rare abductions were, the streets no longer seemed quite as safe as before.

Every family worried about their independent daughters, and estate agents in London ruled out allowing their female staff to meet any client alone; some suggested that they shouldn't be sent out to meet 'strangers' at all. This was an impossible situation for any fast-paced working environment: the lifeblood of their business relied on viewings and fitting around tight time commitments. It seemed like such a backward step; this was, after all, at the height of the 1980s boom years. The whole of the capital had been unnerved by the disappearance of the young woman, though, and for the first few weeks afterwards there was a new air of caution about.

Something about the unusualness of a daytime disappearance bothered the investigative team too. Surely a fit young woman would put up a fight if someone tried to force them into a car? Although she was only 5ft 6in, Suzy was a keen windsurfer and strong enough to at least scream out and resist an attacker for long enough to raise the alarm. Why did she not create a scene? Was it possible that Suzy knew this Mr Kipper?

What added to the puzzle was that Suzy's driving seat had been pushed back, as if someone with longer legs had driven the car. As it was a company car, the police checked with Sturgis and the negotiator with whom she shared the vehicle, who confirmed that Suzy drove with the seat closer to the wheel. It was easy to imagine a male driver adjusting her seat but less easy to explain why Suzy would allow a 'client' to drive her car to Stevenage Road. Negotiators are accustomed to taking clients from one viewing to another, for instance if they ask if Sturgis have any other similar properties to view. In fact, there was a Sturgis 'For Sale' board up in Stevenage Road, but Suzy did not have the keys for that property.

What would induce Suzy to move from her appointment in Shorrolds Road, back to her car, and for the client then to drive her nearly two miles away to a property to which she did not have keys? She was ambitious certainly, sales commissions are vital to negotiators, but these events didn't seem logical. If the client asked to be driven somewhere nearer a tube or train station, that would make sense. But Stevenage Road is much farther from a transport link than Shorrolds Road. Perhaps he suggested that she drive him nearer to where his car was parked. Odd that it should be 1.7 miles away, but perhaps he gave a plausible explanation. But to allow him to drive? That would set off alarm bells with any woman and it would be easy for someone with Suzy's confidence to say, 'I'm really sorry, Sturgis doesn't allow it.'

There are two possible explanations as to what happened. Firstly, Suzy had already been physically subdued and was being moved to Stevenage Road and into another vehicle. Witnesses on Shorrolds Road reported hearing a scream or a yell, but 28 July coincided with school holidays and screams could have come from any child playing outside. If Suzy had been bundled into her car, semiconscious, that could account for the hurried way her abductor parked, yet workmen on the street told police they saw nothing of note all day. The only other explanation for the journey, and for the driver's car seat being adjusted, could be that Suzy knew the man.

It was routine for any investigation of this nature to examine the men in the victim's life closely and now the police addressed this aspect of the case. Was the man she met a client at all? Was 'Mr Kipper' a pseudonym for someone Suzy knew, someone she might be arranging a property deal with? That could explain why she had not filled out an index card at the office. Suzy had a boyfriend, but it was clear that there had been other men in her life and it was even hinted that she may have been involved with a married man. The police urged anyone with a connection to Suzy to come forward.

With hundreds of names to check on the Sturgis lists, and many more names in Suzy's diaries, the investigation had turned into the largest missing persons case since the disappearance of Lord Lucan. There was still enormous coverage in the press, Suzy was a nice middle-class girl and there was an ongoing public clamour for the case to be solved. This was part of the difficulty facing the investigative team: it had such widespread publicity that the incident room was inundated with calls from members of the public, but the vast majority of people who got in touch did not have pertinent information. People wanted to help, but the theories and sightings of 'Mr Kipper' were bogging down the efforts to follow Suzy's trail.

For the Lamplugh family, the impact of Suzy's disappearance

was devastating. It is impossible to imagine the anguish of a parent or sibling, struggling to account for a loved one's last moments, wondering if she was alive or dead, fearing the very worst and praying that as the minutes, hours and days pass, some glimmer of good news will arrive. Caught in a terrible limbo, both wanting and fearing to hear from the police, ordinary family life destroyed in the space of a single Monday afternoon. Letters and cards flooded into the house; other neighbours could not look them in the eye. Every waking moment plagued with questions: Where is she? Why Suzy?

The Lamplughs are a close family and while tragedy can tear many a family apart, they found a way to support each other through their lowest moments of despair. As days became weeks, and the family had exhausted themselves exploring every avenue and making all possible appeals, two things became apparent. Firstly, there was a real possibility that they would never find out what had happened to Suzy. Despite police assurance that 99% of missing persons cases are solved within a year, her family had to face the fact that Suzy might never be found.

Secondly, the family found that beyond a police enquiry, there was very little other support available to them. There was no coordinated missing persons helpline or organisation set up, only a network of Salvation Army volunteers, but they were not in a position to communicate fluently across the UK. Also, there was precious little advice for families and young women still out in the workplace and worried about the likelihood that something terrible could happen. Police assurances about a statistical unlikelihood was not enough. Should you place restrictions on your life for the sake of personal security? If so, what practical steps could you follow to keep yourself safe without giving in to irrational fears?

It is testament to Diana and Paul's resilience and determination to help others that the Suzy Lamplugh Trust was born in December 1986, just six months after their daughter's disappearance, and created specifically to address personal-safety fears. Diana Lamplugh became a familiar figure on our screens, always a measured and sympathetic presence and a provider of valuable insights into how young women could protect themselves.

At the core of the Trust lies a simple message, as Diana would later say: 'We all want to live free and active lives. We also want to feel safe and secure wherever we are – at home and out and about. Despite the lurid headlines, the average person's chances of physical attack from a stranger are very low, but there are active skills and strategies you can use to help you reduce the risk to your personal safety.' Not giving in to hysteria, not constricting lives, but practising simple measures that would help thousands in the years to come. Simple advice now that is second nature to many, such as telling a friend or colleague details of who you are meeting, or at what time and when you should be expected back. Or carrying your keys and phone in your pocket so you can give up your handbag quickly if needs be. Simple steps, but always true to Suzy's maxim: 'Life is for living.'

The Suzy Lamplugh Trust was not the only charity to arise out of the case. Two sisters, Janet Newman and Mary Asprey, were neighbours of the Lamplughs and Mary's son had even attended nursery with Suzy. They were troubled to learn that no central helpline was available for the families with missing loved ones and began to fundraise so one could be set up. For some years, the National Missing Persons helpline was run from a spare bedroom and it was not until 1993 that a permanent home was found for the charity. Despite reuniting thousands of families over the years, the charity, which is now called Missing People, still has to fight for funding from year to year.

Both charities are positive proof that ordinary people can make a huge difference to the lives of many and the police continue to give active support to the aims of both. Yet neither could address the biggest stumbling block the investigation faced: Suzy had vanished and all lines of enquiry had run dry. Somebody had got away with murder.

DS Nick Carter was facing retirement and the unhappy realisation that this would be the only murder investigation of his career that would remain unsolved. The workload for the police was huge: tracking and eliminating possible suspects was immensely time consuming and could require hundreds of written police statements. Forensics had secured all possible evidence as best they could, but Suzy's car had not turned up any suggestive links to a possible abductor.

Strange coincidences permeated the case too. One cropped up in early New Year 1987. A man in St John's Wood noticed that an expensive BMW, with Belgian number-plates, had been abandoned near the street that he lived. He suspected it was stolen, as it had been left for weeks and later the window had been smashed and the stereo stolen. He thought the owner should be contacted and considered making an offer to buy the car. The Belgian AA helped trace the owner's details – it was listed under the name of a Mr Kiper.

Sightings of a BMW had cropped up in several witness accounts on Shorrolds Road. One man had even claimed that he'd seen a woman arguing with a man before she was pushed into the car. But the accounts varied. One lady said that two men sat in a large black BMW that day, yet at the same time, someone who knew Suzy through her work with Sturgis swore that she saw her driving up Fulham Place Road, in her white Fiesta, at 2.30 on the afternoon of her disappearance. Police are accustomed to witnesses struggling to accurately recall details, but as the BMW came up time and time again, it was not to be dismissed.

The press got hold of the Belgian link and made some quick assumptions. Perhaps Suzy could have met this man, a diamond dealer, during her time with the QE2 during the stop-offs in Hong Kong, somewhere the Belgian Mr Kiper visited. They went into overdrive when it became known that Mr Kiper was not his real name, but his mother's maiden name. The diamond dealer was David Rosengarten and the press swiftly pointed out that he looked like the police Photofit of Mr Kipper.

By the time that detectives had flown to Belgium, the UK tabloids were already staking out 'Mr Kiper's' apartment. Any cross-border investigation relies on the police and the justice system cooperating and the process can be slow. But Mr Rosengarten wanted to talk to the British police, as he was now being hounded at every turn by British tabloid journalists. It had reached the point where he had to be guarded by Belgian police officers and he wanted the madness to end.

Mr Rosengarten was adamant that he'd never met Suzy Lamplugh. Although it wasn't initially clear why he'd elected to use his mother's maiden name, he was quick to explain that it was just something he did from time to time. But, in the end, it took just one piece of evidence to bring this line of enquiry to a shuddering halt; something that proved that on 28 July not only was Mr Rosengarten not in London, but his BMW was actually being serviced, in Antwerp: he provided garage receipts and paperwork, proving that he wasn't involved in the abduction.

For the Lamplughs, hope had once more turned hollow. There would be many more moments where they would imagine they'd come a step closer to finding Suzy, only to be pushed back. They had been swamped with psychics and mediums, each arriving at scenarios where Suzy was trapped in an airless room, or held underground, all bleak imaginings but hard to ignore as they offered hope – hope that the dream could end, that they could smash through any building and find her still alive.

Any grief-stricken family finds it impossible to accept that, outside their situation, life moves on. For the police, other cases demanded their attention. A phenomenal number of man-hours had already been spent on the Lamplugh investigation. Yet the investigation team was hampered not only by the volume of information and a lack of a clear sequence of events, but something far more problematic – they did not have a body.

It is very difficult to pursue a killer without evidence of murder. As the weeks passed, the police became increasingly conscious of the fact that the likelihood of Suzy still being alive was very slim – and told the family so. In abductions where a stranger is involved, the chances of a victim surviving after the first twenty-four hours falls dramatically. This wasn't a kidnap-and-ransom scenario. The investigative team weren't certain, but surmised that Suzy might have been abducted by a serial sex attacker who had then sought to dispose of her remains. The other possibility was that Suzy knew her attacker, a disgruntled ex-boyfriend perhaps, but again, her chances of surviving an abduction would have been small – she would have been able to identify him, after all.

Not being able to trace Suzy frustrated hopes of finding her killer, as a body can reveal a very great deal. Not only can a corpse help to build a DNA profile of the offender, but the nature of the attack and the manner of disposal all help to reveal a vital picture. In the act of concealment, murderers reveal themselves.

At around this time, the remains of a young woman were found in Sussex. It was a dreadful call for the Lamplughs to receive but not knowing Suzy's whereabouts was also a burden. Perhaps now, this would be the start of some answers. The police did not reveal the full nature of the attack the young woman had suffered, but did reveal that her skin had been partially removed. When a pathologist carried out a full examination, however, it was clear that the young woman had been pregnant or had had a child at some point.

Diana was sure that it could not be Suzy, feeling that even if her eldest daughter had chosen to have a termination, she would have known. Proof positive that it wasn't Suzy came through blood tests. The Lamplughs were resigned to continue their search and the police were left to open the file on another young victim and to hunt for a murderer.

It seemed to the Lamplughs that they had been forced into

contact with another world, a hidden world that lay below the surface of their prosperous and happy life. It is easy for a happy family to imagine that theirs is the only reality, a home where the happiness of children comes first, where the focus is on their success, where a career in London will lead to prosperity and recognition. Yet there are other lives out there too, people for whom degradation and abuse is commonplace. Someone had hunted down Suzy and it was impossible to know what she had suffered. Someone was watching and targeting young women. And someone had taken and mutilated a young woman and hidden her remains in Sussex.

After a year, the enquiry into Suzy's disappearance wound down. It would not be closed, but resources were needed elsewhere. This was a difficult time for the family but, in truth, every avenue had been explored. In many instances this had demanded hundreds of hours of police time, for example when they attempted to trace a wide range of BMW owners. For the police, although those involved in the case were committed to finding Suzy's killer, practical steps now had to be taken. The family had to engage in some practical tasks themselves, but for them the police's decision was heartbreaking. They had to clear Suzy's flat, sort through her possessions, collect her photographs and begin to come to terms with the fact that she would never again walk through the door.

Inevitably, no matter how much routine took over their lives once more, all it would take was a single phone call to throw them back into grief and despair. Psychics would still call to say that they had had visions of Suzy; well-wishers got in touch with theories of their own; members of the public claimed that they'd spotted Mr Kipper in Scotland, or Wales, or sometimes abroad.

Despite the tireless and positive work the family undertook, Suzy's disappearance took its toll. Tamsin was only a year younger than her sister and has subsequently talked about the nightmares she has suffered: 'horrific nightmares – lots of death and stabbing, always happening to her'. Diana has admitted: 'If something like this happens to you, you never actually get over it.'

Years went by. Diana and Paul busied themselves with the Trust and Diana in particular was in demand as a public speaker. Life does go on. The other Lamplugh children settled into their adult lives and would become parents themselves. That brought more sorrow, of course: the knowledge that Suzy would never meet her nieces and nephews, or have children of her own.

In 1994, Suzy Lamplugh was officially declared dead, but the case on her disappearance was not closed. The family would keep in touch with the investigation team and each time the remains of a young woman was found, would wait anxiously to hear the results of DNA tests. The wait went on. If Suzy had been abducted by a stranger, the police were sure that he would have carried out previous attacks on women of a similar to profile to Suzy's. It was a sound assumption, but it did not necessarily throw up any potential suspects and could even mislead the investigation.

Michael Sams illustrates the point. He came to police attention in the early 1990s and one of his crimes in particular made many people wonder whether he could have been responsible for Suzy's disappearance. Sams had been a good middle-distance runner at one point, but had picked up an illness that led to the amputation of one of his legs. He married but later divorced and set up home in Nottinghamshire with a workshop attached, where he ran a power-tools business. He had an extreme fantasy life, and felt a need to dominate women, but he also harboured a twisted greed that would lead him not only to kidnap women but to demand a ransom for them too.

The first case that the police would later be able to trace to Sams was the disappearance of Julie Dart in 1991. Julie was only eighteen at the time and had been working in the red-light district of Chapeltown in Leeds. Sams attempted to abduct her, but his plan went badly wrong and in his rage, he raped, battered and strangled her. Julie's boyfriend received a letter, one week after her disappearance. It was a ransom demand. The police were called in but in the week that followed, Julie's body was discovered, wrapped in a sheet and dumped in a field in Grantham. At some point, Sams had taken Julie to his workshop – tiny fibres found on the sheet matched those from the carpet Sams had installed there. Yet it took some time before he was traced (nearly a third of prostitute murders remain unsolved) and by then Sams had become central to the case of another missing estate agent whose plight had gripped the nation.

Stephanie Slater was twenty-six years old and, like Suzy, had been showing a prospective buyer around an empty property, a typical 1930s semi-detached home in the Great Barr area of Birmingham. She met the middle-aged Sams outside and suspected nothing until the moment he blocked her exit in the bathroom. There, he pulled out a knife and attacked her.

Terrified and bleeding, Stephanie was bound and bundled into Sams's red Mini Metro and driven to his workshop. There, she was forced into a coffin Sams had made and placed inside a wheelie bin. She was warned that if she tried to escape, she would be electrocuted, as Sams had threaded an electrode down her trousers. Stephanie's hands were bound and held above her head; she would suffer permanent back damage from her mistreatment. She was sexually assaulted and doubted that she would survive her ordeal.

The similarities between the two cases is striking. But there was a crucial difference. Stephanie's abductor contacted the estate agent she worked for and demanded a ransom of £175,000. As the days passed, the police were sure that Stephanie was no longer alive but her boss, Kevin Watts, arranged to deposit the money as instructed and, remarkably, she was released, close to her house but in a deeply traumatised state and unable to see after spending eight days and nights blindfolded. It would be the start of a very long road to recovery for Stephanie Slater.

For Sams however, it was the beginning of the end as with Stephanie's help, police were able provide enough information in a reconstruction shown on *Crimewatch* for Sams's ex-wife to come forward and identify him. Police raided the workshop and found the coffin and the wheelie bin, plus enough concrete DNA evidence to link Sams not only to Stephanie's kidnap but to the murder of Julie Dart. He was imprisoned and speculation ran rife as to whether this man had also abducted Suzy. But the police could find nothing concrete to link Sams to the Lamplugh case. No ransom demand had been made by Suzy's abductor;

ultimately, although the victims were both estate agents, it was their vulnerability that was key, the opportunity to lure a woman into an isolated environment where she would not expect an attack. It was yet another coincidence in the case, and it would not be the last.

Information continued to drip feed in, either directly to the incident room or to the Suzy Lamplugh Trust. One name came up: an ex-girlfriend of a convicted rapist and killer claimed in 1989 that she'd been told where Suzy was buried. Gilly Paige said that she had been in a relationship with John Cannan and that once, when they were out driving, he told her that he'd killed Suzy and buried her in a Norton army barracks in Worcestershire. The police interviewed Cannan, who denied any involvement in Suzy's disappearance. But ten years later, another 'secret' source, very possibly a prison informer, again raised the possibility of a link to the ex-army barracks. It was enough to provide the impetus to review the case once more and in May 2000, it was officially reopened. A new appeal for information was sent out and fresh information arose. Painstaking work was carried out in the months that followed and pieces of the puzzle started to slot into place. John Cannan had previous convictions for rape and in 1989, was serving a life sentence for the brutal rape and murder of a newly wed twenty-seven-year-old woman called Sandra Court. The day before Sandra's disappearance, Cannan had attempted to abduct another young woman in a car park, at gunpoint. She managed to escape, but Sandra was not so lucky. Her body was not recovered for many months; badly decomposed though it was, it was still clear that she'd been left naked and with severe head injuries.

Cannan had been spoken to previously by police and his similarity to the Photofit produced from witness statements back in 1986 was striking. Although older than the suspect the police had thought they were looking for, he looked remarkably like the slim, handsome, dark-haired man described by witnesses. Just as significantly, police gave added weight to two witness descriptions of Suzy and her abductor. These witnesses described not a dark-haired Suzy, as seen in the photograph used by the UK press and TV, but a blonde-haired woman. The police learned that Suzy had had highlights put in her hair the weekend before her abduction. On the day of her disappearance, she was fair-headed. They placed her with a man who looked just like Cannan.

The other significant sighting was a dark BMW. It was established that Cannan had access to a BMW on the day; previously, he'd worked in car dealerships and had arranged use of the car through an acquaintance. The police thought they'd hit pay dirt when they were able to trace the second-hand BMW to a garage in north London. The hope was that even though fourteen years had elapsed, Forensics might still be able to find tiny traces of DNA to link the car to Cannan and Suzy. It wasn't to be, but this wasn't the end of the team's interest in Cannan.

Previously, Cannan had stated that he was in prison on the day that Suzy had been abducted. In fact, he had been released from a Wormwood Scrubs hostel three days before Suzy's disappearance, after serving five years of an eight-year sentence for a brutal rape. While inside, he was known to other prisoners by his nickname: Kipper. The police felt confident enough now to start a search of the former barracks, yet it would prove far from straightforward. The site had not been used by the armed forces for some time and a private housing development now covered much of the ground.

On 4 December 2000, Cannan was arrested on suspicion of kidnapping and murdering Suzy and the Lamplughs' hopes were raised. A search of Norton Barracks began a week later, using specialist teams of forensic archaeologists and trained police dogs. They were hopeful of a breakthrough, but as the days passed they were to be disappointed.

The case against Cannan seemed to be running out of steam and he remained adamant they he had no involvement in Suzy's disappearance, but it was far from the end of the twists and turns to the investigation. The following year the police began to speculate that there might have been a mix-up in name of the barracks. Lying 100 miles away in Somerset was Norton Manor Royal Marines barracks. There was more than a coincidence in the name at stake: the Marines barracks lay only eight miles from the field where Cannan dumped the body of Shirley Banks in 1987. Again, though, they found nothing and they embarked on a painstaking check of the Lamplughs' DNA against almost 800 unidentified bodies held on file. No link was made.

More disappointment was to follow. The police had forwarded their file on John Cannan to the Crown Prosecution Service. It detailed a good deal of circumstantial evidence, but the CPS decided that there was not enough evidence against Cannan to take the case to court. This was a bitter blow and the Lamplughs expressed their dismay publicly. They had to content themselves with the knowledge that Cannan was not free to walk the streets and prayed that it would remain that way.

Suzy's case fell off the public's radar for some years after that, but the Lamplugh Trust continued its work, holding thousands of community meetings and distributing millions of leaflets giving advice and information about safety in the workplace, home and when out socialising. Diana was tireless and Paul recognised how important it was that his wife should have a focus, particularly once the police had told them that, after Cannan, they were not hunting for another suspect. During the following year, 2003, however, the family were to be tested by a new tragedy.

Paul and Diana were attending a charity seminar and Diana was due to speak. At one point, she turned to her husband and said, 'I can't see my notes,' whereupon she collapsed and was rushed to hospital specialising in neurology and neurosurgery. Initially relieved that at least his wife had survived this attack, Paul was then told she had suffered a massive stroke and a brain haemorrhage. Diana underwent two emergency operations but when she came round, her family realised that she had lost all memory of Suzy and the events that had shaped their lives. And after the attack, Alzheimer's Disease set in.

Diana will require long-term care for the rest of her life. The Alzheimer's means that even when she is at home, surrounded by pictures of Suzy, she does not recognise the girl with the bright smile. It has been a huge blow to her family. Fortunately, she does recognise her husband, although they cannot share in their memories of a life together. Paul has talked poignantly about his life now: 'Diana doesn't remember Suzy, that is all gone – what happened to Suzy. Of course, it was very hard to come to terms with that, but then it means that the pain of what happened has gone as well.'

The Lamplughs have each had to adjust to life once more. On a practical level, the work of the Trust has been handed over to a new management team. Emotionally, the family passed a milestone in 2006 at the twentieth anniversary of Suzy's abduction. Paul issued a statement saying that the family had moved on with their lives. He said: 'None of us has forgotten Suzy and what a lovely person she was. But I just know Suzy would have said: "Come on Mum and Dad, come on everybody, you have done what you can, get on with your lives" and that's what we've done.'

Throughout this ordeal Paul Lamplugh has shown admirable fortitude, but he knows full well that the family are still held hostage by the mystery of what happened to their eldest daughter. It takes very little to rake over the coals of their heartache and the nation's curiosity, as they were to find once more to their cost in 2006.

This time, the events unfolded a long way from Fulham and the streets Suzy was familiar with in London. It happened suddenly and brutally on the back streets of a Suffolk town. As Kerry Nicol waited for her daughter Tania to return home on 30 October, she had little idea that her family were about to be catapulted into the media limelight, much as the Lamplughs had been twenty years earlier. When Tania failed to come home that evening, Kerry contacted the police and after forty-eight hours, the public were asked for help in finding her daughter.

Tania's home life was soon being scrutinised, but her circumstances seemed nothing like Suzy's. She lived at home with her mother and younger brother on a housing estate outside Ipswich; her father had left the family home when she was a child. Tania harboured hopes of becoming a pop star, but at the time of her disappearance her mum thought she was working in a café. She wasn't. Tania, only nineteen years old at the time, was battling a drug addiction and unbeknown to her family, was funding her habit through prostitution. The police learnt that she had been working in the red-light district of the town on the 30th, but that nothing had been seen of her since.

It is not unusual for drug addicts and working girls to go missing, often drifting off the radar of families and towns, only to begin life elsewhere. But Kerry Nicol was sure that something else had happened to her daughter and when news reached the police that another working girl had gone missing, they took note.

Gemma Adams, aged twenty-five, was reported missing by her partner after she failed to return home from work. Gemma worked in the same red-light district and with no sight of Tania for two weeks, word went out to sex workers that they should exercise caution and report anyone acting suspiciously to the police. Unlike Tania, Gemma came from a stable and wealthy home: she'd grown up learning to ride ponies and play the piano and attend college. But she shared one thing with Tania that would lead her to walking the same streets: she was addicted to heroin.

Her body was found by a member of the public in a stream called Belstead Brook on 2 December. Tania was still missing, but her family now feared the worst. A murder enquiry was launched and specialist teams began searching the brook and surrounding area. Four days later, police divers discovered Tania's naked body, two miles downstream from that of Gemma.

In the meantime, the police were dealing with a report of another missing prostitute. Anneli Alderton was last seen alive boarding a train from Manningtree to Ipswich and was a familiar face in the red-light district. After the death of her father, Anneli had struggled with grief and run into the wrong crowd; by the age of thirteen, she was addicted to crack cocaine. She become a mother and tried to get her life back on track, with little success. At the time she went missing, she was three months pregnant.

A motorist called the police to report seeing what looked like a mannequin in an area of woodland at Nacton. The police discovered Anneli's body, her arms outstretched in a crucifix pose. Worse was to follow. This was the 10th of December; that same evening, just after midnight, twenty-four-year-old Paula Clennell disappeared. Again, to feed her drug addiction Paula was working as a prostitute. Her body was discovered two days later, in woodland near Ipswich. And as a police helicopter searched for Paula, they spotted twenty-nine-year-old Annette Nicholls, lying dead within a few hundred metres of Paula. Like Anneli Alderton, she had been placed in a crucifix pose.

By now the police, town and nation were gripped by the realisation that a serial killer was at large. Tania Nicol (19), Gemma Adams (25), Anneli Alderton (24), Annette Nicholls (29) and Paula Clennell (24). Five young women whose tragic lives had been snuffed out in only six weeks. The police warned sex workers to stay off the streets but although there was a slacking off in business, the need to raise money still left women standing on street corners, waiting for trade.

Two hundred officers worked on the case and thousands of

calls poured into the incident room. The press labelled the killer 'the Suffolk Strangler', as it was evident that asphyxiation was the cause of death in some (though not all) of the women's deaths. Part of the investigation involved looking through hours of CCTV footage from the town to see if any of the women could be seen on the nights they disappeared. One breakthrough came when a PC examining these tapes spotted Tania Nicol getting into a dark-coloured Ford Mondeo late on 30 October 2006, the night she vanished. A vehicle identification specialist tracked the same car driving around the red-light district of Ipswich on three separate dates. Each night coincided with the disappearances of three of the victims.

Then a man called the police to say that he'd heard 'banging noises' next door and was concerned about his neighbour's behaviour. The man was a forty-eight-year-old fork-lift truck driver named Steve Wright. His partner worked night shifts at a call centre and he was known to drive around the red-light district picking up women; he drove a dark-coloured Ford Mondeo. On 19 December, he was arrested and careful forensic work established that the dead women had tiny fibres on their bodies that matched Wright's clothing, car and home.

Charged with murder, Wright admitted to using prostitutes but claimed that the DNA evidence linking him to the women was no more than coincidence. The jury at his trial did not believe him and he was found guilty of murder. It was during his attempt to explain why he frequented prostitutes that the detectives involved in the disappearance of Suzy Lamplugh sat up and took notice. Wright said that he began paying for sex while serving in the Merchant Navy and that it had become a habit with him. He then added: 'Because it was a young crew on the QE2, it was quite normal really.' Steve Wright knew Suzy: they worked on the QE2 at the same time. What was more, an ex-girlfriend of Wright had told the police that she noticed how he'd flirt with Suzy and tried to pick her up. In a diary, she noted that Wright was on shore leave at the time of Suzy's abduction.

The press went into overdrive. Here was a convicted killer with a firm link to Suzy, someone who'd shown an unhealthy interest in her and who'd been snubbed. Could this be the link the investigation had been lacking for twenty years? The police informed the Lamplughs that they would formally look at the case again and once more, the family wondered if they would at last have answers as to what happened to Suzy in her final hours.

But Wright's ex-girlfriend was mistaken. He wasn't on leave at the time Suzy was abducted and what was more, could prove he was elsewhere at the time. Another dead end. More experienced officers were not surprised, though. It seemed unlikely that Wright was involved. He targeted women who were very different from Suzy and struck time and time again over a short period of time. What triggered his murderous rage will never be known, but it was doubtful that he would have been dormant for twenty years if he had abducted and killed.

Wright's background does share a certain pattern with other serial killers. The women in his life spoke about his 'Jekyll and Hyde' qualities: he could present a calm demeanour but dissolve into uncontrollable rage if challenged. He'd been violent and controlling and had a deep-seated sexual rage. His mother had walked out on him when he was a young child and, much later, a Thai girlfriend had fleeced him of thousands of pounds, so it was easy to see how he could have built up angry feelings towards women.

Wright was known to the police and they had his DNA profile – not for an assault but for theft, from a pub he had been working in four years earlier. Wright's background and behaviour added to what was already known about serial killers in general, but it did not point to a link with Suzy Lamplugh.

There is another convicted killer that is frequently mentioned in connection with the Lamplugh case: John Cannan. He has complained bitterly that he has been tried and convicted by the media, fed by comments made by officers, but it is worth looking again at the case against him.

He has a history of sexual violence against women. He murdered Shirley Banks and had attempted to abduct Julia Holman. He was released from a hostel attached to Wormwood Scrubs prison, only a few miles from where Suzy was last seen, four days before her disappearance. On that day, he had access to a black BMW, through his links as a former car dealer. His nickname while in prison for an earlier assault was Kipper. He was a good-looking young man, with black hair swept back, just like the Photofit of Suzy's killer.

The reinvestigation of the case, headed by Detective Superintendent Jim Dickie from 2000 until his retirement six year later, uncovered something else too. During the original investigation, the police had concentrated on eliminating all the men with real and actual connections to Suzy: boyfriends, ex-boyfriends, colleagues, ex-colleagues, friends, clients, right down to a man she had bought her second-hand car from. They'd missed one thread, however, though it was hardly a thread at all. Suzy had told her mum that she was being bothered by a man who claimed he was a successful businessman from Bristol.

Suzy was probably 'bothered' a great deal, as she was very pretty and accessible, and a detail as sparse as that given by Diana Lamplugh could go nowhere. But DS Jim Dickie and his team learned that Cannan had posed as a businessman several times before. He was a good talker and he'd charmed his way into several women's lives, women who remained unaware, as Steve Wright's girlfriends had, that this man harboured very dark and destructive urges. In fact, the judge at his trial for the murder of Shirley Banks summed up Cannan's nature rather succinctly. He noted: 'You are extremely attractive to some women. But under that there lies a most evil violence and horrible side to your character.'

John Cannan is campaigning for his release. His case reached the High Court in 2008 but a senior judge said that he considered the thirty-five-year tariff, before parole could be considered was 'fully justified'. The attack on Shirley Banks was one of many Cannan had committed against women. Over the years, his use of violence had escalated.

The High Court judge questioned whether he'd ever be safe for release. Retired officer Jim Dickie was more forthright: 'Cannan will reoffend. He should never be released. If you look at his profile, I have no doubt he will strike again. He has been released from prison before and committed crimes. He is a danger to the female population.'

For now John Cannan remains behind bars but he is not

the only man in the UK to nurture murderous intent towards young women. For women everywhere, life is a balancing act, measuring irrational fear against sensible precaution. Perhaps it was Suzy's indomitable mother who articulated our worries best. She wrote: 'Suzy's abduction has brought to the surface a realisation of the often unwitting hazards and dangers faced by the increasingly adventurous, ambitious and skilled women setting out with determination to conquer many new fields in today's world.

'In my experience, women want to be able to work on an equal basis with their male colleagues, but to do so they need to be equipped with an awareness and knowledge of how to survive.'

There is evil aplenty in the world, but ultimately if we submit to fear, and let it affect the way we live our lives, it will be the final triumph for men like Cannan. Whatever happened to Suzy was brutal and terrifying but we should never forget her belief that life is for living. Were she here now, she'd appreciate the motto of the Trust set up in her name. It reads: 'From The End is a Beginning'. Suzy is still to be found, her killer still remains unpunished. But her spirit, and that of her family, remains undiminished.

CHAPTER SIX
KATE BUSHELL
STRANGER DANGER

A girl walks up onto an unmade pathway, sheltered by a hedgerow on her right and the grounds of a disused guide-dog training centre, on her left. There are only a few minutes of daylight remaining on this late November afternoon. She is walking with a Jack Russell on a lead and opens a wooden gate that leads onto a path running through a field. There are trees lining the brow of the hill ahead. Who is waiting for her? It is a question her family and the police have struggled with now for twelve years.

As parents, we are quick to judge. When news breaks of a terrible murder or abduction, it is hard to resist running a stream of questions through our minds. Would we have let our child walk a deserted pathway at that time of night? Would we leave our child unaccompanied? Yet we also accept that, as children reach their teens, we have to begin the process of letting go. The bonds may loosen but our fears do not recede.

When thirteen-year-old Milly Dowler was snatched while walking home from school, a convulsive wave of fear arose that ensured the story did not leave the headlines for weeks. Milly was simply walking home. At the time parents imposed curfews, urged their children to call at all times and began driving their teens to school, but as the months passed, they began to ease off on those precautions. People always do. Normality returns and life moves on. And predators know this.

Ronnie Howard, who was an undercover policeman for twenty-three years, came to understand the way some paedophiles work. While working undercover in a prison, he'd even met two men who had shown him a list of schools they intended to target. They would watch and slowly build a picture of which children were allowed to walk home alone. Fortunately, Howard was able to alert his colleagues, so those plans were foiled. He is now retired, but his view on the subject remains bleak: 'Sadly, I would estimate that most streets in Britain have a paedophile lurking somewhere.'

All parents feel the tension between wanting to give their children steps towards independence and wanting to keep them at home or accompanied at all times. It is sometimes an impossible balance to strike. Parents are told that teenagers have to learn to assess and manage risk for themselves, that it is central to developing as a mature and responsible young adult, but at the back of any parent's mind is the fear that something could go wrong. Terrible things happen and you want to be there, protecting your children, at all costs.

Parents watch the clock, they listen for the key in the door and the familiar sound of shoes been thrown off; only then do they relax. Living in a quiet and relatively crime-free area does help build a sense of security. Exwick is such a place, it is a quiet part of a quiet town – what could possibly go wrong there?

KATE BUSHELL

Kate Bushell was fourteen years old, a talented pupil at St Thomas High School in Exeter. She was a keen musician, came from a close-knit family and hoped one day to gain a place at Oxford University. Her family were unremarkable, except perhaps for the fact that they were evangelical Christians. Her father Jerry had even left his role as a local government officer to work part-time as a gardener and devote the rest of his time to charitable work. Kate attended church regularly and would have done so the day after she left her neighbour's house with Gemma, a Jack Russell terrier.

Kate's mother, Suzanne, was a child minder, and Kate had a brother, Tim, who was two years older than her. They lived on Burrator Drive in Exwick, which is about two miles from the centre of Exeter. It is a popular road of typical 1970s semi-detached homes. One of the attractions of Burrator Drive is its proximity to fields and countryside. A walk down Exwick Hill brings you onto Exwick Lane. It leads to an unmade track that snakes past the guide-dog home, or you can you walk through a gate and onto a path that cuts through a field, over a stile and back down to rejoin the lane. A simple walk of no more than twenty minutes or so, popular with dog-walkers from the nearby housing estates.

Dog-walking was a new pastime for Kate. Her family didn't actually own a dog, though, so a neighbour agreed that Kate could take Gemma for a walk from time to time. That Saturday afternoon, with all her homework completed, she asked if she could take Gemma to Exwick Lane. It was around 4.30pm and getting dark, and Kate promised to be no longer than twenty minutes. Her mum agreed because, as a fourteen-year-old, Kate expected to be allowed these small freedoms.

Five o'clock came and went. At first, Kate's parents were simply annoyed. Then it was 5.30pm and the Bushells began to worry that there may have been an accident. What if the dog had been knocked over, or Kate had run out into the path of a car trying to follow Gemma? And in the darkest corners of their minds they began to fear the worst.

'Stranger danger' is drummed into children at school from nursery age. By six, children are expected to know not to approach a stranger sitting in a car, who might call them over. The hardest part is explaining when a child asks, 'Why would someone want to steal me?' Parents have to balance the need for caution against provoking unnecessary fear in their child. The numbers of such incidents are small, yet every week of every year a stranger attempts to abduct a child. 'Because there are bad people who want to make people sad' sounds like a weak answer, but it is the only one most parents are prepared to give their children.

The call came through to the local police station at 6.44pm. Jerry Bushell was asking for police advice and support. His fourteen-year-old daughter had not returned home after walking a neighbour's dog; he had looked for her, but there seemed to be no sign of Kate. Police forces across the UK deal with tens of thousands of missing persons calls each year in the UK. The volume leads to callers being profiled. As Kate had no history of running away, did not come from a troubled home and had always acted responsibly, officers were sent to the area to join the family's search straightaway.

Almost two-thirds of missing children are found within the first few hours. That was the hope the family and the police held onto as the search went on. Perhaps Kate had bumped into a school friend and had been distracted. Jerry and Suzanne had driven around their estate, but there was no sign of their daughter. It was dark now, cold too, and Jerry set out on foot; Suzanne waited at home in the hope that Kate would walk in and give a simple explanation as to why she'd caused such a panic.

Out on Exwick Lane, the ground becomes muddy and uneven yet it is not a spot that feels isolated. It is only half a mile or so from Kate's front door and there are plenty of other houses that overlook parts of the Lane. But the proximity to street lighting and homes is deceptive. If you know the incline of the field, the bushes and hedgerows, it is easy to stay out of sight.

The moment, when it came, was shattering. Kate was found by her father, Jerry. She was lying on her back, near the stile, Gemma waiting at her side. Even in the darkness, something felt terribly wrong; her stillness made it certain that this was no accident or fall. How else to explain why Kate lay motionless with her Reebok joggers at her knees? Kate's long blonde hair was spread out, her body lifeless. She seemed to bear no other injury apart from the one on her neck, though that shocked them all – Kate's neck seemed to have been slashed.

Nothing made sense. It would only have taken Kate ten minutes or so to walk to the Lane, a few minutes more to reach the stile. The police calculated that the attack had happened more or less immediately: someone had been waiting and had approached the teenager from behind.

The priority was to clear the scene. Jerry was escorted back to the family home, to Suzanne and Tim. The police are trained on how best to break terrible news to families yet in truth, there is no 'good' way to do it. When a homicide happens today, it is standard practice for a force to appoint a Family Liaison Officer (FLO). The role of an FLO is one of the most demanding in policing. Each is a trained investigator, selected by the Senior Investigating Officer heading up a murder enquiry. The officer will help the bereaved by keeping them informed about the progress of a case, but is also tasked with gathering evidence and information. That may sound cold or contradictory, but as the overwhelming majority of victims know their attackers it is a crucial role.

Family Liaison Officers were formally introduced after the Stephen Lawrence Enquiry highlighted the poor levels of support some families received during homicide cases. Stephen Lawrence was murdered in 1993 but the Enquiry did not reach its findings until December 1997 – one month after Kate's death.

A number of police officers were on hand in the days that followed, but no one knew what to say. Everyone felt that losing a child to such a violent and sudden end would be devastating and that any words would sound empty. But they saw in Jerry something they did not expect. An acceptance. His faith maintained him and even though the whole family were shocked and grief-stricken, that faith would continue to be a crutch he and the family would lean on over the following weeks and months.

Grieving is a process but for the families of a murder victim, it is especially painful when they realise that they too, are being considered suspects. It is a necessary part of any homicide investigation but it was quickly established that the Bushells had sound alibis accounting for their movements that afternoon.

Kate had a happy home life and there was nothing to indicate that anyone she knew would wish her harm. She was a regular fourteen-year-old schoolgirl; her life was uncomplicated. Within the first few days, it became clear to Devon and Cornwall Police that they were dealing with the hardest of homicides to solve – a 'stranger' murder. Clearance rates for 'domestic' murders stands at over 90 per cent, in 'stranger' murders, that figure drops to 30 per cent.

The first few hours and days of a murder enquiry are crucial and with no obvious suspects, the net of potential suspects grew wider and wider. The difficulties were immediately clear. The manner of Kate's death left more questions than answers. She had not been sexually assaulted, but her jogging bottoms had been pulled down. There was ample opportunity for a determined rapist to act but there was no evidence of assault. Yet the fact that her clothing had been interfered with suggested there could have been a sexual motive to the crime.

Kate's case did not fit into the expected behaviour for a sexual predator. She was killed but not molested. Perpetrators commonly escalate the severity of their attacks if left unchecked. Canadian serial rapist and murderer Paul Bernardo is typical. In the mid 1980s he began by groping women from behind, before graduating to ever greater violence and murder by 1990. If a predator begins to molest girls or women, the police are aware that the offender can become increasingly dangerous. Not that jail sentences reflect that concern. Some are caught. Men like Fred West, who found himself in court charged with assault in 1973. He walked away with a fine of £100, only to go on to abuse and kill with increasing depravity over the next twenty-one years.

Although the nature of the crime suggested that it was not a typical sexually motivated attack, the police were advised that this could not be ruled out. That meant that all known sexual offenders in the region would be considered as suspects. Even in a small and quiet city like Exeter, the numbers of registered sex offenders is surprisingly high. Each would have to be traced, interviewed and if appropriate, eliminated as a suspect.

The severity of the wound inflicted on Kate also meant that police would have to consider violent criminals. No weapon was found at the scene and surrounding area. In fact, the knife with which Kate was murdered has never been traced. Yet the nature of the attack gave the police some indication of the knife used. It had to be large and very sharp. Kate was not stabbed. A knife had been inserted into her neck on one side and sliced outwards. It required considerable strength and precision and it was the only wound inflicted.

Again, this did not fit the usual profile of a frenzied attack. The case of Abobakir Jabari, jailed for life in 2008, for the murder of nineteen-year-old Lidia Motylska, is rather more typical. The thirty-nine-year-old Jabari had disapproved of his flatmate, Ajeen Jabar, dating Lidia, a Catholic Polish girl. He lured her into an alleyway near his flat and strangled her with a cord from his tracksuit bottoms. Jabari then cut her neck from ear to ear, penetrating deep enough to sever her spine. He claimed in court not to remember the attack, only that he lost his temper. During the course of the assault, he also stabbed Lidia in the chest and stomach. Sexual rage may been a factor in the crime; it is likely that it was only one of many distorted emotions that fuelled Jabari's violent attack.

Jabari knew the victim and his knife attack was prolonged. Whoever killed Kate, however, did so with one efficient stroke. He did not stay at the scene for long. In fact, the brevity of the attack meant that Forensics were left with very little DNA material with which to build a profile, and this would prove increasingly frustrating as the months turned to years.

No case is built on forensic evidence alone; in some instances, it can even help to muddy the picture. At one stage, purple fibres were identified on the limited amount of material that the perpetrator could have touched. However, after further exhaustive work, it was established that the fibres had been left accidentally by a lab technician during an examination.

Even if tiny traces of DNA are found at the scene of a crime, it is not always guaranteed that they can be identified as particles of blood, skin or semen. We leave microscopic traces when we interact with people every day and those traces have to be eliminated in an investigation. With the traces that are left as unidentified, two problems arise. Firstly, the source could be unrelated and innocent – someone brushing past you on a bus, for instance. Secondly, they can't point to who left them. That is only possible if a person already exists on a database as an offender.

And so, although advances in DNA profiling have been extraordinary, cases are still built on traditional police work – identifying key suspects and engaging in the painstaking work of building up evidence of their movements. It is the vital first step and forensic work can then be the second step. If a suspect is identified and their DNA places them at the scene, the Crown Prosecution Service will know they have a robust case to prosecute. If either step is missed, cases can collapse.

The team investigating Kate's case were faced with a dilemma. Once known sex offenders and violent offenders were factored in, the staffing hours required to take statements and then check them ran into the hundreds. Imagine a known sex offender gave an account of his day on 15 November. He claims he went out in the morning to buy a paper and later went to the petrol station to fill up but spent all afternoon at home. As a detective constable, you would have to check each movement, taking statements from shop assistants. That takes hours and if anyone has moved out of the area, which is not uncommon when a case runs into months, it can take an entire day. And that 'action' may be only one of hundreds that must be carried out; time ebbs away.

But if any known offenders were omitted, a known suspect may be overlooked. It is hard to overstate the lessons that all police forces learnt in the wake of the Yorkshire Ripper investigation. Peter Sutcliffe was spoken to nine times over the course of the murder inquiries, before his arrest for the unrelated offence of driving with false number-plates.

Process determines whether a case stands or falls should it reach court. No officer wants to cut corners. Set against this is the certain knowledge that as time passes, a case turns 'cold'. People's memories fail, the pressure builds with the risk that the offender will strike again and the FLO has to tell a grieving family that no one is in the frame for an arrest.

Despite hundreds of staffing hours in what became one of the largest murder hunts in the history of Devon and Cornwall Police, key questions remained unanswered. For a start, there were the reports of a blue van. Police had canvassed the area and asked for any witnesses to come forward. The information they received made repeated mention of sightings of a blue van. In some reports it was an Astra; in others, an estate or hatchback. It was spotted at around 5pm near the stables on Exwick Lane and police released the description of a man described as white, around thirty or forty years old and between 5ft 9in and 5ft 10in tall. He was thought to be wearing jeans and had dark, collar-length hair. This man was never traced.

Neither was the driver and passenger of a similar van that was driven into a scrapyard near Exeter, at around 2.30pm, on the same day that Kate was murdered. The driver – in his late thirties, about 6ft tall, with a stocky build – asked for replacement seats for the Astra GTE. The passenger description was similar to the man spotted in Exwick Lane at 5pm. Again, the van and the occupants never came forward.

There were other sightings too. Some would prove straightforward but of no further interest; some would lead to the hope of a breakthrough. There was the 'running man'. He was white, around 5ft 11in tall, aged around thirty to thirty-five years old, of medium build, with short brown hair and a moustache. He was wearing a blue sweatshirt with a wet patch on the chest area, which may have been sweat. It is doubtful that he was a jogger, however, as he was thought to be wearing jeans.

There was also the man in a three-quarter-length coat, seen

walking parallel to the track on which Kate's body was found. Neither of these two men has been identified.

Then there was the itinerant man, with salt-and-pepper hair, who it was thought could be living rough in the area around Exwick Lane. This theory was backed up by local reports that a man had jumped out of bushes, scaring women who were walking by, in the months leading up to Kate's murder. Because of the nature of the knife attack, the idea that the attacker might be a homeless ex-military man gained some currency. The mysterious itinerant was never traced, though.

Police felt that the murderer would have been familiar with knives, even if the idea of a man living out in the fields near the Lane eventually lost momentum. The investigation was interested not only in military techniques but also looked at the possibility that whoever the attacker was, he had knowledge of the methods used in slaughterhouses. The investigating team singled out the way the murderer had used the knife. Most attacks with a knife involve stabbing and so it was natural for them to look closely at the method used to kill the schoolgirl. It would not be without precedent either. Fred West had worked as a delivery man in a slaughterhouse; forensic scientists noticed that as he dismembered the young women who passed through his hands, West's knife marks mimicked those he would have seen at the abattoir.

Nothing concrete came from enquiries about military and abattoir personnel, but when a 'hide' was found in the area near where Kate had been killed, there was a sense of renewed hope that the killer had left a trace after all. Police had discovered a makeshift den. It was not very sophisticated, but what lay within made the team believe that they had made a breakthrough. Hidden in plastic bags were a number of elaborately folded pieces of toilet tissue, many in a figure of eight. Semen traces were found on the tissue. Forensics began work and so did criminal profilers.

This was some four months after Kate's murder and police were keen to get the view of specialists such as offender profiler Dr Richard Badcock. He would later come to the public's attention after the arrest of Dr Harold Shipman. The forensic psychiatrist assessed Shipman's fitness to be interviewed by police and later the Hyde GP wrote to the General Medical Council to complain about Dr Badcock. (Not surprisingly, the complaint was not upheld.)

All Dr Badcock had to provide was an assessment, but in criminal investigations, the role of the offender profiler extends to providing police with views on the perpetrator's likely age, psycho-sexual make-up, status, and likely future behaviour.

The figure-of-eight tissues led to many theories about obsessive urges and need to control, but the profilers were inadvertently leading the investigation into a dead end. Police work pieced together who might have been using the hide and it eventually turned out to be a young man who lived fairly close by. He would masturbate at home but worried about being discovered. By taking the 'evidence' out of his home, he hoped to save himself any embarrassment. Taken to Heavitree Road police station for questioning, he must have rued the day he arrived at his plastic-bag plan. It quickly became clear that this was not the man responsible for Kate's death and is indicative of the fact that profiling must always be viewed dispassionately and only as part of the mix of investigative work.

Other lines of enquiry were pursued. The police put out an appeal to hotel and B&B owners asking them to forward the details of a man who may have stayed with them in the months up to and after the murder but who left without paying his bill. One description turned up of a man in his mid-thirties, 5ft 8in tall, and with short, brown, receding hair. He may have arrived in a blue Transit-style van. As with other leads, however, this man was never traced.

The frustrations were obvious. Despite hundreds of statements gathered and a long list of known offenders, the men in the early witness statements had still not been identified. They may have had no connection to Kate's murder but until they were formally spoken to, they could not be ruled out.

It was coming up to a year since the schoolgirl was killed. The police were no closer to an arrest than they had been in the early hours of the enquiry. Some serious crimes are never solved and it was possible that Kate's name might have to join the awful roll call of those who would never see justice.

Lyn Bryant left her home in Truro just after 1.30pm to take her Lurcher, Jay, for a walk. It was mid-afternoon on 20 October and Lyn was heading for a familiar route, along the Ruan High Lanes. Like Kate, she was unaccompanied. Although forty-one years old, Lyn looked much younger. She was petite, only 5ft 1in, and had short, dark-brown hair. The last time she was seen alive she was passing Wayside Garage and on her way into the Lanes, past a chapel.

Again, although they are only a mile or so from Lyn's home, the Lanes are isolated and people can walk them unseen by anyone else. An hour later, a holidaymaker found Lyn's bloodstained body lying near a gateway into a field. It was less than three hundred yards from the chapel. The news spread quickly throughout the region and the fear that there was a killer targeting lone females arose once more.

It was a terrible moment for the Bushell family. Jerry: 'When I heard the news of the latest murder I thought, Oh no, not again. We had hoped no other family would have to go through the same. We must pray it is the same person who has carried out the killings because we do not want two of them out there.'

Jerry had hit on the very question puzzling the police. Although the murder took place in Cornwall, not Devon, the area is policed by the same constabulary and the killings were inevitably linked. But there were significant differences between the two. Unlike Kate, Lyn had been able to grapple with her assailant and she had fought doggedly to try and defend herself. She had stab wounds to her neck and chest and the final blow came to the back of her neck, probably as she fell forward unconscious. Whoever walked away from the scene would have been muddied as well as bloodstained.

It was a bold attack, as it was still broad daylight at the time. Like Kate, Lyn had not been robbed or sexually assaulted but there were enough significant differences in the way both women were attacked for police not to formally link the deaths. It had to stay front of mind that it was not dog-walking that was the common factor but isolation. Both attacks were opportunistic. Women feel safer walking in unpopulated areas if they are with a dog but, in truth, they are still vulnerable.

As with the Kate Bushell enquiry, no clear suspects emerged

from Lyn's life. She was a happily married mother of two girls and there was nothing in her life that would have provoked such a violent attack. Once more, this was a 'stranger murder' and like the Exeter CID, the team in Cornwall mounted a huge investigation.

Eventually, almost 23,000 names would enter the database dedicated to the enquiry, with over 12,000 vehicles traced and detectives would follow through over 10,000 'actions'. It was a vast and wide-ranging investigation, and most of the men aged up to seventy in the area would be questioned about the afternoon of 20 October. Like the team in Devon, however, the Cornwall police were left with no clear suspects.

Lyn had been seen talking briefly to a man in his mid-thirties just outside the chapel. A man with short, dark hair, with bushy eyebrows and a square jaw; he was wearing a light-coloured top. The police never traced him. As might be imagined, public concern at the time was considerable: a relatively quiet part of Britain had launched two murder inquiries into two brutal attacks on lone females, without the killer, or killers, being caught.

It certainly wasn't due to a lack of effort or commitment. Both enquiries lacked that one substantial breakthrough that would lead to who was responsible. It would not be someone who knew Kate or Lyn, it may not even be someone connected to the south-west of England, but what police officers feared was that it would be someone who would have the compulsive need to kill again.

It would not take long before the police were notified about an attempted abduction, and the parallels with the two previous murders could not be ignored. It was New Year's

Eve in 1998 and a mother and her teenage daughter were walking their dog in a country lane near Newton Abbot, in Devon. As they made their way to the lanes, they were passed by a man driving a blue-grey Vauxhall Cavalier. A few minutes later, he returned – and this time he deliberately drove into the daughter's legs.

As the mother attended to her daughter, who had been knocked to the ground, the driver appeared, wielding a knife, and threatened to kill the girl unless both females followed his instructions. The women were ordered into the back of the car and the driver set off into a nearby field. Showing incredible presence of mind, the seventeen-year-old girl grabbed the driver's neck from behind and managed to force him to stall the car.

Both women attempted to run from the car but the driver lashed out with the knife. The mother bravely defended both herself and her daughter, and her hands were badly cut as a result; she would later need surgery to repair the damage inflicted on her hands. In the struggle, however, both women were able to break free and ran to a nearby house to raise the alarm.

The press began to speculate that there was a serial killer at work in the region and once more, residents had to reassess their routes as dog-walkers. This time, the police were heartened that the description they issued of the attacker brought some sound leads. The description did not seem to match those of the men the police still wished to interview from the night of Kate's murder. He was described as between thirty-five and forty with short, fair hair and a fair complexion, of average height but well built.

Within five days, forty-three-year-old Graham Anker, of no fixed address, was arrested and charged with kidnapping. He was thought to be sleeping rough in a tent near Torquay and it was hoped that here was a link to the murder of Kate and Lyn Bryant. After a DNA swab, Anker was eliminated as a suspect, though he proved to be a serious and repeat offender in his own right. Ten months later he was found guilty of kidnapping and wounding at Norwich Crown Court. As he also had a conviction for rape, and this was his second serious offence, Anker faced a mandatory twenty-year sentence.

Long-standing 'cold cases' are periodically reviewed by teams of senior detectives and it was clear that Kate Bushell's murder would be considered in the next round of reviews. Senior officers have finite resources and have to balance ongoing casework with cases those that remain unsolved. The Kate Bushell case would not be closed, but the team working on it had been scaled down. The hope was that a new development, such as the arrest of Graham Anker, would provide a vital new lead.

There can be little doubt that whoever killed Kate would not have been able to hide all traces from family or acquaintances. Whoever it was could have changed or disposed of their clothes after the murder, may have acted in an agitated manner, may have changed their vehicle, could have had an obsession with knives and so on. No one truly slips into the night. The killer will be known, and known well, by someone. If his relationship with that person breaks down, perhaps that individual would have the courage to call the incident room and speak to an officer.

However, police inquiries sometimes attract calls from

vindictive former partners or acquaintances. It is not unheard of for officers to be told that 'someone I know did it', only to find that the lead is bogus and is simply the result of ill feeling. Another curse for any investigation are the people who come forward to confess, often making heartfelt apologies for a crime that they could not possibly have committed. That is why investigations always hold back key pieces of information from a murder site; details that only they and the killer will know.

The next link to Kate's murder came at the height of summer and, again, involved a dog-walker. A forty-six-year-old woman was walking her dog, Topsie, near her home in Salcombe, Devon. The married mum of two became aware that a man who'd got out of his car nearby had now begun to follow her. Although it was still light at 7.30pm, she was conscious of the fact that there was no one else around. Turning to look at him, she caught sight of an object he was holding in his hand. It was a six-inch blade.

The man had been following her for about 300 yards. She later said: 'When I saw the knife in his hand I thought, Oh no, he is going to kill me. I know in my heart he would have attacked me if Topsie had not been with me. She is very protective and I am sure she saved my life.' Happily, Topsie, an Alsatian, sensed that her owner was in danger and barked until the man fled. The police issued a description of the would-be attacker – white, aged about forty and clean-shaven – and again weighed up whether there could be a connection with the murders of Kate Bushell and Lyn Bryant. Nothing firm emerged, however, and the man was never traced.

It seems alarming to note that despite the superficially quiet atmosphere of rural areas, there are a number of reports from these locales every year of men looking to abduct or attack women. Some predators are attracted to rural isolation. The number of spontaneous attacks by strangers are small, yet they cannot be dismissed. Precautions can have an impact on crime statistics. The numbers of car break-ins have fallen, for example, as cars are fitted with alarm systems and better security measures. But the numbers do not waver from decade to decade, and there has been no 'golden age' of policing or crime. In fact, for as long as crime has been recorded, the number of predatory attacks have proved fairly constant. The police urge women to think about their routes, think about how to protect themselves – with an attack alarm, for example – but the bleak reality is that every year some women will lose their lives to violent crime.

It should be said that most victims of violent crime are young men, usually drink or drugs are involved, and that men are six times more likely to be killed than women. Street brawls aside, however, the picture is different.

The thought that a killer or killers are still on the loose is what troubles the Kate Bushell investigation. It is possible that Kate's killer will not strike again. Officers involved with the case know that there are two reasons why violent offenders don't re-offend. First, they may be dead. All suicides in the six weeks after Kate's murder were examined by the investigation team. It is not unheard of for a killer to act out a fantasy and then find themselves unable to live with the reality of the situation and end their lives.

Second, they could have been imprisoned for another offence. This is where modern forensics is invaluable. Once an arrest for a violent or sexual offence has been made, DNA can be put on a central database and police officers can review cold cases against the new profile. David Newton provides one example of such a case.

In early July 1997, a sixteen-year-old girl and her eleven-year-old brother went to collect frogspawn in Primrose Valley, near Leeds. David Newton was waiting. The boy was made to lie in nearby bushes and his sister was savagely attacked and raped at knife-point. It was a horrific ordeal and despite an extensive investigation by West Yorkshire Police, the perpetrator was not found. The file remained open and police feared that he would strike again.

When he did, it was nine years later, in June 2006. A fifty-two-year-old woman was walking her dog at Ilkley Moor, an area popular with dog-walkers and runners. Walking alongside the Panorama reservoir, she was knocked to the ground. Her attacker threatened her with a knife but she fought back and incredibly, the blade of the knife was snapped from the handle. She used it to fight back and managed to cut his side and scratch his face with her nails. Her screams also alerted another walker who called the police but she was still beaten savagely by her attacker, hit repeatedly around the face and strangled until she lost consciousness.

Taken to Airedale General Hospital, the woman was able to provide police with a description of her assailant, but it was the forensic traces left on her clothing than would prove the vital link. They matched the profile of the attack on the sixteen-year-old girl from Leeds nearly ten years earlier.

Again, despite a huge and high-profile investigation, a year passed without an arrest having been made. The police suspected that this rapist was probably involved in other violent attacks over the years and were determined to find him. The team decided to make an appeal on BBC's *Crimewatch* and appeal for new leads. They knew that the man had left Ilkley Moor with a bleeding cheek and hoped that a wife or family member might have concerns and now be ready to come forward.

Appealing to loved ones is a risky strategy – they are just as likely to be in denial or to provide an alibi as they are to speak to the police – but Detective Superintendent Paul Kennedy, who was leading the investigation, had been advised that this was a man who could well behave violently at home too. With that in mind, Kennedy was direct in his statement: 'We have highlighted before that these were very violent and brutal attacks and that the person responsible has possibly been violent in a relationship before.

'We have also mentioned strangulation as an aspect of the Ilkley attack. We particularly want to hear from women who may have been in a relationship with someone they suspect might be this man.'

It worked. Names were offered up to the police and a fresh round of leads was followed up. It wasn't until June 2008 that the net closed around David Newton. Police questioned Newton yet the fifty-five-year-old father of four was very relaxed during his interview, so much so that the detective talking to him doubted that this was their man.

He differed radically from the description the fifty-two-year-old victim had provided too. She had described a man of around forty years old, 5ft 9in tall, toned and athletic, with short, brown hair. Newton was much older, with no top teeth,

5ft 6in tall, a ruddy complexion and a pronounced beer belly. Nevertheless, a DNA swab was taken and Newton was sent on his way.

It was only when Forensics called to say that they had an exact match with the attacks made on the sixteen-year-old girl and the Ilkley Moor attack that the police realised that they had spoken to the man who was almost certainly guilty of those and other offences. In the meantime, however, David Newton had gone into hiding.

A nationwide hunt began. As Newton was a long-distance lorry driver, the investigation team feared that he could be in any number of places familiar to him throughout the UK. West Yorkshire Police took the unusual step of releasing Newton's picture to the media, as well as details of the Land Rover he was driving, asking the public to look out for him. They stressed that Newton must not be approached as he was a violent offender and urged that should he be seen, that any witnesses ought to dial 999 immediately.

West Yorkshire Police also called Detective Superintendent John Clements at Devon and Cornwall Police. They knew that Newton had a sister in the area and that he'd worked there as a delivery driver. Devon and Cornwall Police have strong links with hotels and guesthouses in the two counties, and once a few calls are placed owners contact each other in a cascade effect, so all are on stand-by. Newton first checked into a guesthouse in St Ives on Saturday, 28 June, but left the following day. The police knew that he had stayed in camp sites in the area as a holiday-maker in the past and so these were also searched. In the end, Newton was caught after checking in to another B&B in Hayle, some five miles away.

A police team arrived and he was arrested, then taken back to West Yorkshire.

A few days later, Newton appeared at Bradford Crown Court charged with abduction, indecent assault and rape. His case would not be heard until October. Newton pleaded guilty to the two attacks.

Detective Superintendent John Clements is now the Senior Investigating Officer on Kate Bushell's case and his major crime investigation team have followed the David Newton case closely. He is aware that Newton spent a good deal of time in Devon and Cornwall over the years and believes it is highly likely that Newton was responsible for other violent and sexually motivated attacks. Could Kate's be one of them?

In the first instance, the limited DNA profile that Devon and Cornwall have from Kate's attacker will be checked against the full profile the police now hold on Newton. A picture of his movements will also have to be pieced together. The attack on the sixteen-year-old girl happened four months before Kate's murder, at a time when Newton was travelling across the UK. It is feasible that he could have been in Devon later in the year.

The sixteen-year-old was raped, while Kate did not suffer a sexual assault. However, the attack at Ilkley Moor was cut short by the victim's sustained resistance and her screams. By the time the woman returned to consciousness, Newton had fled. Is it possible that someone could have disturbed Kate's attacker? In a review of material, Devon and Cornwall aren't ruling this out. Some time ago, a child came to them with a piece of information that they sensed could only be picked up from the time of attack. He was too young to provide any further information but the small detail that he gave, and that the police are not releasing, may still prove invaluable.

All Detective Superintendent Clements will say is that David Newton is still of interest to the investigation. Many years have gone by since Kate was found brutally killed and the team is still determined to bring her killer to justice. The net that was spread wide might just have caught David Newton. And if Newton was not responsible for taking the life of Kate Bushell, it will be cast again.

CHAPTER SEVEN
HARRY AND MEGAN TOOZE
A TRAGEDY ON THE FARM

It doesn't get any easier, despite what well-wishers say about the passage of time, it doesn't heal. The aftershook of a murder can echo through the lives of a victim's family for years but the hardest thing of all is uncertainty; not knowing where a loved one was disposed of or now knowing who to blame. The weight of loss becomes that much harder to bear should you lose faith in the authority sent to help - the police. It may not be common but it does happen and then the victim's family feel cut adrift in a world of loss and confusion - something Cheryl Jones found as her life was ripped apart not just by murder but by a miscarriage of justice. Her story makes for uncomfortable reading.

Cheryl was Harry and Megan's only child and even though her career had taken her away from south Wales to Orpington in Kent, she visited her parents regularly. It was a 400-mile round trip, a journey of over three-and-a-half hours from the flat to the farmhouse where Cheryl had grown up, but it was a journey she and her boyfriend Jonathan had accustomed themselves to over some ten years together.

Jonathan knew how devoted Cheryl was to her parents. He'd helped out whenever he could when farming tasks required an extra pair of hands, such as hay baling. He liked the Toozes. Megan was a quiet soul but Harry was something of a character, Jonathan knew how much Cheryl missed them both and knew that she called them every day.

In fact, this had become more than just about keeping in touch, Cheryl was concerned: Harry had recently had a hernia operation and she worried about his health. Farm work doesn't come with weekends off and paid holidays, it is a day-in-day-out commitment. Harry was still a formidable worker, able to single-handedly lift heavy containers of diesel, even though common sense dictated that he should slow down. But at over 6ft 1in and some 16 stone in weight, Harry didn't understand the concept of taking it easy.

Cheryl knew that he could not go working at Ty ar y Waun indefinitely, yet the idea of leaving the farm was unthinkable. It may have taken all his strength to maintain the five-acre small holding, but this had been Harry's life's work. He had been a labourer on a farm in the Rhondda but when he met Megan he was a driver for a fruit wholesaler. Megan, who was three years older than Harry, was born and raised at Ty ar y Waun. After they married Harry worked on the farm and once his father-in-law became ill, ran it as a full-time concern.

Jonathan knew all about the farm. Cheryl had talked about it when they first met at the University of Glamorgan, where she was studying public administration and he was a business student. Cheryl chose the college as it meant that she could attend and still be only ten miles or so from home. For Jonathan, the journey to his home town was only six miles.

Like Cheryl, he was close to his family and didn't have the desire to leave his home life behind. Jonathan and Cheryl may have grown up only half an hour apart, but in many ways they were from different worlds.

Jonathan's parents, Graham and Pauline, lived in Caerphilly, a few miles north of Cardiff. Caerphilly acts as something of a commuter town for Cardiff and Newport, with rail and road links making it an ideal location for those wanting to live outside the cities. It sits at the foot of the Rhymney Valley and its castle is still an impressive sight but it is not as rural as it once was. In many ways, it is an extension of Cardiff suburbs, which lie only three miles or so to the south.

Graham was a successful buildings and structural surveyor and engineer with a background in architecture. Jonathan grew up the eldest of three boys in a neatly kept suburban home, an experience repeated many times over throughout suburbs in the UK. These homes are safe and respectable and harbour millions of professional, hardworking couples raising families. The suburbs are often derided for their slow pace and clockwork regularity, where cars are washed in driveways on Sundays and children are sent for piano or ballet lessons, but it is a type of conformity that many seek out. It was a lifestyle that Jonathan never rebelled against. A quiet and hard-working young man, he didn't enjoy standing out at 6ft 5in and his thick spectacles and slight build made him even more self-conscious.

Business Studies seemed like a sound degree, something that would lead to steady employment. When Cheryl met him, she sensed straightaway that here was a gentle soul. Jonathan was mild mannered, polite and thoughtful and he and Cheryl slowly became good friends. Cheryl was a different kind of person. Outwardly, she was also shy, quite self-contained and guarded, but it would be wrong to think that she was meek. She was made of sterner stuff. Just as well, for that quality would sustain not only her but also Jonathan in the years to come.

Perhaps Cheryl had inherited a steeliness. Her upbringing was very different from that of the man she came to love. Rural Wales was as much a part of Cheryl as it had been of her family for generations. It is almost impossible to articulate how growing up in a farming community shapes you, in part because it is never spoken of. You learn quickly as a child that life is hard, the land is unforgiving, the weather is capricious and that your livelihood is always under threat from the unknown. It is easy for outsiders to mock farmers. You'll hear that you'll never meet a poor farmer, that they drive battered Land Rovers and hand-me-down clothes despite sitting on thousands of pounds. But that misses a deeper point. Living off the land is precarious. Every farming family will have known times of hardship, will have heard of families ruined and the devastation brought by bad investment or inclement weather, and all will have heard of suicides carried out in moments of bleak desperation.

Depression among farmers is thought to be twice as high as people living and working in urban areas. It is easy to misunderstand why. A few years ago, Paul Flynn, an MP from Newport, made a remark that did not endear him to farming communities. During a radio interview, he said: 'The main reason why there is a large number of suicides among farmers is because they have shotguns handy.' His remark might have caused some controversy but it brought outsiders no closer to an understanding of a life in farming. The gulf remains.

Part of the difficulty with living in a rural setting is the isolation. It is common not to talk to another soul beyond your family and farming neighbours for days and even weeks – in fact, not until you take yourself away from the farm to conduct business, shop and get supplies. When you do meet someone, they are often from the same group of people and seeing the same people over and over again can easily become monotonous. It is common in rural areas for people to say little. It cuts down on the risk of being misunderstood or thought of as difficult. Of course, some people revel in being cantankerous and even downright eccentric and that is accepted as long as behaviour falls in line with that other great demand of rural life: self-sufficiency. You can be as mad as a March hare in the countryside, as long as you are independent and expect help from no one.

There are other problems inherent to rural life too. Everyone, even if it is no more than a handful of villagers, knows your business. It is hard for outsiders to appreciate that this intimacy has continued generation after generation, some families farming side by side for a century or more, with a history of alliances and disputes. And disagreements in a rural community can take root and flourish for years.

There's no doubt that the backbreaking work has its rewards. The landscape gets under your skin, every nuance of the land becomes imbued with meaning and memory. But it comes at a price. You can love the land, but it won't love you back. Those fortunate enough will take to their role as caretaker with ease; others find it a burden.

Outsiders often see only what is on the surface: the striking views and the pretty stone farmhouses, the abundance of greenery and the slow rhythm of the days. They will never be fully accepted into communities, though, even if they spend decades in one location. It is not a question of open hostility, more a difference of character.

Jonathan faced that strange mix of curiosity and indifference. At first he encountered a barrage of questions about who he was, and what his connection was to the Toozes; afterwards, all interest dropped off. A few greetings and nods would be exchanged but that was all. He was 'a Caerphilly lad' and it didn't surprise many that after going away to college, Cheryl would take up with someone like that. He didn't look much use for farm work, which begged the question: what would happen to Ty ar y Waun after Cheryl's parents died?

Harry was one of ten children and so it may well have struck him as odd that he and Megan had only one child. That was just the way it had worked out, though, and it made the family that much closer. He wondered if Cheryl might feel lonely as she grew up, with only her parents and Megan's invalid mother to mix with, but she seemed fine. Quiet maybe, like her mum, but she was a good girl who would always feel at home on the farm.

Living and working in Orpington was a wholly new experience for Cheryl. She could board a train for London and even though you recognised the same commuters, day in day out, no one ever exchanged words. It was the same with the block of flats she and Jonathan lived in. Just because you lived on top of one another didn't mean you got to know your neighbours; people kept their distance. The contrast with home was stark, though not particularly unpleasant.

Despite living far away from her home, Cheryl took comfort in the fact that she would only have to know what day it was to have a fair idea of what her parents would be doing. On Mondays, Megan and Harry would climb into their Land Rover Defender and either drive to Llanharry, where there was a post office and a Spa, or to Talbot Green, about a quarter of an hour away, to stock up at Tesco. As well as the days, the hours had their routine too. Megan was traditional and house-proud, the cottage was kept neatly and she would put food on the table for Harry as regular as clockwork.

Megan would not let Harry know it, but she was concerned. Perhaps it was a symptom of age. Megan was approaching seventy and it was easy to worry more and sleep less. There were still many things to look forward to, however, and she knew from experience that it didn't pay to dwell on dark thoughts. There would be visits from Cheryl and Jonathan and perhaps they'd marry soon and go on to have children of their own.

Harry hadn't been himself. He seemed anxious and remote. Earlier that year, he'd brought home a Luger pistol. Megan didn't know where he'd got it from. He had shotguns downstairs in a cabinet, but something in him made him decide to sleep with the Luger under their bed.

There has been so much speculation about the final few weeks and months of Harry and Megan's lives at Ty ar y Waun that it is difficult to distinguish fact from fiction. The pressing need to come up with clues as to what actually happened at the farmhouse one morning in July 1993 drove many of the well-meaning residents of the village to begin to doubt their own memories. Some kept their own counsel. Others may even have had something to gain from saying nothing at all.

What we do know is that there was a theft. There had been a break-in at Ty ar y Waun the September before, while the family were at a funeral. It was upsetting, knowing that the farm had been visited by a stranger, a thief and a vandal, yet all that was taken was Harry's old shotgun. It was in such a state of disrepair that Harry feared for anyone who used it and he was relieved that it was all that had been taken. There was jewellery and cash in the house, but they were untouched. Harry also heard that there was a break-in at a nearby scrapyard the same night and wondered if the two incidents might be connected. What upset Megan most was that the taps had been left on in the kitchen and the floor was flooded.

Then there were the two sightings of an unknown 'professional-looking' man, aged between forty and fifty, in the area – someone clearly known to Cheryl's parents. The first came in May, when Harry and Megan were said to have walked into a local solicitor's office, in conversation with this man. A similar description was given for a sighting of the man in July; this time he was seen with Harry alone. The sightings were at two separate solicitors' offices and later, staff were able to provide police with a description. There could be an innocent explanation, an arbitrary connection, but this man has never come forward. Perhaps he did not recognise himself from the description given after the deaths of Harry and Megan Tooze. But it is the nature of small villages to have an idea of who everyone is and for strangers to be conspicuous.

That could go some way to explaining why a grey Suzuki 4x4 was spotted too, six days before the couple were killed and again on the day itself. Like the professional-looking man, the vehicle has never been traced. Some of the sightings by witnesses became less positive under close scrutiny. Mrs Gillian Lewis was a passenger in a car driven by her daughter Claire the month before the deaths. As they travelled down the lane past the entrance to Ty ar y Waun, she saw a man in a trench coat, with dark hair, who pulled up his collar and turned away as she put on her glasses to take a closer look at him. Mrs Lewis's sighting would prove crucial in the months ahead.

Police would also be told of a 'furious barney' Harry was said to have had with a stranger some eight weeks before his death, of his anxieties and his plea to an old neighbour to 'Look after Megan and Cheryl.' Disparate accounts of strangers in trench coats, sightings of vehicles and warnings that something was 'wrong' on the farm eventually begin to seem like mere speculation and statements born of hindsight. But with the Tooze case, nothing is as it seems.

When it came, it came out of the blue. Cheryl called her parents on the evening of Monday, 26 July, during the adverts for *Coronation Street*. There was no answer. They would not both be out for long, even on a warm summer's evening, so Cheryl tried again. And again and again, with her fears now rising. What if her father was ill? There was the hernia operation, but he'd also torn his arm recently and a nasty gash had been left from elbow to wrist. Cheryl decided to call a neighbour, who called back to say that the Defender was in the driveway, that the lights were on and that crockery was laid out. With that in mind, Cheryl started to call local hospitals. Had her father been rushed in?

After three hours of calls and no reports of her parents' whereabouts, Cheryl was growing desperate. She asked Jonathan to drive to the farm to find out what was going on. Jonathan did not have to go to work in the morning but she did. Cheryl would wait by the phone. Jonathan set off in Cheryl's Montego on what would prove a long drive. He stopped to call Cheryl from an M4 motorway service station twice before the Severn Bridge, hoping that all was well and that he could turn back. On the first occasion, Cheryl had heard nothing. On the second, she told him that the police had broken into the farmhouse. It was then about 1am, however, so she asked Jonathan to push on. The weather deteriorated and Jonathan had to stop again because of a leaking window. The rain was driving down and that night, even the traffic lights seemed against him, slowing his run on the 'A' roads that led to Llanharry.

When Jonathan arrived, over four hours later, the police had made a discovery. They had found blood marks but wondered if they could be the result of dehorning cattle. They also told him that a neighbour had rung them and that they'd searched for a few hours without success. That was about to change. Jonathan was led to the lounge and told to wait while the police search of the property continued. Jonathan could not process all he'd been told and looked on in disbelief at the lounge he'd sat in any number of times with the family. Looking down at the table, he noticed there were two mugs and a teacup set out; tea had been drunk. He picked up a tomato, he remembered later that it was an odd shape, and sat waiting as policemen came and went. Then an ashen-faced officer came into the lounge and said that they'd found a man's body in the cowshed, covered with old carpets, crates and boxes.

There was still no sign of Megan. Jonathan had no idea how he would break this news to Cheryl. It seemed impossible, but he was sure that he could not tell her over the phone. He asked to drive back to Orpington to tell her in person. Even at this stage, Jonathan hoped that the next policeman to walk through the door would say; 'Don't worry, we've made a mistake.'

But it wasn't to be. In fact, by the time Jonathan reached Cheryl, just before 8am, she had already been called by the police who had told her that they had now uncovered two bodies in the cowshed. It is too easy to think of unsolved murders as tantalising 'whodunnits', forgetting the impact the loss of loved ones can have on a life. Cheryl's world was destroyed in the few seconds it took to relay the news from the farmhouse. She lives with the horror of what happened to her elderly parents every day. She is haunted by dreams where she struggles to save them, to halt the very moment where someone stood and coldly executed them at the farm they had devoted their lives to.

Who could possibly wish her parents harm? As the hours passed, two names came to her. But neither would be the names that the police had in mind.

As with all murder cases, enquiries were carried out. Ty ar y Waun is often described as an 'isolated farmhouse', but that isn't quite the case. In fact, the nearest property, another farm, lies only 35 metres away. Police called there and the family told them that they had been at home for the most part of the previous day. They confirmed that they had heard shots but said that they thought it was Harry shooting at crows, something he would do from time to time.

The other neighbouring farms were occupied by the Hopkins and the Davies families. They gave accounts of their whereabouts and told the police what they could. It was at this point that reports of the man in the trench coat came out, but the initial description Mrs Lewis gave stated that the man was about 5ft 9in tall. Attempts to find the Suzuki 4x4 and the professional-looking man did not yield any firm results, but the police did find out, from the solicitors Harry and the stranger talked to, that the two men had been looking for the will of a 'Radcliffe woman'. Radcliffe was the family Megan Tooze hailed from and historically they had owned a substantial amount of land and farms in the area.

Why had Harry bought the Luger? Something had happened to unnerve him. Police also discovered that Harry had visited the offices of the National Farmers' Union to find out what legal services they could offer him. He'd talked obliquely about 'they're trying to get me out of my house' but did not identify who 'they' might be.

Police enquiries continued. The post-mortem and forensic work had delivered valuable information. A partial palm print and fingerprints had been found on two areas of the farm, prints that could not be matched to residents or family. One was on the main doorframe; the other, on a garden gate leading to fields at the rear of the farm. The murder sites should have revealed so much more, but the carpet that had covered Megan had been lost, a valuable opportunity squandered.

At first glance, it seems odd that once the police arrived, they did not find the Toozes. In fact, this delay lies at the heart of the mystery. The scenario the police imagined unfolding, and the one that they presented in court, went like this. After shopping in Llanharry and Talbot Green, Harry and Megan arrived home mid-morning and Megan began to prepare lunch. Harry was expecting a call and had even laid out a smart white shirt on their bed as if he was expecting to change. Someone knocked, and someone was invited in, led into the lounge and tea was made. Megan and Harry each had a mug and a teacup and saucer was offered to the guest, who drank it with no sugar.

Whoever shared tea with the Toozes then walked out into the cowshed with Harry. When the old man's back was turned, he raised a shotgun and aiming just above his right ear, and from no more than three feet away, blasted him with a single shot. Every bone in Harry's skull shattered with the impact of the shot and he was killed instantly. The killer then left the cowshed, through the only door at the front of the building, next door to the house. He walked past the window of the lounge where he'd just been sitting, past the front door and found Megan fleeing into the front yard. She would have to have rounded the corner and run towards the back of the house to have any chance of escape, but she managed no more than a few yards when the killer blasted her at close range, again a shot to the head, just below the right ear. She fell to the ground.

The killer then moved the bodies. Megan was moved from

the front of the house; there was evidence of a drag mark, and yet the mud found on her shoes and clothing was not consistent with being dragged. Megan weighed over ten stone, but was probably pulled upright and then carried into the shed. Once inside, she was laid face down by the side of a small internal wall and covered with carpet, milk crates and other bits of detritus found in the shed.

Harry had other outbuildings and this cowshed was used for storage rather than keeping livestock. It was packed with items accumulated over the years which is why, at first glance, the police saw nothing but piles of farming equipment, old furniture and tarpaulin. Taking apart one of the piles, a police officer saw a hand and once all the items had been pulled away form the body, Harry Tooze was found crammed into a trough. There were no drag marks in the shed. Harry was probably carried from the position that he fell, to the trough, on the other side of the small wall where Megan was hidden. The murderer then left. There was no sign that he'd tried to clean himself up, no clothing was found burnt or discarded, no gun was left behind; it was as if the killer then simply disappeared.

Cheryl was told that everything that could possibly be done to track the killer was being done and she sat and waited, sure that the truth of what happened on the day would come to light. Days, weeks, then months passed. How could someone walk onto a farm late one morning, kill two people and leave without a trace? In fact, there was a trace from those sad events that day, but it only came to light after a forensic review some months later. In the first few days, the teacup and saucer had been returned showing 'insufficient detail' to identify a print. Four months later, however, one print had been enlarged and the detail was now thought to be clear enough to give an identification. On the top of the saucer was the partial thumbprint of Jonathan Jones, Cheryl's boyfriend.

Shortly afterwards, Cheryl answered an early morning knock at the door of the flat that she shared with Jonathan in Orpington. It was the beginning of a new and terrible episode in her life. In streamed a line of police officers. They were there to arrest Jonathan for the murder of Harry and Megan Tooze.

Cheryl thought she would break. She knew with an unwavering certainty that the police were wrong. There were, of course, some people who believed that she was simply blinded by love. Mrs Gillian Lewis helped the police produce a sketch of the man in the trench coat – a sketch that looks not unlike Jonathan. She revised her description of the man's height too. She thought he may have been over 6ft tall.

The police suggested that Jonathan had time enough to travel to Llanharry, either by train or by hitchhiking, had murdered his girlfriend's parents after sharing a cup of tea, all in the hope that he and Cheryl would come into the estate and savings worth some £150,000. Jonathan was between jobs, and what was more, had recently had to let go of a home he'd bought as an investment in Orpington as he could not keep up the repayments on it. He hadn't told Cheryl that it had been repossessed. He could have stolen the shotgun from the farm the month before; he owned a trench coat and could have been the man spotted by Mrs Lewis, perhaps when he was on a dry run, only the month before. In addition, he took four-and-a-half hours to get to the farm on the night of the killing, plenty of time to dispose of any evidence such as guns or clothing, before appearing at the farm to wait for news of the couple.

Cheryl knew this account was based on circumstantial evidence and was sure that the police would see sense. Jonathan was even more confident. He later said: 'I was expecting to be freed at the magistrates' court, I was expecting to be given bail, I was expecting that the charge would be thrown out at committal, and I was expecting to be freed by the court.' None of that came to pass. On 6 April 1995, Jonathan Jones was found guilty of murder and sentenced to life imprisonment. Stuart Hutton, Jonathan's solicitor, was dismayed by the verdict. And when he looked at the judge, Mr Justice Richard Rougier, Hutton noted something else: Rougier was clearly shocked by the verdict and did not speak for more than a few seconds.

Hutton has over thirty years' experience as a solicitor based in Cardiff and this was not the only case that he had worked on involving the South Wales Police and a miscarriage of justice. Prostitute Lynette White was stabbed to death in her flat in a red-light district of Cardiff in 1988. Three men were jailed in 1990 for the twenty-year-old's murder and they served two years until their convictions were quashed at the Court of Appeal. The real killer, Jeffrey Gafoor, was found fifteen years later, after the case was reinvestigated and fresh DNA was found under paintwork on a skirting board. Gafoor admitted to killing Lynette and was jailed for life in 2003.

It is far from being the only miscarriage of justice that has tainted the police force. As well as those accused of killing Lynette White, the Court of Appeal has seen Wayne and Paul Darvell, Michael O'Brien, Ellis Sherwood, Darren Hall,

Annette Hewins and Donna Clarke all freed after they were wrongly imprisoned for murder. Annette Hewins was pregnant when arrested and her son was later taken from her when he was only nine hours old. They were reunited when she was freed two years later, but she feels their relationship has been irrevocably damaged. She has since said: 'I have no respect for South Wales Police. I hate every one of them. They convinced themselves someone was guilty and ignored any evidence that pointed to other perpetrators. Yet innocent people, and the victims' families, had their lives ruined.'

Stuart Hutton was sure that the police had the wrong man in Jonathan Jones and worked to demonstrate that the central points in the prosecution case were wrong. The drawing of the man in a trench coat looked like Jonathan Jones – but why would he need a dry run when he knew the farm and the journey intimately? If Mrs Lewis had passed him, sitting as she was in the passenger's seat, she would have drawn level with his torso, not his face. She had seen Jonathan earlier at a family funeral and on TV as Cheryl made an appeal for anyone with information to come forward, and it would be easy to make the innocent mistake of mixing up that face with someone seen fleetingly in the weeks before the murder.

Then there's the thumbprint on the saucer. Stuart Hutton questioned Jonathan and suggested that it was feasible that he idly handled the saucer while waiting at the farm; Jonathan was sure he did not. In Hutton's experience, most of his clients would go along with the suggestion, illustrating how there could be a perfectly innocent explanation for the print.

Hutton's next line of questioning added to his sense that Jonathan had nothing to hide. The solicitor was puzzled by the lack of 'drag marks' at the scene. Other than a short one near the site where Megan was shot, it seemed clear that the bodies were lifted and carried. Hutton doubted that a man working alone could manage to carry Harry's weight and said as much to Jonathan. Instead of agreeing, Jonathan thought about it and said that he probably could lift Harry if he really needed to. It was this lack of guile that convinced Stuart that he was not dealing with a killer.

At the trial, the prosecution's case should have fallen apart. The police relied on the 'missing hour' on Jonathan's drive, when in fact it was readily explained by delays caused by calling Cheryl and by the bad weather. They relied on a train guard to identify Jonathan as the man they saw on the platform waiting for a train that could have taken him out of south Wales and on to Kent but, in fact, the guard stated that Jonathan was not the man he had seen. It went on: the print of the saucer was likely to have been placed there when Jonathan washed it after a funeral and Cheryl testified that her parents would never have given him their 'best china', just the mug they'd always had during a visit. Yet the jury did convict. Hutton has an insight as to why.

The other key to the prosecution's case was Jonathan's alibi. He told the police that he was looking for office accommodation on the day of the murders, but no one at the estate agents he called in to could recall him. Neither could the OTIS lift repairmen working on the lifts in the flat. He remembers seeing them and saying something to the three men, but they could not remember him. One also stated that Jonathan must be wrong as he was elsewhere picking up a part at the time Jonathan suggested.

After the trial, Stuart Hutton persuaded the lift maintenance man to retrace his steps and he demonstrated that he could have been there at the time Jonathan suggested. Yet Hutton realised that the jury in Newport simply could not believe that the three men would fail to remember Jonathan. In a rural community, you would remember. In a busy urban setting, a bloke going up the stairs and saying something like, 'There's plenty more to fix in our flat if you like', would not merit you raising your head from your work. But that was hard for the jury to accept. Add to that, the underlying faith the public have the police, the serious nature of the crimes, and ten out of the twelve members felt that Jonathan Jones was the killer.

He isn't. Even after a forensic examination of his clothing and spectacles, there is not a shred of evidence linking him to the murder. The blood and tissue loss caused by the shootings would have been considerable. If specks of DNA could be found under paintwork of a skirting board fifteen years after the murder of Lynette White, the DNA accumulated at the scene of the Tooze murders should have been extensive. Nothing on Jonathan linked him to the bloody events of 26 July 1993 at Ty ar y Waun. But someone, maybe even two people, walked away from the farm, and they would have been covered in the results of their crime.

After the guilty verdict, Cheryl quit her job, moved in with Jonathan's parents and devoted herself to the campaign for his release. It was a long and uphill struggle but the family and their lawyers eventually saw the case reach the Court of Appeal in May 1996. With the material reviewed, the case against Jonathan Jones was dismissed and after losing over two-and-a-half years of his life behind bars, he was a free man. Cheryl stood on the steps of the court and told the press: 'This is a victory for truth and love. But the fight is not over – my intention is to find out who killed my parents.'

With Jonathan free, Cheryl tried to piece together events once more. Think back to the day of the murders. Someone arrived, not necessarily by car although that 'grey Suzuki 4 x 4' was spotted driving towards the farm on the day. Shots are fired. The first, to kill Harry, then the chase to find Megan and kill her in her tracks. The sound from a shotgun carries for miles, and certainly the 35 metres to the neighbouring garden or the 70 metres to the farm heading in the other direction. It is a warm July day, people will be outside. You would require considerable confidence, then, to stay at the farm and begin to hide the bodies.

It would have taken time. Even if there were two people, bodies are difficult to manipulate – particularly Harry's, which was lowered into a trough. Then they were covered, not by one or two items, but by so many that their hiding place blended with the other piles of household and farm materials.

What's more, someone returned to the farmhouse. There was no evidence that anyone had tried to clean themselves up there, using the bathroom and basin for example, but other evidence that did emerge was extraordinary. Someone put potatoes in a saucepan and cooked them, alongside some cabbage. Afterwards, the cooker was switched off at the mains.

The police knew that this scene, suggesting that lunch was prepared, had to have been staged for a number of reasons. First, no peelings were found. The potatoes had not been peeled at Ty ar y Waun, then, but were brought there.

Furthermore, Cheryl swore the potatoes weren't her father's, the couple only cooked the ones that Harry grew which Megan would then quarter and boil. The ones found at the farm were whole and clearly a different variety. In addition, her mother always filled the pot to the brim, as the remainder would go towards chicken feed. The cabbage was also prepared in a very different way to the approach Megan would have employed: she religiously used bicarbonate of soda. There was no meat and the police later suggested that the dog must have eaten it, and yet the Tooze dog was so old it could only manage mashed food. So why would someone go to the effort to suggest that the Toozes had prepared lunch? The logical reason is to suggest a different time of death.

Establishing time of death isn't an exact science. The pathologist was not called out until the following day and arrived at 2pm that afternoon. The bodies were taken to East Glamorgan Hospital and X-rays were arranged for 5pm. Once the areas where the shot could be seen in the skull were established, they were removed to the mortuary. To estimate a time of death, the pathologist looks for the presence of rigor mortis and post-mortem lividity, then takes a reading from a rectal thermometer and, establishing ambient room temperatures plus factoring in the temperature from where the bodies were found, arrives at a time frame.

Professor Helen Whitwell is a consultant pathologist to the Home Office, and spoke at the Dr Harold Shipman Enquiry. Dr Shipman gave recordings of time of death of the patients he killed, to suit his purposes. When asked to explain how pathologists arrive at a time of death, Professor Whitwell said: 'Essentially the time of death is one of those huge mysteries of forensic pathology... There are lots of complicated equations and things that one can use, but they essentially are not of much use apart from very exceptional circumstances.'

With that in mind, it is worth taking note of the last time Megan and Harry Tooze were seen alive. Harry's sister and her husband saw them in the car park of Tesco in Talbot Green shortly before 11am. They talked briefly and the Toozes headed back to Llanharry. Their Defender was seen turning up the track that led to Ty ar y Waun soon afterwards. The police arrived at the conclusion that the time of death was 1.30pm, just before the Toozes should have eaten lunch. Yet they also had a sighting of their Defender driving towards Llanharry as late at 2.30pm. Another farmer told Cheryl and Jonathan's father Graham that he'd seen Harry at around 2pm, although later he did not want to comment further.

Cheryl noted another detail that seemed suggestive to her. The beds at the farm had been made up but, she suspected, not by her mother. Megan was a woman of habit and would not make the beds up until after 2.30pm each afternoon. The bedding would be turned down in the morning to air and then made up in the afternoon. Yet the post-mortem report showed that no foodstuff was found in the stomach contents of the couple. The police believed that this was because they were waiting to eat lunch when the killer arrived. Cheryl knows that her parents had always finished lunch by 1.20pm. She believes the killer, or killers, were there after lunch, sometime after 2.45pm.

Again, this begs the question of why someone would risk staying in the property for so long, placing saucepans on the cooker and making up beds? If it was to suggest an earlier time of death, it may be because they had an alibi for lunchtime, but not late afternoon.

Yet with all this effort to window-dress the property, if the killer had drunk tea with the Toozes, surely they would make the effort to remove the cup and saucer in case any prints or DNA remained on the china?

The jury did not believe her when Cheryl said at Jonathan's trial that her boyfriend would have been given a mug, not a teacup. But not only did she know that to be true, she observed that the cup was not, in fact, the 'best china'. That was another set, from another cupboard. The cup placed on the table that day was a decorative item, one of Harry and Megan's wedding gifts. That suggests one of two things. Either the killer was ignorant of that fact, as they were of all the other Tooze cooking and domestic habits, or perhaps more dramatically, Megan left it out as a sign. If this was a wedding gift, could she have brought out the cup to remind someone of the long bond they had with the family? Perhaps she even sensed that she and Harry were in danger and used the cup to alert Cheryl, telling her daughter who had been present on that fateful day.

This is pure speculation, but the many discrepancies and loose ends of the case lend themselves to endless conjecture. Cheryl cannot remember who gave the tea cup to her mother, but she did recall that at a family funeral two years earlier, the sheer numbers of visitors meant the cup was used and that Jonathan was tasked with carefully drying it after it was washed.

Was there a conspiracy of silence? Once the Lynette White

murder case collapsed and the three wrongly imprisoned men were released, more damning detail from the original investigation emerged. Not only had the police focused on the wrong men, as they had with Jonathan Jones in the Tooze case, but witnesses claim that they had been intimidated too. One, Mark Grommek, admitted lying during the original Lynette White murder trial, claiming he'd seen the three men outside Lynette's flat. Grommek admitted charges of perjury in 2008 and was jailed for 18 months. Yet the judge, Mr Justice Maddison said: 'You were seriously hounded, bullied, threatened, abused and manipulated by the police during a period of several months leading up to late 1988, as a result of which you felt compelled to agree to false accounts they suggested to you.'

Stuart Hutton knows the Tooze case is remarkable. Firstly, because it represents a miscarriage of justice, and secondly, because the trial judge, Mr Justice Rougier, wrote to the defence team and the Home Secretary after the verdict to say that he had been troubled by 'significant doubt' in the case. For a judge to write such a letter after a verdict was unprecedented. Yet the extraordinary features of the case do not end there.

Once Cheryl Tooze had access to her parents' post-mortem report, she was to face a new and shocking twist. The first part of the report covers the pathologist's arrival at the scene and features general observations about where the bodies were found. Megan was then examined and the cause of death was recorded: 'Death is due to a shotgun injury to the back of the head damaging the vital centres of the brain, with extensive bony injuries to the head and face.' Then Harry's section begins and within the first line, Cheryl was troubled. It reads: 'This was an elderly man about 5ft 7in tall weighing 84kg clothed.' Harry was over 6ft tall, even allowing for the effects of ageing.

The discrepancies didn't end there. The man was described as having mid-brown hair when what little hair Harry had left was white. At 84kg, the man was a little over 13 stone; Harry was nearer to 16 stone. The coronary arteries of the heart were described as 70 per cent blocked, which implies he would have suffered with angina, chest pains and breathlessness; Harry suffered from none of those complaints. He had, however, gashed his arm in an accident six months earlier and was left with a livid scar. This was not noted on the report, although scars as small as 1.5cm on a shin were. By the end of the report, Cheryl was no longer sure that this was the post-mortem of Harry Tooze at all.

This doubt inevitably provoked more questions than answers. If it wasn't Harry, who was it? Could it have been someone who'd threatened Harry and a fight had broken out? The pathologist did record a fresh bruise on the jaw, consistent with blunt trauma, so some physical force had been used before the shotgun was employed. Yet even then, more questions were raised. If Megan had been shot first, and Harry reacted, why did he not call the police and Cheryl? Why would he not come forward, even if he ran in fear, once he saw Cheryl's appeal for information and Jonathan's subsequent arrest for double murder?

Despite the efforts of Cheryl and her in-laws to have the post-mortem reviewed, the Coroner's court have elected not to do so. The case was reinvestigated by Detective Chief

Inspector Trefor Evans in 2001. Cheryl was sure there would be a breakthrough after a holdall was discovered with a set of shotgun barrels along with two shotgun cartridges in a disused mine shaft close to the farm. At one stage, Mr Evans talked to Cheryl and told her that he was close to an arrest. None was forthcoming, however, and DCI Evans retired shortly afterwards, yet another frustrating end to a hopeful development for Cheryl and Jonathan.

The case in now in the hands of a single officer, Detective Inspector Gareth Heatley. South Wales Police chose not to answer questions for this book, but did issue a statement. It reads: 'South Wales Police can confirm that the team investigating the murder of Harry and Megan Tooze has been scaled down. The decision has been made because all lines of enquiry, and forensic opportunities relating to the case, have now been exhausted by investigators. However, it is important to stress that the enquiry has not been closed.'

Cheryl does not believe that all lines are exhausted and she, Jonathan and her father-in-law Graham are still campaigning to find out who was responsible for the death of Harry and Megan Tooze and hope to establish if that really was the body of Harry Tooze found in the cowshed of Ty ar y Waun. Cheryl never saw the bodies and never formally identified them.

Some cases raise more questions than answers. Someone knows what happened that day, though it is far from clear who. Harry had run-ins both with relations and neighbours. And that isn't all. One of the neighbouring farms has a name that is close enough to that of the Tooze farm to suggest the possibility that they were murdered by mistake. Yet as we have seen, something about Harry's behaviour suggests that he was a worried man at the time. The visit to the Farmers' Union and the purchasing of a handgun points to a man who feared something or someone.

The South Wales Police say that the enquiry is not yet closed and as with the murder of Lynette White, they may still find the real killer, or killers. Finding and jailing Jeffrey Gafoor was a triumph for justice.

Each development stirs up yet more anxiety and grief for Cheryl. Even now, she thinks she sometimes catches sight of Harry, watching the son she and Jonathan went on to have. The boy reminds Cheryl of her father. She runs towards the man but never catches up with him.

Cheryl's faith in the police and the legal system was badly shaken over the imprisonment of Jonathan and the knowledge that her parents' killer is yet to be found. The press, the courts and the police learned that Cheryl Tooze was unwavering in her efforts to prove Jonathan's innocence and secure his release, and she achieved it. Who knows what she can still achieve?

CHAPTER EIGHT
JILL DANDO
THE GOLDEN GIRL

After a year-long investigation, two arrests, a trial and successful prosecution, the team at the Met led by Detective Chief Superintendent Hamish Campbell had to watch as the man they were convinced had shot and killed Jill Dando walked free. Barry George had served seven years of a life sentence and his release was greeted with as much press coverage as his arrest, some eight years earlier. The case intrigued all who followed it.

Some believe that George could never have been involved in murder and that Scotland Yard blundered into a miscarriage of justice. Others thought that the police had the right man all along. But there is one thing that everyone can agree on: Jill didn't know her killer. When she was pushed down onto her knees outside her front door one April morning, she was executed by a stranger. Beyond that one clear moment, the picture becomes darker and darker.

'Stranger' murders are hard to investigate because they are random. With no connection to the victim evident, the police are left relying on physical evidence such as DNA traces on a weapon or the victim. It can help trace an assailant if they have offended on a previous occasion, and if their profile is held on a criminal database. Other evidence can come from CCTV, piecing together movements and even identity, perhaps by tracking a vehicle registration number.

Without physical evidence, investigations fall back on witness accounts. The process of asking questions door to door has long been integral to investigations, but it can only ever provide part of a picture. Witnesses are vital, and yet the Jill Dando enquiry found, as all enquiries find, that accounts are fragmented and unreliable. No two witness statements will ever be quite the same. What's more, accounts change. One witness talked with Barry George on two occasions over the space of three days. First, he said that George had blond hair. Later, he changed his description to 'mousy'. George has never been anything other than dark-haired. No matter how well intentioned the witness, memories are unreliable.

In a worst-case scenario, an unbalanced individual will strike out at a victim they have chosen but have no link to, are seen but not apprehended and leave no traceable DNA material at the crime site. This was the situation that faced Detective Chief Superintendent Hamish Campbell with the murder of Jill Dando, and it was not for the first time. Although he did not realise at the outset of the enquiry, this case had echoes with another 'unsolvable' case his team had encountered.

Two years earlier, twelve-year-old Katerina Koneva was sexually assaulted and strangled at her home in west London. Her parents had arrived from Macedonia to escape the conflict there and their daughter was thriving in her new school environment. Her father Trajce was on his way home from college but when he arrived he could not open the front door. Looking through the window, he saw that a chair was being used to block it. He could see his daughter's school bag but then he also noticed a pair of men's black shoes.

He was frantically trying to smash through the door when a man jumped from the window and into the garden. Trajce called out and confronted the man. 'It's difficult to put into words, but I remember the way the man looked at me,' he recalled later. 'He was so cool. He just looked at me and ran away.'

Trajce gave chase – some forty-six witnesses say that they saw the desperate father in pursuit. The attacker got away, though, and by the time Trajce raced back to his daughter, the twelve-year-old was dead. She had been raped and then strangled, a cord tied around her neck. Despite the number of eyewitness accounts, despite CCTV images and despite fingerprints and a strand of hair found near Katerina's cardigan, the identity of her attacker remained a mystery.

Campbell and his team were determined that the hunt would go on even as the years passed; a reward of £20,000 was posted, but no new information came to light. The team knew that this kind of offender was sure to attack again. During the course of the enquiry, sightings of the man came up several times and one girl, the same age as Katerina, had even been followed home by someone who could have been him. She managed to get through her front door and hid as her pursuer rang the doorbell. The girl had the presence of mind not to answer it and, in time, he gave up and went away.

It seemed as if the trail had run cold but as suspected, the assailant struck again, this time, attacking a young Korean student who was waiting for a friend outside a tube station.

The man struck up a conversation and said that he could help her find accommodation. Instead, luring her to his flat in Acton, west London, he attacked her and tied her up. She was able to talk her way out of the ordeal, pretending to befriend him and promising that she would call him the next day.

Once free, she went to the police and her attacker was arrested. The case came up at the Old Bailey in 2003 and there, the name of Andrzej Kunowski was revealed. He was Polish, forty-six years old and a tailor. After being found guilty of rape, he was sentenced to nine years. The police were aware that DNA samples taken after his arrest, matched those found at Katerina's home. Once they contacted their counterparts in Warsaw, Poland, they found out that Kunowski had been charged with the rape of a ten-year-old girl there and had fled to Britain in 1996. He'd attacked almost thirty girls and women by the time he was jailed in Britain. In 2004, he was tried and found guilty of the rape and murder of Katerina Koneva and was jailed for life.

It took over six years before there was a breakthrough in the Koneva case and it took more than police diligence to make it happen: it came about because Kunowski committed another crime and was caught. Not many cases take years to solve, but they do crop up. And when they do, officers know that no matter how proficient they are in tracing, investigating and eliminating leads, at some point they need a bit of luck. As DCS Hamish Campbell made his way to Gowan Avenue on Monday, 26 April, only a mile away from where Katerina had been killed, he didn't think that this would be another difficult case. In fact, he imagined that this murder would be solved as the vast majority are: quickly.

Campbell was highly regarded, a veteran of criminal intelligence and anti-terrorist branches with over twenty-five years in the job. A methodical investigator, he would marshal resources to ensure that his investigations stayed on track, he was happy to use external officers to review findings if necessary and no matter the complexity of a case, he knew how to keep a cool head. He would need to. Because as he stepped out of his police car, he stepped into the most high-profile and expensive investigation in the Met's history and a circus of publicity that would threaten his career and the reputation of his department.

All DCS Campbell was aware of at that point was the rumour that it was Jill Dando who'd been attacked. This came through in the first call to emergency services, from a woman who'd dialled 999 at 11.43am. On the recording, she'd asked for the Ambulance Service and said: 'Hello, Ambulance, I'm walking down Gowan Avenue... 29 Gowan Avenue. It looks like there's somebody collapsed.'

'I'm sorry, which area?'

'Fulham, SW6.'

'SW6, Gowan Avenue.'

'And, confidentially, it looks like it's Jill Dando, and she's collapsed on her doorstep. There's a lot of blood.'

The call handler asked the woman to establish if the lady she was calling to report was breathing. It is part of standard procedure as vital minutes are lost while an ambulance makes its way to an address. During these first few minutes, many injured and ill people can be saved if a passer-by can carry out simple steps, such as putting the patient in the recovery position or checking that they haven't swallowed their tongue. Call handlers are trained to talk people through techniques but it was clear that this caller did not want to approach the injured person. She sounded distressed. Another woman's voice could be heard in the background, talking about blood coming from the victim's nose. The caller is heard again:

> 'She's got blood coming from her nose. Her arms are blue.'
> 'Right, can you just…'
> 'Please…'
> 'Sorry, it's very important, I'm sorry to push you. I just need to find out if she needs… if she's breathing. Could you just ask somebody for me, please, or check yourself?'
> 'How does one check?'
> 'Right, is the lady's chest going up and down?'
> 'Oh my God, no. I don't think she's alive, I'm sorry, I don't think…'
> 'OK, don't worry, don't worry. I'm going to get some help there as fast as I can for you.'
> 'Please.'
> 'It shouldn't be too long. We'll see you very soon. Bye-bye.'
> 'Thank you.'

It is an obvious difficulty for call handlers that they can't see the nature of an injury, but it is a blessing too. Because what Helen Doble – the woman who made that call to the Emergency Services – saw will haunt her forever. She knew

Jill. She wasn't a close friend, but she knew her well enough to say hello and exchange a few words in the street.

Of course, she knew Jill from her appearance on *Holiday*, *Crimewatch* and the *Six O'Clock News* – we all did – but Helen worked in TV too, not that uncommon a profession for a borough like Fulham. She worked in production, and had had a stint on *This Is Your Life*, so she'd had her dealings with 'talent' like Jill. 'Talent' is the name given to presenters, anyone who is the public face of a programme or a channel, as Jill was. It can be a disparaging term. Some researchers and journalists who source and write up stories watch as their words are spoken by someone on screen, for a far higher salary, and wonder what would happen if the autocue broke. But of course, presenters such as Jill are consummate professionals and if that happens and it's a live broadcast, they improvise and make it all look effortless, no matter what is being screamed into their earpiece.

It is a talent, and Jill had it in abundance, but that isn't why Helen liked her and looked forward to talking to her. Jill was simply so nice. She didn't have the ego and the high-handed manner some 'talent' demonstrated. She was down-to-earth and bubbly; you always left her company with a smile on your face. That is why Helen could not understand what she was looking at. When she said 'It looks like it's Jill Dando', it really didn't. That was Jill's house, that was her car parked outside, but the woman slumped against the front door in the porch, with her bag open, her keys in her hand, with her phone ringing, that couldn't be her. There was so much blood. Someone must have stabbed this woman and walked away, knowing she was fighting for her life.

No one imagined it would end this way. Jill was liked by everyone, even those whose contact with her only came via the television screen. She was the golden girl, the girl next door, the girl from Weston who didn't have any airs and graces, even though she'd made it to the very top of her profession. And somewhere between the TV personality, the 'brand' of Jill Dando and the reality of the woman herself, a hard-working presenter trying to juggle a hundred projects and plan her wedding, something evil had crept in and brought her life to an abrupt and violent end.

Jill Dando didn't have a charmed life, although she often talked of how lucky she was and how 'someone up there' was looking out for her. She was born in 1961, some nine years after her brother. Her mother Jean had rhesus-negative blood and, in the early 1960s, second pregnancies by such women weren't encouraged. If a RhD-negative mother carries a RhD-positive baby, the D-antigen in the baby's blood can cause the mother's blood to react as if it were under attack, and in doing so, produce antibodies. In a first pregnancy, the process can be triggered but it isn't harmful, but if a second baby is RhD-positive, antibodies are more virulent and can attack the blood cells of the baby. After 1969, it became common practice to inject the mother with anti-D immunoglobulin and any problems were thus eradicated. But as Jean came to full-term, she knew there was a risk her baby could have jaundice, be deaf, blind or even stillborn. As it turned out, blood type wouldn't prove to be the problem. Jill was born with another serious complication, though: she had a hole in her heart.

Doctors could not operate until she was three years old. In

the early 1970s, such an operation still involved a high degree of risk and her parents were very fearful that they would lose their daughter. After two difficult weeks Jill recovered, yet even as the years went by, her mother found it hard to shake off a need to protect her daughter. They were very close, some friends thought unusually so, more like best friends than a mother and daughter. Jill confided in her mother about everything and they spent hours together in the kitchen talking and laughing.

Jill's brother Nigel was a reporter for the local newspaper in Weston and Jill decided that she'd like to follow suit. She opted not to go to college but to begin work on the *Weston Mercury* as soon as she'd finished her A-Levels. By then, Nigel had moved on to the *Bristol Evening Post*, but Jill stayed loyal to the *Mercury* for five years before moving to Radio Devon, as a programme assistant. There were no jobs for reporters at the radio station when she joined and Jill was happy to change roles and then begin stints as a presenter during morning slots.

She had made the kind of practical decision that many young women would: she didn't have a 'career plan' to follow and simply took opportunities as they arose. Jill's father, Jack, had worked as a printer for the *Mercury* since he was demobbed from the Army in 1946, so he was very proud that both his children had become reporters. But Jill was to find her regional background, her decision not to go to university and her drift into presenting would undermine her in some people's eyes, even as her career hit the upper echelons of broadcasting.

The BBC newsroom was hard-nosed when it came to credentials. This wasn't the view of BBC management, though: what they were looking for was someone who communicated 'brand' values, someone viewers instantly identified with and felt reassured by. But reporters felt differently, and that's where it mattered once you sat down at your desk. In the newsroom, if you weren't razor sharp, a hardened journalist with national and even international experience, you would find it hard to be taken seriously. And the biggest taboo of all was to try and mix a career in 'entertainment' with news. The line was firmly drawn. You chose low- or highbrow, you don't get to flit between the two and expect a newsroom to applaud.

And yet this was precisely what Jill would go on to do. It often made her working life difficult as she was acutely sensitive to the fact that she was thought of as a lightweight. She was perhaps the first news presenter to go on to present lighter formats, such as *Holiday*, along with the *Six O'Clock News*. She appeared on the front of the *Radio Times*, was seen cavorting in a bikini, sipping cocktails and appearing in *OK!*, or in evening gowns, arm in arm with Cliff Richard. Absolutely inappropriate for a news journalist and yet very much a sign of how life as a 'celebrity' in 1990s Britain was changing. Life would never be the same again, in fact.

Jill seemed on top of the world by 1999. Yet scratch below the surface and all was not well. She had been walking a difficult line professionally and she sensed she'd lost her way. The newsroom had thrown their weight behind blocking Jill's appointment to become the face of the *Six*. They just didn't have faith that she could grill government ministers; she was too nice, not intellectually rigorous enough. A few years earlier, in 1996, Jill was thrilled to be voted 'TV Personality of the Year'; now she had to accept that this urge to be popular had damaged her standing in the newsroom. You can't be a personality and anchor the news at the same time.

Jill didn't want to restrict herself to entertainment, though. She enjoyed *Crimewatch* but had to learn that even that was thought of as entertainment by news teams. Jill had campaigned hard for the role on the *Six*, and many in management backed her, knowing how positively she scored with viewers. By the end of 1998 she had to accept that it was never going to be. The job was going to be offered to Huw Edwards. Jill had to ask her agent who he was. She soon found out. Edwards had a first-class honours degree, contributed to *Panorama* and *Newsnight* and was the BBC's Chief Political Correspondent. In the newsroom, it was no contest.

This rejection hurt Jill. Despite her outward confidence, she was plagued with insecurities about her credibility and background. It was something her long-term partner and mentor Bob Wheaton recognised. He was a heavyweight news producer and was well respected. After they met, he felt the need to nurture Jill as he was genuinely impressed by her ability to present. She was unflappable no matter if a 'package', a news story, had been lost. Jill held any programme together seamlessly.

Bob and Jill were more than lovers. He had shaped Jill and her career for eight years. Despite the fact that Bob was fourteen years older, with a divorce and children behind him, Jill had hoped that they would marry and start a family of their own. It wasn't to be. By 1996, both accepted that their relationship had run its course.

Bob was irritated that Jill had not been taken seriously by

BBC news, but it was nothing in comparison to the frustration felt by her agent, Jon Roseman. Jon recognised that the contract that Jill was offered in 1998 was light on substance and felt that Jill's inherent loyalty to the channel was being used against her. He asked her to give thought to the offer ITV had made but in his heart, knew that Jill would not leave the Beeb. She loved the channel, she felt at home there and didn't really care that ITV could be more lucrative. What she wanted was to appear on BBC as often as possible. This need was her Achilles heel.

Jill had been devastated by the death of her mother some twelve years earlier and even though so much time had passed and so many accolades had come her way, there was a loneliness about Jill that all her friends sensed. She felt that all she had achieved at the BBC could slip away and was desperate to cling on, even though her new contract was vague about the BBC's commitment to her. The organisation was her home and rather than play hardball, she preferred to hope for the best. It was a passive side to her nature that infuriated Jon, but he, of course, was there to be the 'bad cop'. At one meeting with BBC executives, Jon was so combative that Jill hid in the Ladies toilet until everything had blown over. She felt incredibly upset by conflict.

The need to feel accepted and liked was at the root of her efforts to be on screen as often as possible. She was winding down her commitment to *Holiday*, it was simply too gruelling, but was desperately hoping that something would come along, a chat show perhaps. No one outside TV would have guessed that Jill was insecure about her abilities and her future. Her viewers only saw her charming and confident persona, and now with news that Jill was engaged to be married it seemed as if her gilded life was continuing as planned.

Her fiancé was Alan Farthing. He knew all about Jill, about her fears and her worries, and saw how it jarred with her natural and exuberant love of life. He felt her professional disappointments would be short-lived; she was too unique a talent. He was sure any career turbulence would be brief, and besides, Jill had made it clear that she longed for children, that TV could take a back seat for some years to come. Yet even Alan had to admit that at first, meeting her was daunting. He had to consciously push past the glitz and veneer of her celebrity lifestyle, to remind himself that a real woman stood behind it all. Because by the time they met, there is little doubt that Jill was a celebrity.

Alan was a gynaecologist and working at St Mary's, the same hospital as Jill's best friend, Jenny Higham. Jenny was sure that here were two individuals who would get on well and she engineered a meeting. Alan was cautious, though, because of Jill's fame. When they first went to dinner, he was bemused to watch people come up and talk to her as if he were invisible. Jill would chat and dispense autographed photos that she kept in her handbag. Plus, being invited supper at Gowan Avenue and finding that fellow guests included Cliff Richard, Gloria Hunniford, or the Countess of Wessex, was unnerving. But Alan quickly saw that Jill was a simple girl at heart, cheerful, caring and unspoilt by fame. He fell for her and Jill was overjoyed when he asked her to marry him in January 1999.

Everyone who knew her said she 'glowed' from that moment on. At last, she'd found the man she always hoped she would, someone who cared for her and would share her future. They searched for somewhere to raise a family and found the perfect home in St John's Wood. They both had homes on the market with sales agreed, Alan in Chiswick and Jill in Fulham. Jill exchanged contracts on her home in mid-April but was pleased that she would not need to move until July, as there was still so much to do. By the end of April, she and Alan would have exchanged on their new home, and they'd be married on 25 September. It was a hectic but wonderful time.

Most of this made the news. Pictures of Alan and Jill were in magazines and newspapers. Soon, they were locked into negotiations for their wedding to appear in *OK!* – Jill believed that getting a glossy magazine on board was the best way to secure some control over what would be a big media event. Her good friend Cliff Richard had allowed *OK!* into his home, so Jill was sure that it could be tastefully handled. Pictures of Alan and Jill were in demand that year; it seemed that the public couldn't get enough of this fairy-tale romance; the golden girl had found her prince. But someone looking on didn't like what they saw at all.

On Monday, 26 April, Jill woke up at Alan's house in Chiswick and despite his efforts to encourage her to stay in bed and enjoy a rare lie-in, she got up and made him breakfast. She was happy to do so and, besides, she was planning a day of leisure. She was meeting friends for lunch at a charity event but all she needed to do for the rest of the day was a few chores, like getting toner for her fax machine and picking up some fish for their evening meal. Alan left for work at 8am and Jill just after 10am. She'd been on the phone chatting to Alan's mother, to Jenny and picking up messages relating to work. Jill loved her mobile, she loved checking in with people every day and catching up with gossip.

She parked her car in Bridge Avenue, Hammersmith, a little after 10.30am, so she could call in at Rymans and pick up what she needed. There, she found some A4 paper she needed but not a toner cartridge, so she made her way to Dixons. She was picked up on CCTV footage there, at about 10.45am, wearing black trousers, boots and top with a buttoned-up red tailored cardigan and a Burberry mackintosh; she had a large black handbag over her right shoulder. She looked for cartridges but couldn't see what she needed and left in less than a minute. The footage would later be played in the Old Bailey; Jill's features aren't clear and yet it is unmistakably her. Her hair, styled almost like Princess Diana's, marks her out. Many people had told her how much she resembled the late princess.

She was back in her car by 11.01am and headed to Fulham and Gowan Avenue. The last image of Jill is of her car, as she headed into Manbre Road at 11.10am. She had less than half an hour to live.

Barry George left his flat at some point that morning but at what time, it is hard to tell. He lived less than a mile from Jill, but in every other respect he could have lived in another world.

Jill had come to live in Fulham because work had brought her to London and Fulham was desirable, packed with period properties and boutique shops and restaurants. She wasn't wedded to Fulham and had talked about moving out of

London to raise a family, but for five years it had been ideal as her time was split working in town and flying out of Heathrow. George hadn't chosen Fulham, he'd simply drifted there, after a spell in prison. He'd had a troubled childhood growing up only a few miles away in Shepherds Bush. His mother and father had separated when George was eight years old and he had struggled at school.

Growing up, George was assessed as having special educational needs and had proved disruptive in class. He may well have struggled with Attention Deficiency Hyperactivity Disorder (ADHD) as well as epilepsy and found it hard to form friendships. After a fracas where it was reported that he hit a teacher, George was sent to a specialist boarding school called Heathermount. Matters didn't improve there and George later claimed he was repeatedly bullied. He had two sisters whom he saw little of; the eldest was Michaelina, known as Michelle, who later married and moved to Ireland with her husband and children. The other was Susan, who like Barry suffered from epilepsy.

George left school without qualifications but at this point, scored the one real triumph in his life. Under his own steam, he applied for a job to be a BBC messenger and was accepted. That was May 1976 and he worked there until September. George can quickly recall the dates even now; it was a period of stability in his life and the one time he secured full-time employment. It isn't clear why he left. He loved the job and it is possible he was asked to leave.

George found dealing with stress difficult and it could affect his behaviour. In 1980 he had dealings with the law, for the offence of impersonating a police officer. George had applied to join the Met some time earlier but had been rejected. The letter that informed him of this featured the Met's crest and George cut it out and made a fake warrant card with it. He'd used the card to pose as a detective in Hammersmith but, after he gained entry to a woman's house in nearby Kingston, she'd become suspicious and called the police. When arrested, he gave his name as Paul Gadd, the real name of Gary Glitter. He was charged and, at Kingston Crown Court, was found guilty and fined.

It was the start of his efforts to pose as an authority figure: later, he would pretend to be a member of the SAS and would immerse himself in the world of military paraphernalia and firearms. He would also fail in his attempts to qualify as a serving member of the Territorial Army. It is interesting that George's father had served in the army as part of National Service, and had been a prison officer, a fire officer and a special constable. It's likely that George had a fixed idea of what represented masculine roles in society and by aping them, he felt he could assume that authority for himself. After his father walked out, George had only limited contact with his family. Even though he lived only three miles from where he was born and grew up, George was cut adrift.

After 1980, the nature of his offences took a dangerous turn. He began indecently assaulting women. At first, these were no more than bungling attempts to grope women he'd start talking to. One hit him with her briefcase when he lunged at her, another alleged that he'd tried to put his hand up her skirt. He was given a three-month suspended sentence and the next time his name appeared, or that of his alias Paul Gadd, it was in a very different setting. By then, George was a stuntman. Initially, he posed as a karate expert and claimed he could smash through forty-seven tiles with a single blow. Then a new name-change brought an altogether more incredible incident.

George was now Steve Majors. The name was an amalgamation of two names: the character Steve Austin from *The Six Million Dollar Man* and the actor who played the role, Lee Majors. And George was about to attempt a stunt that would certainly require 'the technology' to put him back together again. Filmed by a regional TV programme in 1981, he attempted to roller-skate down a ramp and jump over double-decker buses. When asked why he was so confident of success, something of George's fantasist personality was revealed. He said: 'Because I can trust my knowledge and the knowledge of the universities throughout the world that have been involved in the calculations.' Mounting a huge ramp, George descended at speed but with no elevation and smashed into some boards, the buses untouched. He broke his leg and dislocated a vertebra in his spine. If a life was ever reflected in a visual metaphor, this was it: an unbalanced act fuelled by fantasy, ending in disaster.

He joined Kensington and Chelsea Pistol Club, but his application to become a full member was turned down. Soon afterwards, he attacked and attempted to rape a woman as she walked to her parents' house in Acton, west London. Eventually, he would face trial for the offence, but not before being caught hiding in bushes outside Kensington Palace, residence of Princess Diana. When discovered, he was kitted out in military regalia complete with rope and a knife. He said he was on a training exercise, but the police quickly surmised that he was a fanatic. At his flat, they found more military gear, his SAS equipment and magazines on guns and explosives. It was for attempted rape, and the earlier sexual assault that he received his prison sentence of thirty-three months. At this point, the authorities should surely have been alerted to the fact that here was a somewhat disturbing individual.

By 1985, George was released and living in a hostel. While there, he was known to have at least two imitation guns, possibly three, which he'd show off as part of his new persona, Tommy Palmer. A real-life Palmer did exist: he had taken part in the SAS raid on the Iranian Embassy during its siege in 1980 and was later killed on active duty in Northern Ireland in 1983. George adopted this new identity as part of his unhealthy fantasy life and bought a respirator, one of the distinctive head-and-face masks used by special forces when they took back the Embassy. George would sometimes pose in the mask, with his replica 9mm pistol.

It was in 1985 that he moved into Crookham Road in Fulham; a year later, his sister Susan died after an epileptic seizure. George did not attend the funeral. His life seemed to be spiralling out of control once more. He was held over another rape case and his father had ended all contact with him, now convinced that George represented a danger to his new family. Yet, in 1989, those who knew him were surprised to learn that George had married. His bride was Itsuko Toide, a Japanese student. But the marriage was not to last: in a little over a year she returned to Japan, leaving George alone once again. He was to admit later that he found rejection very difficult to cope with.

Life in George's Crookham Road flat reflected his unusual

personality. He rarely threw anything away and the space was filled with magazines, newspapers and photographs, many of which he used to support his changing identities. As well as Tommy Palmer SAS, he would pose as Barry Bulsara, alleged cousin of Freddie Mercury; George had even mocked up a picture of himself and the Queen singer together. Many people would later come forward to the police to tell of their encounters with George, his rambling stories of life with celebrities and his mock 'I can't tell you any more' modesty. Clearly, to survive in a fast-moving and uncaring capital city, George felt that he had to impress listeners and a connection to celebrity seemed to him the likeliest way to achieve that end. He was right. Anyone he'd spoken to remembered his stories; it's a sign of our times that to brush up against fame is seen as noteworthy. Jill knew it too. She was used to being stuck in traffic on the Fulham Palace Road and noted that other motorists would point at her, wave and get on their mobile phones to tell friends who was in the car next to them.

London is generally ill equipped to deal with traffic and in its Victorian suburbs, such as Fulham, even more so. Houses on Gowan Avenue can command prices of over £1 million, but none come with parking. There is a free-for-all as residents park on the road outside the houses and it is not guaranteed that you can park anywhere near your front door. But on 26 April, Jill did just that – there was a space right outside her house.

That same day, George wanted to visit the offices of HAFAD, the Hammersmith and Fulham Action on Disability. He needed to find out about help for his growing list of physical ailments and complaints. The charity's offices were on Greswell Street, about a mile away. The easiest route, by car, would be to head down Fulham Road and right onto Fulham Palace Road, left onto Finlay Street, up Woodlawn Road and Greswell Street is on your left. That sounds convoluted, but it's straightforward if you know Fulham and would only take about five minutes. George didn't drive, he was on foot and most pedestrians would avoid the busy Fulham Road and Fulham Palace Road. Much easier to cut through residential streets, such as Munster Road and down Gowan Avenue.

Parked outside her house, No.29, Jill had enough time to drop off the stationery and Dover sole she'd bought and pick up any mail and messages. She'd spent more time at Alan's house than her own over the last few weeks, so there were bound to be letters to pick up. She opened her gate, walked the few steps along the distinctive black-and-white period tiles that characterised the homes on the street and went to open the white-painted front door. She had her keys in hand. Her mind would have only been focused on the few chores to clear before changing for the charity lunch at the Lanesborough Hotel. She didn't see the man waiting in the porch-way until it was too late.

It had been a busy morning on Gowan Avenue. Not just the usual rush of commuters making their way to their cars or the underground; there were also visitors staying with relatives and waiting for taxis to pick them up, people cutting through the street on the way to the bus stop, drivers using the road as a cut-through, mums taking toddlers for a walk. At any time of the day, Gowan Avenue was busy. It was something that Jill liked about the street, it made her feel part of a neighbourhood. The idea of living behind a 'gated community' never appealed to her. Safe, maybe, but somehow airless and impersonal.

From nowhere, the man grabbed Jill and held her arm tightly, pulling her hard onto the ground. What raced through her mind? Was she being mugged? She screamed, once, then felt a paralysing fear. If he'd waited a moment longer, the door would have been open and he could have pushed her inside the hallway. Who knew what her ordeal would be then? Take the bag, the phone, car, whatever you need. Although Bob Wheaton grew up in Zimbabwe, he had a better instinct for London than Jill ever would. He'd warned her before, any number of times: 'This is London. This is a big, bad place.' He was right. The gun, pressed so hard to her left temple, muffled the sound of the single shot.

George made it to the HAFAD offices but it wasn't clear at what time. It could have been late morning or early lunchtime. Staff member Susan Bicknell told George that he didn't have an appointment, but that she could arrange one for the following day. He ignored her and carried on talking, making complaints about the way his health problems were being handled. Susan knew George had mental health difficulties too and tried her best to usher him out of the office after twenty minutes or so. She looked up at the office clock and saw it was 11.50am.

By that time, Helen Doble had called Emergency Services and an ambulance had made its way to Gowan Avenue. Hamish Campbell would arrive around half an hour later, just as the ambulance was leaving, racing to Charing Cross Hospital. There was a small crowd of neighbours and police officers made sure they kept their distance but Campbell noted that in their frantic efforts to save Jill, the paramedics had trampled over the scene. They had moved Jill's body and had walked through the blood loss, which was considerable. Later, all but one footprint would be identified. Every effort to reconstruct how Jill's body had been found would be thwarted. Neighbours, passers-by and paramedics gave detailed accounts; none matched.

Alan Farthing was busy in surgery that morning and his phone collected messages as he worked, asking him to please call, that it was about Jill. Jon Roseman, Jill's agent, left a message and when Alan called, Jon asked if Jill was with him. Alan said no, that he was at work, but Jon's tone worried him. Jon said that he was hearing rumours that Jill had been attacked outside her home. Alan was sure it must be a mistake but said that he'd call the local police station to check. Calls were on divert to Kensington but the duty sergeant there took Alan's details. As soon as he put the phone down, the ward sister paged him. Two officers were waiting to talk to him. He still wanted to believe that it was a mistake.

Standing in Gowan Avenue, Hamish Campbell didn't think this would be a troubling case. If it was true that the victim was Jill Dando, then her personal life would be combed through and the attacker would surely come to light. An ex-lover, her current boyfriend, someone with a grudge. They would trace whoever did this. In fact, police officers should be with her fiancé by now, so they could begin to build a picture of Jill's life.

Alan was taken to a police car at the back of the hospital.

He was struggling to process the rumours and the fear that they could be true. Sky News had reported that Jill was dead and her brother Nigel called Alan, partly to let him know what had hit the news wires, partly in hope that Alan would say that it wasn't true. All Alan could say was wait, we don't know. He was being taken to identify a body. Perhaps it wasn't Jill. A wave of hope washed over him. Then came the awful realisation that someone was certainly dead, someone had been attacked, and even if it wasn't Jill the lives of someone's friends and loved ones were about to be shattered by this terrible and random event.

Barry George hadn't finished with his day. He wanted to get to another charity, Cancer Colon Concern, near Earl's Court. He walked from HAFAD back onto Fulham Palace Road and into Traffic Cars, a minicab firm. He was hoping to get a free ride. Controller Ramesh Paul told him to forget it but then George's luck changed: a cab had to pick up a parcel not to far from the charity, so he could get a lift after all.

It was quite a week for Barry George. The Monday visit to HAFAD wasn't the only one he'd make that week. He returned on Wednesday and made a nuisance of himself, demanding that staff remember his visit at the start of the week. He asked people to remember what he had been wearing on Monday and was agitated and aggressive. It was this second visit that made the staff think of him, as the investigation into what had happened to Jill dragged on. After leaving HAFAD, George appeared again at the cab office. Once there, he demanded that Ramesh recall details of his visit two days earlier. Barry George seemed to want to make sure that he was visible on the 26th. But why?

Alan identified Jill's body. Until the very last moment, he felt that it could not be true, that he was being walked through a scene that someone would soon bring to an end. It had to be a mistake. Only hours earlier, he'd kissed Jill goodbye at home and they'd made plans for the evening. But then he saw her. Jill, lying with a thick towel wrapped around her head. It made the scene more unreal, as if she'd stepped from the shower. At this point, Alan was still unaware that Jill had been executed with a single shot to the head. How he got through the next few seconds, hours and days, he isn't sure. The oddest thing was that he did not have to tell anyone that he'd lost Jill. Everyone knew.

In the media storm that followed, Alan would be swallowed up, analysed, his every gesture dissected by a hungry media looking to fill pages and news slots on a rolling basis. Theories of possible suspects would hit the headlines – Serb hitmen, disgruntled crime bosses, crazed loners – all were explored alongside pictures of a grieving Alan. In the fevered speculation, it was easy to lose sight of Jill. It took the man who loved her, who'd planned to spend his life with her, to remind the world of the true story behind the tabloid headlines: 'I cannot think for one moment what could go through someone's mind when they do such a thing to such a beautiful, caring and well-meaning person such as Jill.'

But it had gone through someone's mind. Over and over. Every angle explored, hours of planning, the desire to extinguish Jill Dando fanned by fantasy and preparation. Why?

Start at the beginning. That is where Serious Crimes Units look – at those who knew her best and may even have wished her harm. It was no easy task. There were literally hundreds of names in Jill's contact book – all had to be TIE'd (Traced. Interviewed. Eliminated). Could the killer be her fiancé, an ex-boyfriend, a jealous wife or the girlfriend of one of Jill's men? There were quite a few men in her past, more than Jill's girl-next-door persona suggested. No more than any other professional, single and successful woman working in London, perhaps, but not as few as her viewers might have guessed. Each had to be found and spoken to, but all came back with a similar picture of Jill. She was very fondly regarded by all who knew her, a kind, bubbly woman who could not inspire malice in those who knew her. And there's the rub. There were far too many people who thought they knew her, even if they'd never shared a spoken word.

Stalking is not a new phenomenon. From time to time, details of such cases appear in newspapers when celebrities bring the matter to court. In 2008, a 37-year-old former psychiatric patient, Jack Jordan, was found guilty of stalking Uma Thurman. Over three years, he'd harassed the actress and her family, sending a disturbing series of cards, emails and letters, stressing that they should be together. Jordan later claimed that he never intended to upset or frighten Thurman. 'In a misguided way,' he declared, 'I was trying to give her an opportunity to meet me and give myself an opportunity to meet her.' This is a typical example of a troubled mind latching onto to a celebrity figure. The stalker is drawn to a characteristic the celebrity embodies, beyond an obvious sexual appeal, such as confidence, charm or talent, and it becomes the focus of their fantasy life. In that life, the celebrity and stalker are friends, or lovers, or the stalker is protecting the celebrity, acting as bodyguard, and they have a unique and exclusive bond. It allows the stalker to act out an important desire: to be seen as special, or chosen, and removed from their ordinary life and an ongoing struggle for acceptance.

It begins simply enough, with letters of admiration. When a signed picture arrives from the celebrity, a link is forged. Some stalkers imagine that when a celebrity is on the screen, coded messages are being passed to them alone. An elaborate but wholly fictional relationship is built in the mind of the stalker, a focus that can take up hours every day as information on the celebrity, their family, their home, their movements, is compiled. But something happens. A perceived slight, a rejection of some sort and adoration quickly changes to anger. All the rejection the stalker has ever faced, the toxic mix of resentment and loneliness, now has a new focus. How dare they reject me? I am the one person who can make them pay.

Some tales of celebrity stalkers are truly shocking. In 1998, Jonathan Norman, then thirty-one years old, was found guilty in California of stalking the film director Steven Spielberg. Prosecutors alleged that had intended to tie up the director and rape him in front of his wife and family. Norman's car was stopped; in it, police discovered handcuffs, razor blades, tape and photographs of the director, his wife the actress Kate Capshaw and their seven children. The rage some stalkers harbour knows no bounds.

In 1989, Robert Bardo shot and killed actress Rebecca Schaeffer on her doorstep. Her case changed the law in California in an attempt to prevent stalkers finding the home addresses of celebrities. Bardo had hired a private investigator, who'd simply made a request to the California

Department of Motor Vehicles for Miss Schaeffer's address. Rebecca was only twenty-one years old when she died and had only opened her door as she was expecting a script for *Godfather III* to be couriered to her.

Bardo had written to Rebecca Schaeffer on several occasions. And it is a characteristic common to stalkers that would trouble Hamish Campbell's team. Unlike Bardo, anyone living nearby would not have to hire a private investigator to find out Jill Dando's address, as it was fairly well known in Fulham. George would later claim that he had no idea that Jill lived within a short walk of his flat, but during the investigation, the police were contacted by a woman who recalled a conversation with George in which he'd boasted of his connection to the presenter. But the problem for the police would not be whether George knew where Jill lived; it was what Jill meant to him. After his flat was raided and everything removed, no files, no pictures, no letters to Jill were found. There were a few newspaper cuttings about her, but they were primarily items written after her death and of the stacks of papers and magazines found there, articles about Jill only made up a small percentage of the items George hoarded.

Yet George had been brought to their attention because of his bizarre behaviour around the time of Jill's death, such as his repeat visits to HAFAD and the minicab company. 'Why?' would be a question Hamish Campbell and his team would ask themselves over and over again. Unlike many other unsolved murders, so much publicity surrounded the case that few people would be left unfamiliar with the major characters by the time of Barry George's trial, retrial and release.

Originally, George was characterised by the media as a stalker and a gun fanatic. His ex-wife told a tabloid newspaper that, although they had had a very tempestuous marriage, she did not believe that he had killed Jill Dando.

Once the Crown's case against George unravelled, however, he was painted as an innocent victim, a loner with a low IQ, airbrushed into the role of killer by an incompetent police force. The real killer was out there and the police had failed Jill and her family.

With George's release in 2008, the Met had a decision to make. Should they reinvestigate? In August that year, it was announced that Commander Simon Foy, head of the Yard's Homicide and Serious Crime Unit, would lead a review of the case. It would be an enormous task. Over 2,500 witness statements and 3,700 exhibits would be sifted through and the Met would launch an appeal for new information.

Everyone knows about the gun. Within hours of Jill's death, Forensics had established that she had been shot by a single round of 9mm calibre. Two things set it apart. It was the less common .380 ACP (or 9mm short) and would have to be fired from a suitably chambered pistol. Armed criminals in the UK rarely use the short, perhaps as few as 5%. The 9mm of choice is the more powerful Parabellum. The second detail was that the cartridge had been 'crimped': small indentations were made by hand, possibly by using a gun-maker's tool or simply by applying a hammer and nail. Why had that been done?

Perhaps it had been done to secure a better grip in the barrel of the gun. This was a more significant finding. The gun will have had a smooth rather than rifled barrel. That meant that it began life either as a decommissioned gun that had been re-commissioned, or it was a starter pistol that had been converted, or it was a 24in barrel that had been cut down. That meant the user either had a certain working knowledge of guns and was able to machine it, or knew how to get access to such a gun. After extensive debate, the police felt that it was most likely to be a reactivated weapon. But nothing was ruled out, Campbell was too cautious for that.

Despite media protestations, the police were not incompetent. The investigation carried out by Campbell's team was thorough and holds up to scrutiny. Verifiable facts were few. In the hours, days and weeks that followed Jill's death, they were flooded with public calls and 'sightings', confessions and hoax calls and they worked methodically through the hundreds of people who intersected Jill's life. There were at least 140 people who came into contact with Jill who could be described as having an 'unhealthy' interest in her – not uncommon for an attractive and well-known presenter.

The press did not help. Many man-hours were devoted to tracking down a 'utility stalker', a man who'd contacted gas and electricity suppliers to Jill's house prior to her death, posing as her brother and attempting to fish for details. Who was this man trying to forge a connection to Jill via her home, fantasising that he was her older brother, an intimate and protective figure in Jill's life? Profilers had a field day. This was exactly the type of behaviour someone with an unhealthy fixation on Jill would display. After exhaustive enquires, the utility stalker turned out to be a tabloid journalist, simply working angles to dig out information on Britain's 'Golden Girl'.

Major enquiries throw up strange coincidences too. One man, entirely absent from Jill's life, contacted her after a six-year silence just six weeks before she died. Jill spoke with him two weeks before her death. He had been arrested for stalking another woman. Yet after he'd been traced and interviewed, he had to be eliminated. Here was a suspect pool of over a thousand, each demanding huge resources, and the weeks, then months, were ticking by.

One of the essential roles a senior investigating officer plays is strategic. They have to keep enough distance to recognise when an investigation is losing its momentum. With an enquiry that generates a massive response, it is often the case that the investigation team can't see the wood for the trees. With limited forensic details, with the facts as they were known yielding little, Campbell established criteria to help his officers filter the deluge of calls and leads that came in.

First, do potential suspects have access, or have they had access, to firearms?

Do they have an interest in firearms?

Have they been identified by more than one source?

Do they have an obsession with Jill?

Do they look like the e-fit?

Do they have a criminal record – particularly in connection with firearms, violence, contract murder, or stalking?

Barry George indeed fitted some of these criteria. He may not have been known for an obsession with Jill, but he was certainly obsessed with fame. He did not come to police attention until nine months after Jill's death. When he did, it was part of the TIE. His name cropped up more than once in HOLMES (Home Office Large Major Enquiry System), one as early as three weeks after Jill's death, but his details differed on each occasion. Some did not give his name; some gave the wrong address. HAFAD had contacted the enquiry, because of George's return on the Wednesday after Jill's death, in such an agitated state. But no one in the office could agree on the time George had been there, a detail that was crucial if the police were to build a timeline around him. Yet it was still enough for DC John Gallagher to interview Barry George and in doing so, set off a chain of events that would lead to his arrest and ultimately, his conviction.

DC Gallagher left messages at George's flat in Crookham Road. He was never there to open the door it seemed, and it was not until they waited for George when he went to collect his benefit money that they caught up with him. George said that he had not left his flat on the day of Jill's death until 12.30pm or later and that he'd walked to HAFAD by going west through Bishop's Park. After his visit to the minicab office, he'd got a lift to Colon Cancer Concern and then had gone straight home, where he stayed until early evening. It was then that a neighbour told him of Jill's death. He'd never met her and didn't know where she lived. He said that he'd been taught to fire a rifle in the Territorial Army but declared that he had not used a firearm since that time.

George was taken to his flat by the police and asked to find the items he'd been wearing on the day. The items were handed over, including the coat. The clothes and Barry George's physical description also matched enough witness statements from Gowan Avenue on the day of the murder to allow the police to search and remove items from his flat.

Among the many boxes of items that came out of

Crookham Road were notes of condolence written about Jill. George had walked around Fulham getting people to sign them. In each, George would write how his cousin, Freddie Mercury, had been interviewed by Jill and that he'd been present at the interview, as Freddie's cousin, Barry Bulsara, and so he felt moved to write something about her now. In fact, Jill had never interviewed the lead singer of Queen.

With the military paraphernalia, pictures of George posing with firearms, his past convictions for violent and sexually obsessive behaviour, his proximity to the murder scene and uncertain alibi, his stalking and SAS-style antics outside Kensington Palace, it was hard to ignore Barry George as a suspect. Hamish Campbell noted in his log that this was far from 'wholly compelling', though. It concerned him that searches of George's flat did not uncover a hoard of obsessive material about Jill. Nevertheless, George scored highly on the criteria Campbell had created for the investigation and so he asked his team to focus on either eliminating George or gathering enough evidence to prove a firm link.

The link, when it came, remains controversial to this day. To get George's clothes photographed to hand out to teams sifting through witness statements, DC Gallagher had them shot at a studio used by the Met. Firearms were also sometimes photographed at this studio. They had been taken out of plastic bags, designed to stop any cross-contamination from other items or rooms. Three weeks later, the clothes were examined by forensic experts and the all-important breakthrough came: a single particle of firearm residue had been found in the pocket of George's overcoat.

So much was to be written about this single particle after

the court case, it is important to remember what it meant at that moment. For a start, it did not mean that it was residue from the scene – the forensic report made that clear. All that could be stated with certainty was that it was consistent with residue from a similar gun. Bearing in mind that so few criminals use the type of gun and bullet used to kill Jill, it was significant. Although it was only a single particle, other convictions had been successfully made on forensic evidence as slight as this.

What the police did not have was a direct forensic link that placed George on the doorstep of number 29 Gowan Avenue the morning that Jill was killed. There were no hairs or fibres that showed that he had waited, hidden at the doorway. But the firearm residue, coupled with what the police already knew about Barry George, was enough to secure his arrest on 25 May 2000.

Over the next few days, George was interviewed by the police and provided a name in connection to his ownership of guns: David Dobbins. He was someone George had shared a hostel with in the mid-1980s. It was the type of accommodation where the residents are effectively homeless and are allowed bed and breakfast but have to absent themselves during the day. The police traced Dobbins, along with other residents, and all confirmed that they were acquainted with the suspect at a stage where George was claiming to be Tommy Palmer of the SAS. They saw his guns, more than one and possibly as many as three, and at one point, 'Palmer' had charged into rooms firing blanks, dressed in his military garb. Later, with George now accommodated at Crookham Road, Dobbins would rob his old friend of two of these guns. If, indeed, there had been two: the police wondered if there could have been another gun, particularly after the two stolen ones were accounted for.

Barry George's trial would not begin until May 2001, a year after his arrest. During that time, he'd been held on remand and rumours spread that the Crown Prosecution's case was slight, at best. There were only three areas to build on. First, witness statements. The majority of witnesses described someone who looked like George, similar height, similar build and similar complexion. Crucially, though, there were more than enough who did not.

There was the light-haired 'sweating man' who ran to a nearby bus stop, there was the 'running man' on his mobile phone wearing a green suit and there were the sightings of two men sitting in a Range Rover. There was enough doubt for the defence team to undermine confidence in witness accounts. Residents on Gowan Avenue illustrated the difficulty the police and later the prosecution would face: at least three said that they were 'sure' it was George they'd seen at the time of Jill's death, but not sure enough to be absolutely certain during the ID parade of a year later. 'Fairly sure' would be all the defence needed to damage their evidence.

Similar problems faced the Crown's second line of attack, namely tracing George's movements that morning. George had said that he had not left home until after 12.30pm. As Jill was attacked at just after 11.30am and if George was lying about when he left, it would give him enough time to kill. Later, he changed the time he said he'd visited HAFAD to around 10.45am. This would cut into the possibility that he could have been on Gowan Avenue during the 'kill time'. As it was, the defence were about to make hay with the conflicting accounts of HAFAD staff.

The remaining piece of evidence for the prosecution was the firearms particle. Again, Michael Mansfield for the defence did all he could to undermine any faith the jury could have that this meant George was guilty. It could have got into George's pocket from a firework, or from the dry cleaners, or more likely, from the photographic studio the police used. The case hung by a thread and many reporters were sure that George could not be found guilty beyond 'reasonable doubt'. Yet when prosecuting counsel Orlando Pownall declared that the fact evidence was circumstantial did not make it inferior, perhaps that tipped the balance for the jury. After three months of argument, Barry George was found guilty.

The defence team was surprised by the verdict and immediately announced that they would appeal. In the meantime, George began his life sentence and Jill's friends and family carried on with the impossible task of trying to understand why she was hunted down and killed.

The difficulty of imagining the kind of person who would stalk and then kill someone of such light and beauty has led to any number of alternative theories to explain Jill's death. The possibility of a Serb gunman hired to assassinate Jill was raised by Michael Mansfield during the trial. The theory was that because Jill had fronted a fundraiser for Kosovan refugees, and because the Serb Broadcasting House had been bombed by NATO a few days before her death, her execution might have been a state-sponsored revenge killing. It's unlikely. For a start, if Serb operatives were at large in the UK, why not place a bomb at the BBC? Why not kill the editor of *The Sun*, a paper that had tirelessly mocked 'Slobo' Milosevic and had called for military action against him?

Serb hitmen do exist – one killed the moderate Serb prime minister Zoran Djindjic in 2003. He and his security detail were sprayed with bullets, fired by a sniper from a nearby building. Although Michael Mansfield stated that his theory had been based on a police intelligence report, the death of Djindjic and even that of the man who was supposed to have ordered Jill's death, 'Arkan', explains why the police did not exhaust themselves chasing this lead. Arkan was leader of Serb paramilitaries responsible for many war crimes in Kosovo. In 2000, he was assassinated by Dobrosav Gavrić, a police officer on sick leave, while he sat in a hotel foyer. Again, a number of bullets were discharged, not just one shot. The police had sought advice from special forces and those with experience of assassinations carried out during The Troubles in Northern Ireland. All had said the sequence of events that led to Jill's death did not bear the hallmarks of a professional hit.

This laid to rest the idea that Jill had upset a 'crime family' during her time with *Crimewatch* too. The criminal underworld had no interest in drawing attention to themselves, and nothing to gain by risking a paid hit on a TV presenter. And a professional hit would not have been carried out this way. No.29 Gowan Avenue was too exposed, there was very little cover at Jill's front door, unlike Alan's home at Chiswick. More than one shot would have been discharged, and not from that gun, with that bullet; in a professional hit, there is no room for error.

In some ways it is easier for us to imagine her killer bearing a grudge based on greed and criminality, such as a disgruntled gangland boss angered by exposure on TV, than it is to imagine a loner acting out a final act in a fantasy. But it doesn't add up. It is far more likely that Jill was killed by someone who was acting out an assassination, not by a genuine assassin.

It now falls to Commander Foy to sift through the ruin of an investigation, cold from the passage of time, and hindered by a thousand lines of enquiry leading nowhere. It is a monumental task and police officers find themselves inclined to agree with the freed Barry George when he stated that no one would find Jill's killer now.

Someone killed the Golden Girl, though; someone knows the true sequence of events all those years ago. Could it be the work of a deranged mind at a point of personal crisis? Jill was marrying, was 'leaving' him behind, just as he'd always been left behind by others before. *She'd 'promised' that she wouldn't, that what they had was special and that they'd be together. How could she do this? She had to realise that it must stop. All of it.*

When the police sought the advice of firearm specialists, one further reason for not selecting 29 Gowan Avenue for an assassination attempt became apparent: Jill was so rarely there. As Helen Doble had remarked to herself in the weeks before Jill's death, you just never saw Jill there any more. Only Jill and Alan knew that she planned to call in and get her post that morning – unless she was watched leaving Alan's house, but that would have meant she was followed through a meandering shopping trip as she picked up stationery and fish. On foot and in the car, Jill's last minutes on CCTV were pored over by police officers; no one was observed tracking her. It was fate. When Jill decided to check in at home, when she pulled into Gowan Avenue and saw the parking space, when no neighbour was on the street to stop and chat with her as they often did, it was an ill-fated window of opportunity that coincided with the fragile mind of a killer who may not have even known he would kill until that moment. *There she is getting out of her car. I knew it. It has all led to this moment. This was exactly how it was meant to be.*

Richard Hughes was Jill's next-door neighbour and had been working from home that day, tracking early stock market activity. He hadn't had a chance to talk to Jill for weeks, since he saw her and asked her when it would be best to visit the Bahamas. He heard her open her gate and walk up her path; he heard her scream. Later, he told the police it was the kind of scream you make when you have been surprised by someone, a shriek of recognition. Hearing the gate being closed again, he glanced out and saw a man in a dark coat, with dark hair, walking away, towards the Fulham Palace Road. It looked like he had a phone in his hand. He turned his head to look back only once, as if he were checking something. Satisfied, he turned away and carried on walking.

It was over. She'd screamed in surprise, in recognition, when it was already too late. Jill's charm and good fortune, her huge talent and the warmth she inspired in everyone, was devoured in one moment by someone who had known only failure and rejection. Perhaps that was the recognition. A moment of bleak terror when someone so full of light acknowledged a consuming darkness.

The search goes on. It is possible to live a life of secrecy and isolation in London, but it is not possible to live without a trace indefinitely. The Met review, sifting through the thousands of pages of Hamish Campbell's investigation, will have heard about the collapse of Sky's news presenter Kay Burley. She interviewed Barry George after his release in August 2008. Although they have not met since that interview, she became concerned that he might have developed an obsession with her. In October 2008, Kay Burley fainted at work due to stress. She approached the police with her concerns and security around the newsreader was subsequently stepped up.

There might be nothing in it. No more than an over-cautious reaction to a new reality, a world where being a celebrity means being the unhealthy focus for a small number of unhinged minds. But Kay's life offers eerie parallels with Jill's: she is only a year older and grew up away from the hubbub of London's media circus – in Kay's case, Wigan. By eighteen, Kay was working on a local paper, the *Evening Post and Chronicle*; like Jill, she moved to local radio, then regional TV. She got her national break at TV-am in 1985 as an occasional newsreader, just a few years before Jill would start work on the BBC's *Breakfast News*. She lost her mother too, to breast cancer, and decided to take part in the reality show *Dancing on Ice* to raise funds for Macmillan Cancer Care. It's Kay's appearances outside the newsroom that have undoubtedly added to her appeal among viewers, and she's been voted 'Most Desirable Woman on TV' by a TV listings magazine any number of times.

Barry George insists that he has not been stalking Kay Burley. He has admitted cycling to the TV studios in west

London, to ask for a copy of the interview tape, but he is certain that he did not make a request to see the presenter at that time. There is certainly no evidence to suggest that he had developed an unhealthy interest in her.

But still, despite more than twenty years in the public eye, something scared Kay Burley, terrified her to the point of collapse. The fear is always there, that there is someone or something in the darkness, looking to emerge and consume the light.

CHAPTER NINE
JANINE DOWNES
ALL WOMEN COUNT

Two young women stand outside The Harp Inn on Shakespeare Street in Wolverhampton. It's a cold February night and they shiver in clothes that won't keep out the worst of the weather. The smaller of the two is wearing jeans and a thin Nike tracksuit top. She is tiny, not quite 5ft tall, and it's hard to tell what age she might be. Janine Downes is, in fact, twenty years old, but her actual age would be glossed over in the years that follow. Some reports would say she was nineteen, some twenty-three.

The other girl is wearing boots with no socks and a short skirt. She has her bleached blonde hair tied up in bunches. It's to make her look younger, even though she is only sixteen years old. She knows what the punters like. The girls lean close together, sharing a pack of cigarettes. As the smoke rises into the night sky, you can hear them laughing; they are always sharing jokes, and turn to look at the dark saloon car that is crawling towards them. Looks like business.

They both approach the car. The sixteen-year-old leans in to the window as it is wound down, but the man isn't paying attention to her; he's looking past her, to the small girl with the cropped red hair. 'I want her,' he motions. This surprises Vicky, the girl with the bunches. She knows she's the prettier of the two, as well as the youngest. She steps aside. They usually work together, both getting into the car. Not that punters want to pay for two: mostly they choose one and then the other girl will sit and wait. It's safer that way, though. Plus, in truth, it's good to warm up for a bit.

This punter is adamant: only one girl. Some of the men are wary of being robbed; some don't like to be watched. They agree a price: £20 for full sex, but it has to be with a condom, the girls aren't stupid and won't risk infection. They are not drug users, so they don't feel the pressure to earn quick money just to feed a habit. These girls have other dark and terrible pressures in their lives, but drug use isn't one of them.

Vicky turns away. She's looking up the road for the next car to drive slowly kerb-side and knows she'll meet up with Janine in an hour or so. She doesn't watch as the car pulls away, doesn't study the driver's face, doesn't hug Janine goodbye. Almost twenty years later, Vicky will relive those same few moments and finds that they are harder to face as the years pass, not easier. She was the last person to see her friend Janine Downes alive; she was Janine's last link to this world.

Sometimes, the most enduring friendships are those forged in the hardest of times. Vicky's life now is unrecognisable to the one she shared with Janine, but she has never forgotten the unique bond they shared. Two working girls together. Vicky survived because Janine showed her the ropes and taught her how to laugh. For many years, Vicky had little to laugh about.

Neglected as a baby, her mother eventually walked out on her when she was two years old. She didn't know her father and was soon shipped off to her grandparents. She had an older brother and sister but can barely remember them; it was never clear where they were sent.

Her grandparents tried as best they could, but there was an unhappiness in Vicky that she could not evade. Perhaps she could run from it. Vicky began to leave home regularly and by the time she was nine, her grandparents had had enough. She was put in care.

It is ironic that residential children's homes are called 'care' homes, as all too often care in such places is conspicuous by its absence. It is a hard truth but even today, some professionals take up the role because access to children holds a certain evil attraction. Vicky was groomed by a care worker. He allowed her to sit in his flat in the day, she felt special for the first time in her life. When he began to touch her, she felt she could not say 'no'.

Vicky went to a foster home aged thirteen and for the first time found herself living in a stable and happy household. The next two years were two of the best she'd known, but life there began to unravel because Vicky and her foster-brother fell in love. He was, of course, no blood relation, but seeing how close Vicky and her son had become, Vicky's stepmother asked her to leave.

She drifted into a hostel in Sellyoak, working when she could, but she had little idea what to do with her life. A new girl moved into the hostel, she was barely 5ft tall and can't have weighed more than 8 stone but Vicky was amazed to see how she handled herself. She would take nonsense from no one. Janine had a razor-sharp wit and she thought nothing about giving anyone who crossed her a tongue-lashing.

She was more than tough, though. Vicky found that Janine would make her laugh but that she cared too. She must have seen something vulnerable about the younger girl and took her under her wing. Both smoked constantly and they'd find ways to scrape together any spare change and buy cigarettes. Despite their endless hours talking, Vicky gradually came to realise that she knew very little about her new friend, only that she was originally from Wolverhampton; Janine would rarely talk about her past.

Vicky sensed Janine was hiding something, despite her lively demeanour. Her nails were bitten to the quick and she could often seem on edge. One evening, she said to Vicky: 'Come with me, I've got something to show you.' They went out to the streets, near a cricket ground, Vicky watched as Janine approached a car that had pulled up ahead of them. 'I'm going to earn some money,' she said.

Vicky wasn't sure whether she was going to laugh or cry, she could not believe what she saw when they got in the car and Janine told the driver where to pull over. Janine turned her face away from the punter; she never let anyone kiss her and even if they tried to kiss her neck, she pulled farther away still. She looked detached, just waiting for the married man on top of her to stop heaving, just waiting for it to end. She zipped up her jeans, took the £20 and they got out of the car.

Janine was soon laughing again. 'Don't worry about it,' she told Vicky. As the nights passed, Janine never expected Vicky to cross the line and start working too, but it was almost inevitable. 'What if they don't bring me back?' she asked

Janine. But Janine had a way of reassuring her. They were just sad blokes looking for a quick thrill. And it was true, the punters were a fairly sad lot. Many were married, old and unkempt, most were lonely.

It was common to get in the car and charge £20 only to have them talk and not even touch you. That was easy enough. One guy would even take Vicky home to his neat semi-detached home and take photos of her. Nothing pornographic, just her sitting in his room, like she was his girlfriend. He'd look at them after she'd gone, imagining they had some sort of life together. He'd pay her well too, £50 or £60, and give her chocolate, a bonus from the Cadbury's plant where he worked. It was the one place Vicky could take her boots off, and rub her ankles, her boots having ripped the skin off from too many hours standing and walking in the cold.

A few months later, Janine asked Vicky to go with her to Wolverhampton. Janine never explained why they should leave Sellyoak, she just said that she had friends there and that they would let them stay in their flat. It seemed a better prospect than staying in the hostel and so Vicky agreed.

Arriving in Wolverhampton, Vicky was upbeat. Perhaps this would be the start of a new life. She and Janine could live by their own rules rather than the hostel's, they could get jobs and put the past behind them. The sixteen-year-old had no idea that Janine's 'friends' were pimps and that henceforth the two of them would face new and frightening levels of damage and abuse.

The set-up was simple. The girls could live in the flat, alongside another six girls or so, but they had to pay their way. Food and shelter and money for condoms and basics would be provided, but if their earnings slacked off they'd be badly beaten. To an outsider, it is hard to understand why any girl would agree to such terms. They'd sell their bodies and virtually all the cash would go to the pimps, who'd spend it and spend the rest of their time smoking dope.

When Vicky arrived, she was greeted warmly, told that she'd be looked after and assured that Lee, a tall and powerfully built black man, would make sure that she settled in OK. At first, that's exactly how it went. It was a kind of belonging. Lee was warm, funny and affectionate, hugging the girls and making them feel that things would be fine now. 'We look out for you,' he assured Vicky.

Gradually, things changed. Money was tight; why didn't they go out and earn? Vicky could hardly protest. She'd earned money this way before and so she and Janine were out on new ground, near the Walsall Road. First they would go to The Harp and have a drink, then by 9pm, they'd be outside waiting for the inevitable approach of a saloon car.

One of the men who hired Vicky was a policeman, though she and Janine were sick of the police. From time to time, they'd run through a sweep of the area; the red-light area was fairly packed, so the vans would fill with girls who knew that the next few hours would be wasted and they'd have to explain to their pimps why their earnings were light that evening. Vicky and Janine must have been picked up nearly twenty times, but even that didn't stop Janine seeing the funny side. In one police photograph, she's looking to the right, her eyes lit up, her mouth barely suppressing a smile. It's all part of the game.

Going back to the flat with less cash than usual was a problem, though. Lee and his friends wouldn't accept that the girls had simply had a quiet night. Try and explain and you would get a slap. Janine knew how to play them, though. The girls would make enough for the night and hide £20 for themselves. A couple of times, she'd even rob a punter as Vicky serviced him. Then she'd burst out laughing and shout, 'Run!' She used to find the sight of an exacerbated bloke huffing and puffing out of the car truly funny. Most would just let it go, they certainly wouldn't go to the police – after all, what would they tell them?

Janine and Vicky shared what they had and supported one another, but there was no escaping the many bleak moments they faced. Life in the flat could change quickly; sometimes the pimps would demand sex too, and sometimes Vicky wondered whether she and Janine would ever be able to break the cycle they were locked in to.

It was a Friday night, the most lucrative night of the week, and the girls were getting ready to go out. Janine didn't have any clean socks, so Vicky passed her a pair of her own light-blue ankle socks. She thought about all the things Janine had done for her during their year-long friendship; she remembered how shocked she'd been to see Janine stand up in the bath back at the hostel and shave off her pubic hair. It was to prevent picking up lice and Janine laughed when she saw Vicky's eyes widen. Now Vicky thought nothing of it and wondered how she would have coped without this tiny woman at her side. Janine was afraid of no one and Vicky felt safer with her than she ever did with Lee and all his swagger.

Like so many other things in the girls' world, the offer of

protection was a lie. Lee and his gang never left the flat. They'd send their girls out and then sit, smoke and watch TV until they came back in, after which they'd count their money and either praise them or give them hell. If a punter did look like he could turn nasty, it sometimes worked to say, 'You better not touch me, my pimp is watching,' but in truth the girls hit the streets alone and if the police moved them along, the risks could be even higher.

The facts are straightforward. Prostitution is never safe, but girls are safest working from a house; they are six times more likely to suffer a violent attack if they are in cars or an alleyway. If they can't work in a serviced house, then visibility is the next best thing. A well-lit area with CCTV cameras helps, but not always. Cameras didn't save the Ipswich girls.

Murderer Steven Wright would drive into Ipswich's red-light district, close to the home he shared with his partner, to seek out his victims. Fortunately, however, his car was eventually picked up on CCTV. At his trial in January 2008, for the murder of five women, two witnesses identified Tania Nicol, one of Wright's victims, from the footage, as she approached his car. In the final reckoning, nothing will stop evil men from preying on working girls. They are too easy a target, thought of as disposable, despised and uncared for. It seems that no matter how much light there was in someone like Janine, there will always be those who seek to extinguish it.

It was about 9pm when the dark-blue Mondeo pulled up and the driver asked Janine to go with him. Vicky was in the habit of not focusing on faces, she found it easier that way. She looked in the car, nothing gave her cause for alarm; she thought she'd meet Janine back near The Harp soon. It could take as little as ten minutes or, if the punter was a talker or having problems getting an erection, it could be an hour. That was always a danger point. Men often became angry if they couldn't get erect. They'd blame the girls. They'd never ask themselves what the hell they were doing, picking up girls who were abused, or addicts, or both. Girls who despised them. Perhaps the realisation that they are really the whores gnaws at them and provokes their rage.

Vicky was picked up too, but was soon back outside the pub. She smoked and she waited. Janine wasn't usually gone for long. This time, though, hours passed. Vicky knew that Janine would not got back to the flat without her, but by midnight she was on her way back there to check. Lee had no idea where she was. He was unconcerned – only the flicker of irritation that she might not be earning registered on his face. Sometimes, the girls would stay out all night, but not often. Once or twice, Vicky had stayed with the Cadbury's man but there was no regular in Janine's life that Vicky could think of. She handed over what she'd earned and went to the room she shared with Janine.

The knock was unmistakable. It could only be the police. The flat was known to them, they'd been there several times before. Lee shoved Vicky and another girl out onto the balcony, locked the door and drew the curtains. He answered the door but Vicky could hear everything. She heard a male voice saying: 'We've found a body. We think it is Janine Downes.'

Vicky could hear everything but could take nothing in. It couldn't be Janine, she always knew what to do, nothing could have happened to her. The police asked questions, and there would be more to come, but Lee was evasive. He was an old hand and told them little information of any use. They left and there was a moment when nothing happened. Even Lee knew they were on dangerous ground. This was more than a loss of income. The balcony door was yanked open and Lee started screaming at the girls. He was shoving Vicky, yelling: 'Get in the fucking bedroom!'

Locked in, Vicky crawled onto the bed, the ache worse than anything she could remember. Perhaps they were wrong. Perhaps Janine would knock on the door. Lee would be furious but Vicky would be happy to take any slap he could give in his mindless rage just to see Janine walking in and smiling once again.

The day wore on. No one approached Vicky. No one seemed to know what to do. The pimps were angry but clueless. Their one thought was to clear themselves of any involvement should the girl really turn out to be Janine. Vicky did not sleep. Images of the car, of Janine being chosen, of her stepping inside, kept crashing through her mind. Try as she might, Vicky could not recall a single feature of the man's face.

She knew she had to get out of the flat and she had to call the police; but she also knew that if any of the pimps guessed what was on her mind, she'd be beaten and locked up again. Vicky held back all she felt, fixed a casual, unconcerned look on her face and asked Lee if she could come out. She went into the kitchen and said as there was no milk, she'd go and get some. Lee said that was fine, but told her not to be long. Walking away from the flat, pain inched through Vicky's body. The nearest phone box was a minute's walk away but nausea slowed her every step.

She made the call to the police and even with her back pushed against the cold glass, she could not stop shaking. Very soon, sirens cut through the February air. It wasn't just one patrol car either: Vicky saw the road fill with vehicles and within three minutes of making the call, she was being driven to the police station.

The police knew that Vicky was a vital witness and she was questioned at length. An incident room had been set up and Vicky was told a few of the facts as they were known. Janine had been found the day before, just after 9am on Saturday, 2 February. Her partially clothed body was concealed behind a hedgerow at the edge of a lay-by on the busy Wolverhampton to Shifnal road, the A464. It is about twelve miles from where Janine was picked up and the road runs parallel to the M54, possibly the road the driver then took to take him anywhere in the West Midlands.

Janine's small body had been savagely used. She was naked from the waist down and had been sexually assaulted. She had been killed elsewhere, possibly in the car, and drag marks were found in the frost on the ground, indicating that she had been pulled from where the vehicle would have parked to where she was abandoned.

A ligature had been tied around her neck and she had been strangled. But it was the damage inflicted to her face and head that shocked the investigative team. She had been repeatedly beaten with a sharp, jagged weapon until her features were obliterated.

To sustain such an attack, the murderer's mind would have to have been distorted by rage. No ordinary loss of temper could have provoked such an assault; this was a man who had coldly selected Janine, perhaps because her small frame suggested that she would put up little resistance. He had then driven her to a spot where no one would be able to hear them. Then he had unleashed all his violent impulses on her. This cold-blooded murder had been carefully planned.

Vicky was asked about Janine's relationships but, in truth, she had none outside the flat. She was asked about their relationships with Lee and his fellow pimps, and Vicky answered the questions truthfully. She was then asked if she knew that Janine was a mum. This hit Vicky hard. Janine had never mentioned children. She remembered the times that she had seen Janine get changed; her stomach betrayed no signs that she had ever carried children.

The majority of working girls are mothers, but Vicky had no idea that Janine had young children somewhere in the city, little more than toddlers. What had stopped her mothering them? What had stopped Janine telling Vicky about them, when they had shared so much? It was too much to take in and as Vicky was left alone over the following few hours, her sense of grief and loss grew sharper. Did she truly know Janine at all?

There was no clear idea what to do with Vicky now that her statement had been taken. She could not return to the flat and the pimps, as they were sure to react violently when they heard she'd talked to the police. Moreover, she was the last witness to see Janine alive. She may not be able to recall the killer's face, but the killer would know her.

Of course, the man in the dark-blue car may not have been responsible for the murder. It is possible that Janine returned to Walsall Road and was picked up by another punter before

Vicky's return. But so far, no one had come forward to say that they had seen Janine after the time she left Vicky's side. The focus had to remain on the driver of the Mondeo.

Once news of what had happened to Janine, and Vicky's disappearance, hit the streets, rumours started to circulate. What if Janine knew the identity of Gail Whitehouse's killer? Had he come back for her? Twenty-three-year-old prostitute Gail had been killed a year earlier and police now became concerned that a sick-minded predator was out there.

Vicky was adamant that Janine knew nothing abut Gail's killer; she was sure that Janine would have shared that much with her. But as well as scouring the streets and taking statements from other working girls and local residents, the police wanted to question one of Janine's pimps. One was brought in for questioning. This man committed suicide a week after his arrest.

The suicide raised a number of questions. After a brutal murder, police regularly look at suicides in the weeks that follow, as it is not unknown for the perpetrator to be overwhelmed with guilt and decide to end his own life. Vicky has never understood why this man chose suicide. Was he responsible in some way for Janine's death? Or did he fear being accused of the murder?

While Vicky knew the pimps were violent, none of them would damage their business by killing off an asset. Whoever did what they did to Janine was in a frenzy and despite turning over what she knew of this particular pimp in her mind time and time again, it didn't seem likely that he could have been responsible. Yet the question remains for Vicky: was suicide the action of an innocent man?

Had there been a plausible link from the pimp to Janine, if his DNA had been discovered under her fingernails, for example, no doubt the police would be content to clear up the murder swiftly. As it stood, days turned to weeks and no one was in the frame.

It was decided that the city was no longer safe for Vicky. She was told that she would be relocated, to a town many miles away. She was also told to change her name and never to talk about what she knew or had seen. Only seventeen years old, Vicky was driven by a female police officer to a town where she was unknown and advised to start her life afresh.

How this young girl with a shattered life was expected to live was not their concern. Remarkably, however, Vicky did more than survive. It took her years to recover, but she went on to marry and have children of her own. If you met the pretty mother, now in her thirties, you would never guess that she has seen the very worst of human behaviour. She shelters her children from the life she knew. They are safe with her, in a loving home that is a testimony to her spirit; she has created the kind of home life she never knew.

Motherhood has brought her happiness, but has also made her realise that Janine must have been very damaged to leave her children and take to the streets. Vicky knows with perfect clarity that nothing – nothing – could take her from her children. She also knows that she cannot forget her friend and would never wish to. She wants to be able to look Janine's killer in the eye and ask him, why? He is out there. Crawling through a world Vicky's children do not know exists, but a world that takes very little to reveal itself.

A darker world lies beneath the surface of everyday life. Hidden mostly, when it breaks through, our collective shock and outrage seems to grow with each new atrocity. When a child goes missing; when a girl is snatched from the streets; when a young woman is found in a makeshift grave – we wonder what the world is coming to.

In truth, it is the world as it ever was. It takes very little effort to peel back a few layers of our everyday understanding to confront it. But our attitude to those who work on the streets is often shameful. Rather than look at what causes girls, and boys, to sell themselves, we focus on making sure that it happens elsewhere, out of view. We look to law-makers and those charged with enforcing the law to act, to 'clean up the streets'. We tell ourselves that if a prostitute is killed it somehow is less shocking than if the victim is a respectable member of society, that it is 'part of the game'. We are wrong, and it is only when the stories behind these lost lives become known that we appreciate the true cost of any lost life.

Operation Enigma was launched in 1996 with a simple aim. It would look through the 207 unsolved murders of women dating back over the previous ten years to see if any links between them were apparent. The police were concerned that there could be a serial killer on the loose, hiding his tracks by moving across the country and changing his kill method.

It took a centralised effort to pull the operation together, as police forces are autonomous. The structure of policing allows each to focus on the specific needs of their neighbourhoods; some are urban, some are rural; all are different. But if criminal activity doesn't stay in one area, there is always a danger that, unwittingly, separate forces won't share all the information they have. This happened in the case of Peter Sutcliffe, the 'Yorkshire Ripper'. As an HGV driver, he preyed on women from Manchester to Leeds, crossing police districts, and in doing so helped extend his time at large.

With forty-four police authorities in England, Wales and Northern Ireland, information has to flow smoothly. Another incentive to look at the unsolved murders came from the understanding that a murderer's modus operandi isn't fixed. A killer who asphyxiates one victim may elect to use a knife to attack the next one. It is a myth that killers stick to a 'signature' and two police forces may direct their efforts at what turn out to be one assailant. Peter Sutcliffe attempted to decapitate one of his victims, Jean Jordan, with broken glass and a hacksaw, in an effort to disguise his methods. And so Enigma would also look at whether a prostitute bludgeoned in Manchester could be connected to a jogger stabbed in Cheshire.

Enigma was given impetus by the murder of four prostitutes from across the Midlands in the early 1990s. Gail Whitehouse (23), Janine Downes (20) Tracey Turner (32) and Samo Paull (20) had all been found brutally murdered. Working girls were right to fear that they were being preyed on. What the team found shocked all involved. By using forensic and behavioural techniques, Operation Enigma established an alarming twenty-one 'clusters' – cases with shared characteristics – and asked that 72 cases be looked at again in light of their finding. The Investigative Psychology Unit at Liverpool University had suggested that there could be five serial killers at work in the UK; Operation Enigma uncovered an unsettling picture that seemed to back up this troubling proposition.

The Hannibal Lecter stereotype – a killer with exceptional IQ and finesse – is hardly typical of a serial killer; the reality is usually much more mundane. In the Home Office enquiry that followed Peter Sutcliffe's arrest and imprisonment, Sir Lawrence Byford noted that Sutcliffe was an 'otherwise unremarkable young man'. He was no criminal mastermind. Enigma suggested that at any one time, a handful of men could be trawling the motorways of the UK, hunting and attacking women at random, with UK police forces ill equipped to track them.

By the time that Operation Enigma was concluded in 1998, twenty-six police forces had been advised to review the cases and clusters they'd highlighted. It was difficult to contradict Enigma's conclusion – the possibility that someone was travelling the length and breadth of the country, picking off the vulnerable at will. Two years later, a killing spree that saw three women lose their lives over four days put one name in the frame.

Philip Smith was a fairground worker who'd grown up in and around Gloucester but who had moved from town to town since childhood. He moved to Birmingham in 1999, by which time he was aged thirty-four and a father of three. He had spent some time homeless, working occasionally as an odd-job man or unlicensed taxi driver and eventually moved to a run-down terraced house in Sparkbrook. There, he became a regular drinker at the Rainbow pub in Digbeth and was an unforgettable figure at 6ft 4in and over 22 stone.

No one knows what triggered Smith's explosive episode of

violence in November 2000, probably not even Smith himself. He has been silent ever since his arrest and imprisonment. His one outburst in front of detectives was over cash he'd left at his flat. He angrily asserted that he'd need the money to buy chocolate bars once inside. Regarding his victims, he displayed no emotion at all, although it is certain that he knew two of the women from his time drinking at the Rainbow.

The first was Jodie Hyde. She was 21 years old and was struggling with a drug addiction, principally with sniffing butane gas. Jodie was highly vulnerable. Smith took the opportunity to offer her a lift to a hospital appointment on the ninth of November; he'd recently bought an old Volvo from his landlady's partner and was earning money giving people lifts. Smith persuaded Jodie to return to his house with him and once she was inside, subjected her to a brutal attack and then strangled her, after which he carried her naked body to his car.

He drove to open land at Ackers Trust, an adventure playground. Once there, he rolled a blanket around the corpse, tied it with a rope, covered it in petrol and set fire to it. Officers in a patrol car found the still-smouldering body. Jodie had suffered over 60% burns and could only be identified by her fingerprints.

Three days later, two more horrific discoveries were made. In the case of the first victim, Smith had approached another woman he knew from the Rainbow, 25-year-old Rosemary Corcoran, a single parent. CCTV picked up images of her struggling with Smith outside a nightclub. He forced her into his car and, over the next few hours, subjected her to a beating that left her unrecognisable. Leaving her in a wooded lane in Droitwich, he ran over her naked body in his car and then hastily dumped her corpse. It was found soon afterwards by a man walking his dog. Among her injuries, the pathologist recorded that the mother of three's brain had been dislodged and her jaw had snapped away from her skull.

Smith was still not satisfied, though. On the drive back to Birmingham, he spotted Carol Jordan. She was on her way to work in a care home when Smith deliberately drove into her, striking and fracturing her hip. He bundled her into his car and beat her until she blacked out. The beating continued and so severe was it that Carol, a 39-year-old mother of six, could only be identified later from dental records. Her body was abandoned at Lea Bank, where it was discovered by another dog-walker.

Lost in these horrific details is the impact of the deaths of these women on their families. Men like Smith destroy more than a single life with their deeds. As Tony Jordan, Carol's partner, said: 'She was a wonderful wife and a loving and devoted mother. She lived for the kids. This evil monster has made me a widower and has left six children motherless.'

Smith was arrested in connection with Jodie's disappearance. At this stage, police were treating the three murders as separate cases, but forensic work soon linked him to all three murders. In fact, the forensic material was so overwhelming that during his trial at Leicester Crown Court in July 2001, Smith changed his plea to guilty. Blood from all three women had been found at his house, in his car and on his clothing. When police entered Smith's home, they even found his 44in jeans floating in brown water in his bath, the water discoloured from dirt and blood.

After the trial, the police spokesperson stated that it was 'virtually inconceivable' that Smith had not killed before. His details were duly sent to the National Crime Faculty at Bramshill in Hampshire. Part of the National Police Training College, it exists to help tackle cross-border crimes by coordinating data and acts as an advisory service and centre of expertise for police forces across the country. There were forty unsolved female homicides, including that of Janine Downes, in the West Midlands at the time and speculation arose that Smith could be responsible for fourteen of them.

A review of unsolved cases took the focus outside the Midlands, from County Meath in Ireland back to Gloucestershire. (Smith still retained his Gloucestershire accent.) 32-year-old Carol Clark, who'd been working as a prostitute, had been found beaten and strangled in the Sharpness Docks area of the county in 1993. Earlier still, in 1989, 43-year-old Carol Gamble had been found stabbed, beaten and set alight at her cottage in Stroud.

As well as the areas where Smith had lived there were the regions he had visited while working for the fairground. Devon and Cornwall Police carried out a thorough review to see if he could be linked to the murder of fourteen-year-old Kate Bushell, but found no connection. Smith is still being looked at in connection with other murders and he has been spoken to on several occasions.

Janine's case was reviewed and Smith was considered a suspect for some time but no firm link has been established between him and her murder to date. For now, police are simply relieved that such a dangerous character is off the streets and will remain so for the remainder of his life. It's a chilling fact, however, that Smith was not the only deranged man preying on vulnerable women in the 1990s. Others were at work too.

Alun Kyte is not much to look at. A slight, balding asthmatic, he looked older than his forty-four years. He was known at several hospitals and surgeries as he'd seek medication for a number of complaints while he travelled across the UK. Kyte worked as a lorry driver and a mechanic but he was also a con man, involving himself in everything from petty fraud to cheating drivers out of money by claiming that he'd 're-tuned' their cars. In fact, what he did with the cars he worked on would later help police build a profile of his movements.

Kyte thought himself very smart. He changed cars frequently and even used those he was supposed to be re-tuning to trawl the motorway system that cuts across the Midlands. He drove from Sheffield to Gloucester, from Norwich to Chester, criss-crossing his way, and in some instances putting 1,000 miles on cars, altered the mileometers and then handed them back to unwitting customers.

Much of his time was spent with one aim – to pick up working girls. He had an unhealthy obsession with prostitution and harboured a deep-seated desire to inflict harm. By 1997, he was serving a seven-year sentence for a vicious attack and rape at knife-point on a woman in Weston-super-Mare. Police already knew of Kyte, as he had been reported after attacking a prostitute in 1994. Nearly three-quarters of working girls will have suffered violence for every year they work. The overwhelming majority do not report the attacks to police, anticipating that they would face indifference from a police force regularly charged with arresting them for soliciting. Kyte knew this, but in 1997 he was found guilty of rape.

While serving his sentence in Bristol Prison, he was known to boast of his exploits. Despite his conviction, he was confident he would not be connected with any of his other crimes. He was wrong.

Advances in forensics meant that DNA taken from Kyte's blood sample could be matched to semen traces left on the body of Tracy Turner, a thirty-two-year-old prostitute who worked out of motorway service stations in the Midlands. At the time, police were at a loss as to who her assailant could be. There were reports that she had been picked up at Hilton Park Services near Wolverhampton, but her body was found at Bitteswell, near Lutterworth, 52 miles away. Tracy was deaf and had been raped, stripped and strangled. Her body was found on 3 March 1994.

At first, no connection was made with the discovery, eight weeks earlier, of the body of twenty-year-old Samo Paull. Samo, a single parent, was also a working girl and had been picked up in Balsall Heath, a red-light district in Birmingham, on 30 December 1993. She was missing for three weeks before her remains were spotted, partially clothed and lying in a water-filled ditch near a lay-by outside Swinford, Leicestershire, 38 miles away. Both sites where the bodies of Tracy and Samo were dumped were about an hour's drive from the point where the girls were picked up.

Again, it was DNA evidence that linked Kyte to Samo's death. He denied murdering her but a forensic scientist testified that the chances of anyone else sharing the genetic profile built from the physical evidence left on the two women were 33 million to one. Fellow prisoners also testified against Kyte, telling the jury that he had regularly talked about what he had done to the two women.

Clearly, Kyte still imagined he could talk his way out of a guilty verdict and stated that the DNA evidence must have been the result of consensual sex. He casually told the court: 'You meet people and have sex with them or a one-night stand and you don't remember it.' The jury did not believe him, though, and he is currently serving a life sentence.

As with Philip Smith, police forces across the UK now have the opportunity to review their unsolved homicides with the known profile and movements of Alun Kyte. It is certainly unlikely that Samo Paull was the first woman he killed. Could Janine Downes be another of his victims?

There are similarities between the cases. All three women were found partially naked and certain items of their clothing have never been recovered – in Janine's case, her jeans, trainers and the ankle socks Vicky had lent her. Behavioural psychologists think such theft may be linked to 'trophy-taking', allowing the rapist to revisit, and fantasise about, the killings.

All three were working girls and while Kyte had a sick obsession with them, using girls time and time again, he was also open about his loathing of prostitutes, once declaring: 'You don't pay for those kind of women.' Payment is often the flashpoint for violence. It's common for punters suddenly to erupt into rage when asked for payment after the act. Some feel a sense of entitlement to sex with women and feel that 'slags enjoy it'.

Kyte hinted that Samo Paull had laughed at him during sex, so he throttled her until she stopped. It is unlikely she did, but if she was as smart-mouthed as Janine Downes, a casual remark could have punctured Kyte's over-inflated sense of his own prowess and could have inspired him to act out one of his violent fantasies.

He was known to be violent, was known to have used a knife, known to have frequented red-light districts and then to have driven the girls for miles from the point where he picked them up; he was also known to work in the Midlands during the early 1990s. Kyte cannot be ignored in the search for Janine's killer.

And Janine's name could be just one of many. In the last ten years, as many as seventy working girls have been killed and the numbers of those who have gone missing is even higher. They make up the biggest single group of unsolved female homicides in the UK.

Of course, many killers do end up facing justice. Men like Steven Wright, who embark on intense campaigns of violence – Wright murdered five women in six-and-a-half weeks. Other killers who spread their geographical tracks, who kill over longer periods and who separate the site of murder from the site they abandon their victims, are harder to trace.

The murders of prostitutes are harder to solve, as the potential list of suspects is high. These are very vulnerable women, even more so as police are charged with clearing them away from well-lit residential streets to out-of-town, isolated locations. But there can be little doubt that police and public attitudes add to the difficulty in solving these crimes. The brutal murder of a twenty-year-old mother of two would stir sympathy and outrage; the brutal murder of a twenty-year-old prostitute, less so. There is an unspoken sense that for working girls, violence goes with the territory.

Vicky knows that. When she wrote on an online website about the loss of her friend Janine, she received abuse. Faceless web users mocked her with comments along the lines of 'Slags can't expect anything else' – an eerie echo of the attitudes of the men who misuse them.

Attitudes are changing in the police force too, yet senior detectives will admit that they hesitate before releasing the information that a victim worked on the streets. If they do, they get less press inches and a weaker public response. For the police, behind every spate of prostitute killing there is the spectre of Peter Sutcliffe. It can be argued that the hysteria over his killings and his campaign to 'clean the streets' only provoked widespread panic and outrage after the murder of Jayne MacDonald, a 'respectable' girl of sixteen. It was only after her death that press coverage began to concentrate on the issue that no woman was safe; no such stance had been taken when the victims had been restricted to prostitutes. Morally, it was indefensible. The English Collective of Prostitutes has a simple slogan when it comes to discussing violence on the streets and it captures all that needs to be said: 'All Women Count'.

Women who work on the streets are mothers, daughters and wives. Some will be pushed into that way of life through addiction, others have been marred by abuse suffered since childhood. None emerges unscathed. While we turn a blind eye to the risk they face, it shames us all and men like Alun Kyte will continue to thrive. Until we truly believe that 'All Women Count', all women lose.

CHAPTER TEN
HELEN SCOTT AND CHRISTINE EADIE
THE WORLD'S END MURDERS

There may not be another case quite like the unsolved murder of Helen Scott and Christine Eadie. It left two families devastated and a community shocked and it frustrated the best efforts of two Scottish police forces for many years. Now the police believe the case is solved. But a High Court judge disagreed and the case of the World's End murders now threatens the very foundations of the Scottish legal system.

The police believe that they have identified not one man but two who were responsible for the savage abduction, rape and murder of the two seventeen-year-old friends. The case eventually came to trial in 2007, but the judge presiding at the High Court in Edinburgh, Lord Clarke, suggested that it was too weak to stand. It was thrown out and the homicides that rocked Edinburgh remain, officially, unsolved. One of the accused is dead, the other had the charges against him dismissed, yet the police are adamant that they are not looking for anyone else in connection to the murders. Who is right?

The police were shocked when the trial collapsed, but the

burden was harder still to bear for the families of Helen and Christine. Three days afterwards, Elish Angiolini, the Lord Advocate and Scotland's chief public prosecution officer, told the Scottish Parliament that the trial judge should have allowed the evidence to be put before the jury. The suggestion was that the man the police had charged had been allowed to escape justice. In reply, Scotland's most senior judge, Lord Hamilton, criticised the Lord Advocate for attacking the independence of the judiciary.

This is not an obscure legal spat. It drives to the heart of the ability of the police to track perpetrators of unsolved murders. Despite the highest standards of policing thirty years ago, East Lothian and Edinburgh police forces could not track the killers of two young women – girls who could have been anyone's daughter, anyone's sister. They believe they have done so now through the massive advances made in DNA profiling. Lord Clarke was unmoved, however, and with the European Court of Human Rights stating that police in the UK should not be allowed to keep profiles of everyone arrested for a recordable offence, the advances made in tracking suspects through shared DNA profiles may now have to roll back.

What lies at the heart of the crisis is that the police are beginning to solve cases by using the DNA profiles of *innocent* people to trace a guilty relative. This has massive implications for unsolved cases and while it has put human-rights campaigners and the police on a collision course, serious crimes have been solved using this method.

Here is an example. Three young women were raped and strangled in Llandarcy, south Wales, in 1973 and the hunt for the 'Saturday Night Strangler' began. Someone was targeting young women as they walked home after a night out. Despite a huge and intensive investigation, however, the killer was never found. The case was reviewed again in 2000 and although advances in DNA had allowed a forensic team to build up a profile from material left at the crime scenes, no match existed on the current offender databases

It was a year later that DNA specialist Dr Jonathan Whitaker hit on the idea that the offender might well have had children, who would by now be adults. As we pass on 50% of our DNA to children, that partial match could well exist on the criminal database if any of the children had offended. Sure enough, a name came up, that of car thief Paul Kappen.

His father, Joseph Kappen, had died eleven years earlier. At the time of the murders, Kappen had been spoken to but his wife Christine had provided him with an alibi for the nights in question. She and the children lived in fear of Kappen, a violent man with a long history of petty crime dating back to the age of twelve. His profile was not held on the police database, but by persuading daughter and wife to volunteer a sample, Forensics deduced that Joseph Kappen was the man they were looking for.

The final step was to exhume Kappen's body and by extracting his femur and some teeth, an exact match was made. Kappen had been responsible for a great many other violent rapes too and at last, his name was made public and the families of the dead girls had some small measure of justice.

This case was brought to the attention of police in Scotland. Could this provide the breakthrough they needed in the World's End case after so many years? The team charged with reviewing the case in 2004 began at the beginning...

Looking at the photographs of Helen Scott and Christine Eadie is like staring into a forgotten world. Only three decades have elapsed since their deaths, but so many changes have occurred that the Edinburgh of those days has vanished. It was a time of no mobile phones, no Internet, no CCTV, no personal computers, no DNA-based forensics. In fact, policing at that time had remained unchanged for decades. Detective work was paper based; cards would be placed in index files and cross-referenced for those who worked a homicide. A detective working just after the Second World War would have been familiar with the systems policemen and women would be using thirty years later. Today, officers feel their methods are light years from those of the 1970s.

That is not to say basic detective work is not conducted in the same manner. Witness statements are taken, the laborious task of checking facts and confirming alibis has to be carried out, with all efforts focused on one goal: establish the facts. It is easy to forget that the role of Serious Crimes Units is not to establish guilt, it is only to discover what happened.

Today's detective work still relies on gathering witness accounts and this is usually all that is required when a murder is routine; the perpetrator will usually be known to the victim. It is an approach that is pushed to breaking point when a more rare 'stranger' murder is committed, though. At least police now know that they can fall back on that other pillar of modern detective work: DNA profiling from physical evidence.

Of course, pretty much every aspect of home and working

life was different in the late 1970s; after all, technology had not yet been transformed by the electronic and digital revolution. Christine left school at sixteen and, following a job with the council, was working as a typist for a firm of property surveyors. She'd take notes and type letters on a typewriter. You had to be accurate: mistakes could not be deleted, they'd have to be Tippexed out. To meet up with Helen, her friend since school, she'd have to call her on a landline once she was home and agree, and then stick to, a meeting time and place. No mobiles. No texting.

The contrast between technology today and thirty years ago has a direct bearing on this case. What took place on the night of 15 October 1977 occurred in large part because the perpetrators knew they could strike and leave no trace. There were no cameras to pick up the girls leaving the World's End pub on Edinburgh's Royal Mile. The girls could not text to say who they were leaving with, could not call for help on a mobile phone. Their signal could not be traced to map their route and the vehicle that left the packed streets of Edinburgh could not be tracked as it moved out of town and drove the girls to an isolated spot. When the girls walked out of the pub that October evening, they effectively vanished.

So what was known about their movements that night? Like many other young people, Helen and Christine had been drinking along the Royal Mile on a Saturday night. Binge-drinking may seem like a modern phenomenon, but teenagers in the 1970s acted much as teens today do. Although they were underage, Helen and Christine had drunk at the World's End a number of times; the place had long been packed and was popular with the younger crowd.

By the time they arrived there, around 10pm, they had already met up with a few friends, had drunk a fair amount and had already fallen out over something someone had said, though they had made up again. It was a typically eventful evening, something they'd surely laugh and share anecdotes about over the week, until the next big night out.

Helen had just started a job working in a kilt shop on Prince's Street, just a few moments' walk from the Royal Mile. She didn't view it as a permanent job; she planned to go to night school and gain childcare qualifications. Both she and Christine came from good and stable homes; they were pretty, personable and had everything to live for.

That explains the great shock over their disappearance. Here were two typical teenagers, enjoying a night in the centre of the city, part of a group of friends. Sadly, they were not missing for long. While they remained missing, there was still hope. Perhaps there had been some kind of silly mistake, staying out all night when they knew they had to be home by midnight. That hope vanished the following afternoon.

Less than twenty miles from Edinburgh is the bay of Gosford in East Lothian. It is overlooked by the grounds of a stately home, Gosford House, seat of the Charteris family. A couple were walking on the coastal path shortly after lunchtime when they saw what they thought to be a mannequin washed up on the high-tide mark. As they stepped towards it, however, it became horribly clear that this was no shop-window dummy. It was the body of a girl, naked, bound and gagged.

Once the police arrived, they soon concluded that this was probably Christine Eadie, reported as missing by her family earlier in the day. She had been abducted and murdered, but what of her friend Helen Scott? East Lothian police informed their Edinburgh counterparts that there was no sign of the other teenager. It took another call to establish where she was. This time the call came from a dog-walker, a few hours after Christine's body had been found. Helen's corpse lay less than two miles away, in a field. Like Christine, she had been bound and gagged. She was naked from the waist down, but her coat was still in place.

The news broke and its impact spread widely. The capital was in shock, but then so was the whole nation. Two families were devastated and communities wondered who could be responsible for such a dreadful crime. Although it was not acknowledged at the time, the police were reeling too. As the girls' bodies had been moved, the investigation would now occupy two police forces. Officially, East Lothian would take precedent as wherever a body is found, the local force owns the investigation, but the rural force had little experience of dealing with two high-profile murders, so the bulk of the investigation would have to focus on Edinburgh.

Each force appointed a detective chief inspector to oversee the enquires from the two centres and both reported to Detective Superintendent George MacPherson. From the moment the girls were discovered, the case was high profile and the resources committed to the case outstripped those for all previous investigations. Police from both forces were determined to find who was responsible for the attacks and when the case was periodically reviewed over the decades that were to follow, it was clear that the original investigation was carried out professionally and with the utmost dedication. Yet as the weeks passed and 1978 came around, the teams began to fear that whoever took the girls had simply vanished without trace.

The investigation began, as all investigations do, with a thorough look at the girls' lives, their families, friends and acquaintances. Both girls were popular and well known but as the scores of statements were gathered, it became obvious that there was no source of conflict in their lives that suggested they were at risk from anyone they knew. Police assembled witness statements from the group of girls they were with that night and other drinkers at the World's End. Shortly before they disappeared, they had been talking to two men.

These two men came up in several witness accounts and it was clear the police would need to identify them and question them as soon as possible. They were not regulars at the World's End, they looked to be older than the girls and one of them had short hair. The hair length was significant: this was the late 1970s and most men still tended to wear their hair longer back then.

An appeal was put out for these two men to come forward. They were last seen talking to Helen and Christine and they bought them a round of drinks. When the girls left the bar at around 11.30pm, could they have been waiting for them? They may well have gone elsewhere and have had sound alibis, but they needed to be questioned and eliminated. No one came forward. The team in Edinburgh suspected that these men were married and feared alerting their wives to what they were up to. Or, they had played a role in what happened that night.

The Royal Mile may not have had CCTV, but it did have a young police officer on duty who knew the street well. Policing was still based on foot patrols at the time and officers had to learn their patch inside out. That night, the officer recalled seeing two young girls leave the World's End and head in the direction of Waverley Station. One stumbled and was helped by her friend. A man approached them, probably offering a lift. There was a second man standing a little way behind him. It looked as if one of the girls was keen to accept the offer of a free ride home; the other was not. Eventually, the four walked off together and turned down St Mary's Street.

Could this have been the last sighting of Helen Scott and Christine Eadie? Without CCTV, the images could not be isolated and studied. But the young officer was well used to keeping a trained eye on what was happening around him at this time of the evening. Pubs all closed at the same time and drinkers poured out onto the streets; it was often a volatile time. His experience prompted him to watch the two girls and wonder if all was as it should be. Looking back, he believed that it had definitely been Helen and Christine, and as the years passed, he wondered if he had walked over and broken into the conversation, they might have hesitated to accept a lift and still be alive today.

In truth, the offer of a lift in the 1970s did not seem that risky. Many young girls and women relied on rides from comparative strangers as they left the city centre, even if the driver had been drinking as heavily as they had. Accepting a lift was an unremarkable event. It is likely that the man who approached Helen and Christine knew that. Perhaps he guessed that with their judgement altered by alcohol, this was the perfect way to lure two teenagers into his vehicle. Perhaps he'd even walked into the World's End knowing that and waited quietly, scanning the crowd, assessing who was the worse for wear, whose guard was down and who to approach with a smile and the offer of a free drink.

Enquires in East Lothian fell flat: no one had seen a car or van in the early hours of the morning or any evidence of the girls' bodies being moved. That presented a problem, as the police had no idea of the vehicle involved. Forensic examinations could establish only that the girls had been sexually assaulted, gagged with their own clothing, stripped and bound. Both had been strangled.

Other than the tights that had been used as a ligature, Christine's clothes were never found. Helen's tights had also been used as a ligature around her neck and her belt was used to tie her arms. She was naked apart from her coat. There was a semen stain on the back of the garment, but even the most cutting-edge DNA profiling available at the time could only provide a partial DNA profile. Yet it was enough to allow the police to begin eliminating some of the men they had spoken to.

DNA profiling was very much in its infancy and many of the procedures followed today were not in place during the 1970s. There was a risk of cross-contamination from the officers and lab technicians involved in removing the bodies and bagging up key pieces of clothing, but still, later investigations were impressed with the level of care taken during the first enquiry and they were able to revisit the materials and advance what they knew. The original team also took samples from many of the drinkers at the World's

End and this would also prove of use in clearing a number of names.

The team still had no clear idea of who the two men seen drinking with Helen and Christine might have been. Detectives were fairly sure that two men were responsible for the horrific ordeal the girls suffered, as they guessed that one man alone could not have physically subdued two healthy teenagers.

At first, it seemed that the involvement of more than one man would help the investigation. There was twice the chance that a family member or friend would notice something suspicious, there was a greater chance that mistakes would be made and if one could be identified, the police would have the leverage to make one or both implicate the other. But as the months wore on, the investigation was no nearer the truth than it had been on that first Sunday morning.

Both forces carried out considerable work on the case. The description of one of the men seen talking to Helen and Christine led to one obvious line of enquiry. Edinburgh is a barracks town and so in due course all the soldiers that were in Edinburgh that night were traced and spoken to. This was a mammoth undertaking, as many were in transit and had since left the city for destinations as far away as Germany and Cyprus. But despite the commitment from the detectives involved, nothing of value turned up.

In May 1978, senior police officers had to make the decision to wind the hunt down. It was a blow to the families of Helen and Christine, but they were assured that the case would never be closed. All leads had been exhausted at that point, but any new information would be examined. The case was also periodically reviewed as the years went by. Each time, something else was added to what was known, but still without that vital piece of evidence that would help track down who was responsible for the loss of two young lives.

No one could have guessed that 1978 marked only the midway point in the career of one unmistakably evil man. The name Angus Sinclair may not be as well known as that of Peter Sutcliffe or Fred West, but there is every reason to believe that it should be. By the late 1970s, Sinclair was already a veteran of several horrific attacks inflicted on children as young as seven. Was he one of the men that stalked the World's End pub that night?

One further resource today's senior investigating officers can draw on is behavioural profiling. It can't give you a name, but with enough information of the crimes to study a behavioural scientist can create a profile of the likely criminal. With large-scale enquiries that generate hundreds of names, it can be a helpful filter. The profile created for the Saturday Night Strangler case suggested that the killer would be white and aged between his late twenties and mid-thirties, would have been in trouble with the police since he had been a juvenile, lived locally, had a history of assault, worked in an unskilled role, had an absent father, had a troubled marriage, enjoyed solo sports and would be a collector of weapons.

The profile was almost a tick-list for the dominating features of Joseph Kappen's life. At the time of the Llandarcy murders, he was a thirty-two-year-old bouncer, from a broken home, responsible for a long list of petty crimes, was known for his violent temper and had a wife and children who were in fear of him. But Kappen was not the only man who could match the profile. Hundreds of miles away, Angus Sinclair was an uncanny match too.

Sinclair was born in 1945 in Maryhill, Glasgow. He had a brother and sister who were over a decade older than him and he was only four years old when his father died. Nevertheless, Sinclair did not suffer neglect or abuse as far as anyone can tell and he enjoyed a typical, if tough, Glasgow childhood. He did reasonably well at school, though not much detail is available about his childhood as a whole. There were reports that he was put in care for intermittent periods, possibly for proving too much of a handful for his mother.

He was probably involved in a string of petty crimes after the age of ten but did not come to the attention of the authorities until 1959, when he was fourteen and was accused of housebreaking. This would not have marked him out as a potential serious offender and a great number of boys from tougher neighbourhoods in Glasgow found themselves up in court in their teenage years. The events that made Sinclair different – very different – occurred soon after his release on probation.

It was 1961 and Sinclair was back in court facing charges of lewd and libidinous behaviour. The language sounds outdated, but it was a charge that could be used when sexual assault could not be established, though the police believed that sexually inappropriate behaviour had taken place. This was not about being a sixteen-year-old caught with a fifteen-year-old, and falling foul of the strict rules of the day. Sinclair had assaulted an eight-year-old child.

It's easy to be wise in hindsight, but an assault on a young girl should have alerted the authorities to the likelihood that Sinclair was a dangerously unbalanced personality in the making. Instead, he received three years' probation and was free to walk back to the housing estate he'd left. This was to have a tragic outcome for Catherine Reehill.

Catherine was only seven years old and had the misfortune to live near the same block of flats as Sinclair. He'd watched her many times, for example when she ran errands for neighbours. Only seven months since his last charge, he lured Catherine into his flat with the promise of more money for sweets. He then attacked the little girl with a staggering ferocity; she lost a lot of blood in her attempt to fight him off. He raped and strangled her and threw her lifeless body down the stairwell, intending her death to appear as an accident.

Fortunately, his subterfuge did not pay off. He was questioned several times by police over the next few days and Sinclair's brother persuaded him to make a qualified admission. He said he was overcome with a sexual urge and did attack Catherine, but that the girl had banged her head by accident. He was sentenced to ten years in prison.

Three things were to become clear from this guilty sentence. Firstly, never again would Sinclair be guided by his family into admitting his involvement in a crime. He would become entirely uncommunicative when questioned by police on later occasions. Secondly, he would not make the 'mistake' of leaving a body near his home again. And thirdly, the psychiatrist's assessment that Sinclair had failed to show any remorse, or to understand the gravity of his crime against Catherine Reehill, would not change. Nor would it for any of his victims. Regretfully, that psychiatrist's report was filed and then forgotten.

While serving his jail sentence, Sinclair proved himself a model prisoner. It is not uncommon for serial offenders to adapt easily to prison life and even find themselves put in positions of responsibility, such as working in the kitchens. Sinclair was to learn to a range of skill sets while inside. He learnt how to tie elaborate knots to repair fishing nets. He was also trained as a painter and decorator, in the hope that when he was released, he'd find steady employment.

Sinclair was released from Peterhead Prison in 1968, after serving a mere seven years for the rape and murder of Catherine Reehill. He returned to Glasgow to live with his mother, but was soon working for a painting and decorating firm in Edinburgh. He got to know the city well. He was still being supervised by a parole officer, who noted how many girlfriends the diminutive Sinclair seemed to be involved with. By the age of twenty-five, he had met and married a student nurse, Sarah Hamilton, and the couple moved back to their native Glasgow. She knew nothing of the real nature of the crime that had led to his imprisonment, although she did know that he'd served time inside.

The Sinclair marriage was not a happy one. The couple had a young son, but Sinclair showed little interest in him and spent much of his time out dating other women. When he was home, he demonstrated a violent temper and Sarah stayed with him only to give her son some stability. She came from a large and troubled family and so in some respects expected little from Sinclair. He would move out for long stretches at a time, presumably to live with his girlfriend of the time, but he would always return. Yet even when he was at home, his 'fishing trips' kept him out of the house when he was not working.

Some of Sarah's siblings disapproved of Sinclair, but the Hamiltons were not a family Sarah could return to. There were ten children who'd grown up in a violent household dominated by their alcoholic father. As adults, many of the Hamiltons had problems with alcoholism too. One of them, Gordon, would drink so heavily that it led to a premature death and yet the other drinkers in the family regarded him as different. He seemed arrogant, as if a cut above his brothers and sisters, even though his behaviour mirrored theirs.

If anyone could have made a claim to have been superior it was Sarah, who had worked hard to escape her upbringing and become a nurse. But she only ever sought to help her siblings and tried her best to remain on good terms with them all. It surprised her to see that Sinclair and Gordon got on well. It was no great friendship, but they would go on fishing trips together and seemed to tolerate each other's company well enough.

Another Hamilton brother, the youngest, worked alongside Sinclair at a painting company for some time and, it could be argued, got to know him best. He learned that Sinclair liked to plan and execute robberies and thefts and was not averse to using exceptional levels of violence. This brother was candid with the police when they spoke to him in London after the third re-investigation into the World's End murders began in 2001. By that time, Sinclair was of interest to Lothian and Borders Police, the new name of the force that was an amalgamation of the two older police forces originally in charge of the enquiry.

Sinclair had in fact, come to the attention of the courts long before 2001. In 1980, he was charged with the illegal possession of a .22 calibre gun. It may well have been used during one of his robberies. But what the police found when they dug deeper into the life of Angus Sinclair proved more disturbing by far.

On paper, Sinclair had been law abiding since his release from prison. In fact, when he next appeared in the High Court in Edinburgh, it was to face eleven charges of rape and indecency against children aged from six to fourteen years old. They had all endured horrific attacks but although the cases had been widely covered in the press, they had never been formally linked. This was despite the fact that they followed a similar pattern, the same approach that Sinclair had followed to lure Catherine Reehill to her death all those years ago. Children would be asked to run errands or asked for directions and then would be pulled into alleyways near to the high-rises where they lived and were attacked. For a decade, Sinclair had got away with a terrifying string of offences both as a paedophile and a violent thief. Finally, he faced a substantial jail term.

In 1982, Sinclair began a life sentence and the judge recommended that he serve a minimum of fifteen years. Of course, his victims, all children, were serving 'life sentences' of their own. Once again, Sinclair adapted himself to prison life and rose through the ranks of responsibility. He was thought of as an ideal prisoner and as senior inmate many others would turn to him for advice and guidance. It is possible that despite the judge's request for Sinclair's sentence to be a lengthy one, he could have been back on the streets by the mid-1990s. This time however, the police were not waiting for Sinclair to be released and to re-offend. This time, his past would come back to haunt him and some measure of justice for one of his victims would be served. Everyone in CID suspected that Sinclair was responsible for more crimes than he would ever admit to, but the identity of one of his victims surprised many when it was disclosed.

Mary Gallagher was seventeen years old in 1978 when she was found murdered after a serious sexual assault that took place on some waste ground near a railway station. She had been walking there with an eleven-year-old boy who had run away once he spotted a man staring at them. Mary didn't get away.

This murder came only eleven months after the World's End murders and, as with Helen and Christine, Mary's clothing had been used as a ligature; the attacks were not linked, though. There were sound reasons for this. Mary's attack involved one man; she had not been abducted and removed to another site but killed on the spot. It would take a forensic review twenty-two years later for the police to hit a DNA match. One name came up: Angus Sinclair.

He was tried for the murder of Mary Gallagher in 2001. Passive to the point of boredom, Sinclair listened as the judge told him that this time, he should not expect to be released. He had in fact, already been turned down for parole two years earlier. Clearly, he still imagined that he deserved to be free.

The press now realised that Angus Sinclair was a dangerous man who had been at large for too long. Now other names were added as his potential victims. Names such as Anna Kenny, Agnes Cooney and Hilda McAuley, all from unsolved cases of the late 1970s. Despite an initial flurry of hope, however, there was to be no concrete DNA material linking Sinclair to the assaults and murders.

It would take until 2004 before scientists were able to establish that there had been two traces of DNA left on the bodies of Helen and Christine. At first, detectives had been wrong-footed as one signature had masked the other. It seemed possible that only one man was involved, although for many years his identity could not be traced. During the review, Forensics suggested that the Y chromosome in the DNA be isolated. The Y chromosome is passed from father to son; it does not change and might prove of use.

It did, but in the most unexpected way. While trying to isolate the Y chromosome from the semen stain on Helen's coat, Forensics identified another code. It was a smaller sample, but the complete profile became apparent all the same. The police were now handed two distinct codes. They were both run through the national database and one name came up. It was from the smaller sample and the name of its owner was Angus Sinclair.

Some of the detectives working on the review had heard of him, though not many. After all, he'd been locked away since 1982. A new question now arose: who had Sinclair been in close enough contact with to recruit on such a high-risk abduction and murder? It was clearly planned, but it was difficult to see who Sinclair would have trusted in such a scheme. The other difficulty was in accepting that Sinclair changed his pattern of offending behaviour with the attacks on Helen and Christine. Until then, his focus had been on children. Who had convinced him to target young women?

It is very rare for men to team up to kill. Detectives pored over all they knew about Sinclair and his associates back in the 1970s. Many DNA swabs had been taken over the years as the case was reviewed, as much as to clear possible suspects as to find the culprit.

It was at this point that the Y chromosome from the larger sample hit a match with an existing swab. It was a match for Sarah Sinclair's family. One of Sarah's five brothers must have been with Angus on the night of the World's End murders.

It was a process of elimination and the focus soon switched to Gordon Hamilton, Sarah's brother. The investigation was then faced with yet another new challenge: Hamilton had been dead since 1996. He had become increasingly isolated from his family and had become a heavy drinker. He died aged forty-one and had been cremated.

Final confirmation that the other assailant had been Hamilton was not easy. He left almost no trace. He had no criminal record. Of his life with his family, none of his possessions existed. The police eventually gambled on the hope that as a general handyman, Hamilton had left a trace of himself through his work. They tracked down one of the flats he had decorated, somewhere that had not been touched since, and a room where he'd installed polystyrene coving.

The original team that investigated the 1977 murders would never have believed that it would one day be possible to trace the killer through a small DNA sample he left as he decorated a room, but it was, and the police were now confident that they had their second man. They had Gordon Hamilton's DNA at both murder scenes, but he would never face trial. Perhaps his guilt led him to his drink-fuelled early death.

The next logical step was to try Angus Sinclair for his involvement in the rape and murder of Helen Scott and Christine Eadie. Police were fairly confident that they had enough to convince a jury but first, Sinclair had to be arrested and questioned. By this point, Sinclair had been in prison for over twenty years and was entirely at ease with his surroundings. Despite several in-depth questioning sessions with two highly experienced detective sergeants, he gave nothing away. He had nothing to gain. He knew he was serving a life sentence and was happy to remain silent, adding only occasionally, 'I have nothing further to say.'

It was a composed performance and the police knew that their investigation would have to stand or fall without the benefit of an admission of involvement from Sinclair. The case went to the Crown Office to allow them to prepare the prosecution's case. The defence team for Sinclair also had all the material that the police had gathered over the many years of the investigation.

The trial date was set for September 2007. Sinclair had been charged with the abduction, rape and murder of the two World's End victims. His legal team had over year to prepare their line of defence and it was very simple: Gordon Hamilton was to blame. Sinclair had consensual sex with the two girls and anything that happened to them after that point was Hamilton's fault.

It seems extraordinary that someone with Sinclair's background could be expected to be believed but, of course, his criminal past would not be admissible during the trial. That was something that the prosecution were aware of, but they trusted that the DNA link would prove sufficient. The defence saw the weakness in their approach immediately and their next move was to prove catastrophic to the Crown Office and the thirty-year police investigation.

They made a legal submission to Judge Lord Clarke and suggested that, firstly, the prosecution had no evidence that the girls had been abducted on the night in question. Secondly, that any DNA traces could be explained by consensual liaison. And lastly, as there was no evidence linking Sinclair to rape, neither was there any evidence that rebutted the suggestion that Hamilton alone was responsible.

Judge Lord Clarke spoke to the courtroom. He said: 'I am of the view that the evidence taken at its highest in context of a whole is neutral as to whether or not he [Sinclair] was involved in acting with force or violence against the girls, there having been some evidence of sexual contact between him and the girls in the twelve hours or so before they were killed. I'm not satisfied what the advocate-depute had to say overcame these difficulties in that respect.' With that, the Crown was told that it had insufficient evidence to proceed and the charges against Angus Sinclair were dismissed.

The families of Helen and Christine had to relive their grief once more as the legal and political battle raged on. In many ways, their lives had become shaped by the tragic loss. Morain Scott, Helen's father, spoke about the shattering effect the crime had on his family. He was sure that his wife Margaret, Helen's mother, died an early death brought on from grief over the loss of her daughter, and now he felt justice had been denied. He spoke for many when he said: 'At least had it gone to a jury, you can accept their decision, but for the case to be thrown out after all the hard work that was put in just astounds me completely.' The families felt that they had been handed a legal ruling, not justice.

The case demonstrated the uphill struggle that any unsolved murder investigation faces. It is not enough to have a previous string of convictions, not enough to build a list of probabilities and circumstantial evidence and it is not even enough to place a suspect at a scene with a DNA link.

Anger at the collapse of the trial is still palpable. There have been demands for an enquiry and a series of bitter exchanges about the case at the top levels of policing and the legal system. Helen and Christine's families were dismayed at the outcome but they were comforted to learn later that once the jury were told that they were dismissed they stayed to honour the girls' memory with a minute's silence.

Helen Scott's brother, Kevin, has vowed to fight on and challenge the law of double jeopardy that prevents anyone being tried twice for the same crime. Kevin Scott has said: 'If the new Scotland wants to send a message that it's open to change, a change in the law would be a strong message to send.'

It is a Scotland that Helen and Christine would no longer recognise. The girls would be women in their late forties now, probably married and with children of their own, daughters perhaps, stepping out into a Friday night, full of light and laughter.